Samad Seyidov

The Phenomenology of Creativity

History, Paradoxes, Personality

AuthorHouse™ UK Ltd.
500 Avebury Boulevard
Central Milton Keynes, MK9 2BE
www.authorhouse.co.uk
Phone: 08001974150

Published by AuthorHouse 4/1/2013

ISBN: 978-1-4817-8739-0 (sc)
ISBN: 978-1-4817-8740-6 (e)

Author's Preface

Creativity has always attracted the attention of both scientists and ordinary people. While the former try to find ways to unlock its secrets, the latter are delighted by its beauty, power, and refinement. The epithets often attributed to creativity are also inherent in the distinctive characteristics of supreme, divine, mystical forces. And this is no happenstance, because creativity, as the creation of the new, always bears a trace of the supernatural, incomprehensible, and inexplicable, which goes against the grain of the conventions and rules of generally accepted forms of behavior, thinking, and communication.

By combining the incompatible, by generalizing the seemingly unlike, and by systematizing the chaotic, creativity becomes a kind of sparkle in our souls which turns us into hot flames when we have to shed light on the road to the unknown and which allows us to remain human even when many people go blind in darkness and ignorance. The author will acquaint the reader with a variety of points of view on the nature of creativity and will introduce the reader to the "laboratory" for the study of human thought, with the intention of providing a conception of the ideas and hot topics of ethics, philosophy, psychology, and so forth. The book you are holding in your hands was written from this point of view.

TABLE OF CONTENTS

v

IN LIEU OF A FOREWORD.

The "Curse" of Psychology

Starting a book with a description of a "curse" may not be a great idea, but if, as I see it, such a "curse" exists, then a scientist's duty is to understand it. It is true that historically, scientists were the first to study what seemed sinful, shameful, and even accursed to others. Attempts at scientific explanations of the mysterious phenomena of nature have always distinguished real scientists, who rebelled against the prejudices and illusions of their times. By putting themselves in danger and at times at risk of death, they have selflessly tackled the solution of problems which no one had even dared study before. Copernicus, Galileo, Einstein, Freud, and the many other geniuses who basically founded modern science were not just unafraid of "curses," but energetically and dispassionately studied and analyzed them.

Sigmund Freud, of course, was the most vivid example of this kind of "behavior" in the history of psychology. All of his creativity involved a devastating critique of the then-accepted notions of the psyche, the determination of man's behavior, and the contents of the subconscious. In practically all his works, he discovered and described new aspects of old phenomena that had been quite thoroughly studied before him. We can cite the book *Totem and Taboo* as an example of his scientific "protest." Here he analyzed the traditions, mores, taboos, and even curses of particular peoples, ethnic groups, and individuals, from the standpoint of the totally new psychoanalytical approach.

Another no less vivid example of a scientist's interest in forgotten and often denied human experience is the creative work of Carl Jung, who, in Freud's footsteps, expanded the boundaries of our understanding of the nature of the human psyche. His discovery of the collective subconscious and archetypes, on the basis of a profound analysis of individual human psychology and the historical and philosophical heritage of different (especially Eastern) peoples, established the foundation of a new approach to the study of human mental processes.

"At the beginning of my career as a psychiatrist and psychotherapist," *wrote Dr. Jung,* "I was absolutely ignorant of Chinese philosophy, and only afterwards did my professional experience show me that in my techniques I had unconsciously followed the same secret path which had dominated the best minds of the East over many centuries" (Jung, 2008, p. 10).

Another "courageous" student of human psychology was Alfred Kinsey,[1] an outstanding American researcher of sexuality. His works, which were combined under the general title of *The Kinsey Reports*, had a profound effect on all strata of his contemporary American society. Their impact on social, cultural, religious, family, and other values would be difficult to overestimate, because the mathematical and statistical reliability of Dr. Kinsey's evidence, plus the transparency of their presentation, not only contradicted but undermined current notions of male and female sexuality. In principle, Alfred Kinsey's studies, like Freud's theory, were the original precursors of the sexual revolution that began in the 1960s.

A remarkable example of a unique scientific approach to the "curses" is the work of Natalya Petrovna Bekhtereva, the granddaughter of the great V. M. Bekhterev. As the Director of the St. Petersburg Institute of the Brain, she has devoted her entire life to decoding the mysteries of this organ. In her book *The Magic of the Brain and the Labyrinths of Life, she writes,* "I have tried to avoid touching so-called mysteries, but I have considered it my duty to recount the strange and by no means always explicable phenomena I have encountered in my life" (Bekhtereva, 2007, p. 52).

In all her work, this outstanding neurophysiologist has proved that studies of the brain by the most advanced and progressive analytical methods must not exclude evidence of the scientist's regular encounters with the mysterious and inexplicable phenomena of the brain's activity.

The bizarre and inexplicable are not just produced by the human brain, but also by its product, the psyche. Today this phenomenon, which has drawn a great deal of attention, is still just as hard to interpret definitively as is the psychology which studies it. In fact, it would be difficult to find a field in the humanities as contradictory as psychology. Since the time of its origins, people have been discussing not just specific psychological phenomena, but the

---

[1] *Alfred Kinsey* (1884-1956) is still one of the most controversial figures of modern psychology. His scientific work, personal life, and personal relations have not only become a topic of study for specialists and historians of psychology, but also became the basis for the screenplay of a well-known Hollywood biographical movie made in 2004 (*Kinsey*).

definition of psychology as a science. Whether it is a science of behavior or a science of the mind, if psychology "is understood not as the knowledge of human beings and their life experience, but as a mere science, it will always be known as the dullest and most useless of all the philosophical disciplines, which in its ultimate vacuity has become a kind of hunting ground for mediocre minds and barren systematizers" (Spengler, 1993, p. 477); but if it is not understood in this way, psychology is the highest level of understanding of the human being.

The amount of psychological research has grown from year to year. For example, from July 1, 2006 to July 30, 2007, the number of doctoral dissertations on psychology and related fields in the United States set a record of 37,971,[2] leaving not just physics and mathematics far behind, but also economics, history, and law.

This is not to say that psychological topics are becoming more comprehensible and less controversial. On the contrary, psychologists have demonstrably contradicted each other in attempts to prove the superiority of their own theories and the inferiority of others' theories. It might seem that a process which is totally natural for any other science is taking the opposite direction in psychology right now. In mathematics, the disproof of one theorem and proof of another does not mean the rejection of theorems as a means of proof. A combination of a variety of theorems makes it possible to create a certain concept or system. The situation is completely different in psychology, where the proof of one theory not only results in the disproof of another, but in the rejection, or at least the modification, of the entire conceptual framework of psychology itself.

There are a large number of such examples in the history of psychology, and several of them have already become textbook cases. For example, John Watson, after creating his theory of behaviorism, not only introduced new terminology, but rejected Wilhelm Wundt's concept of *consciousness* in psychology. Or George Kelly, who introduced the theory of personal constructs and not only criticized Freud's search for behavioral determinants, but even rejected the idea of studying motivation, because he believed that the phenomenon itself does not exist.

The possibility of casting doubt not just on a theory, but on its very conceptual framework, dramatically differentiates psychology from all other sciences. In this respect

---

[2] Statistical surveys of the number of dissertations on psychology and related fields have been conducted annually by the American Psychological Association since 1975. The figures cited in this book were taken from the American Psychological Association's 2007 survey, which is available on the APA's website http://research.apa.org/ des-07.html

psychology is similar to philosophy, from whose roots it basically sprung. But in contrast to philosophy, where the study of concepts is essentially a study of phenomena, in psychology phenomena are the source of concepts. Psychologists interpret human phenomena in different ways, at times denying them altogether and at times identifying new phenomena, but always trying to create their own conceptual framework to describe them.

We encounter a strange paradox: *In psychology, one and the same phenomenon may be interpreted in different ways and serve as the basis for the development of often contradictory theories. But the contradictions do not make it difficult for them to co-exist and they may even complement each other.* For example, the discrepancies between the existential and behaviorist approaches to human psychology are practically insurmountable, but these mutually exclusive schools of thought only enrich our ideas of humanity. In a letter to Carl Jung, Freud called Jung's theory "total nonsense" and renounced him as a student. But this did not keep Jung from not only making great discoveries in psychology, but from giving the concepts and terms introduced into psychology by Freud a totally different content. Today, for many of us, the concept of "libido," which Freud first used to describe human sexual energy, co-exists with the Jungian concept of the libido, which means human vital energy directed outward or inward. No one has any intention of rejecting these terms just because they are inconsistent, and conversely, we can see that contradictory concepts complement each other and help us gain a broader understanding of the energetic component of human behavior.

In general, any new trend in psychology tries to refute past notions of the nature of the psyche. As we already mentioned above, behaviorism was a unique reaction to Wundt's introspectionism, while Gestalt psychology was a reaction to the mechanism of behavioral psychology, and so forth. At the same time, the creation of a new school in psychology is by no means a rejection of the old. Now that modern theories of psychology are quite popular for applied use, most scientists would not even think of rejecting the classical ways of studying human psychology. If we compare the number of publications on topics of neurolinguistic programming, as the latest applied trend in modern psychology, with the number of publications on Jungian theory, the results will be approximately the same.[3]

---

[3] We have not conducted a comparative study of the number of publications on neurolinguistic programming and Jung's works, but our systematic observations of new publications allow us to say with a certain degree of confidence that the numbers do not differ significantly.

So what is actually going on? Is psychology developing or is this development just an illusion? Is it progressing, standing still, or regressing? How can we approach the description of human behavioral phenomena, if all existing theories are to a certain extent limited? Why is it impossible to develop an integral picture of the human psychological world, following the example of Newton's or Einstein's physics?

Answering all these questions is not all that easy, and not just because of their complexity, but because the psyche is an ideal world in a real dimension, which no one has yet succeeded in describing and understanding completely. The dilemma of the "ideal and real" is an eternal companion which psychology inherited from philosophy. Every scientist and researcher makes his own choice and expresses his own preferences. Realism is obviously quite attractive, but at the same time quickly leads to "exhaustion." It acts like a drug that you get habituated to quickly, but you need more and more of and finally overdose on; you are then forced to enter the world of idealistic notions and images. The idealization of reality is the "highest level" of realism, which by itself leads to the disintegration of reality itself. In other words, ignoring the psyche as an ideal phenomenon ultimately leads researchers to absolutize any actual existing human phenomenon. When it becomes an absolute, this phenomenon destroys itself, its role, and the reality in which it exists. It is no accident that sex and aggression as absolutes of Freudian theory, after going through all the phases of "realization," have now turned into idealized categories which are often used not just to destroy psychoanalytic theory itself, but for destruction of the human psyche.[4]

Thus, we may conclude that *psychology must not be characterized by an absolute, uniform, invariable criterion for assessing human mental activity and behavior.* But while we may accept this hypothesis as correct, we must be careful not to fall into the trap of relativism. Relativism is just as risky for scientists as absolutism. In fact, practically all psychological publications abound with phrases such as "roughly speaking," "relatively accurate," and "in a certain sense valid." I have had a hard time finding a psychological study where terms such as

---

[4] Today most psychologists, educators, and other scientists who work with children and adolescents are very concerned with the pernicious effects of television and the Internet's promotion of violence and sex. Studies show that the number of crimes committed by adolescents, which has grown geometrically in recent years, may be attributed to viewing violent and pornographic TV programs and websites. Studies by American scientists have confirmed that major changes in the personalities of adolescents, such as neuroses, complexes, habituation to violence, and the lack of moral barriers in behavior and communication, have been aggravated by their acquisition of unlimited information that contains scenes of violence, aggression, and sex.

these were completely excluded. Psychologists often use them deliberately to protect themselves from research results that could be challenged. This approach may in a sense protect the researcher from fierce criticism of his work, but it will not allow him to achieve truly important results. The limitations of this approach are obvious, because an idea that has no factual (real) basis, even if it is reflected in a variety of psychological concepts, is *psychologically relative.*[5]

We have already mentioned that the absolutization of a psychological phenomenon destroys it from within and, by emasculating it, becomes a source of personal and interpersonal tension. No less a danger is posed by psychological relativism, which, by masking a studied phenomenon so thoroughly, makes it impossible to analyze and study it as a unique phenomenon. In recent literature we encounter more and more researchers who have used contradictory approaches in an attempt to analyze and explain a particular psychological phenomenon. The incoherence of these attempts, the desire to come up with an "idea" or something "correct" and to please everyone, is a kind of calling card in psychology. It is true that we cannot say, for example, that Maslow's theory of personality is true and Freud's concept is nonsense, or that Guilford's theory of divergent thinking is correct and Witkin's cognitive styles are a fraud. But in psychology we also cannot allow eclectic, pseudo-integrative approaches to the interpretation of human life and behavior.

We are quite aware that most psychological theories, concepts, and approaches reflect genuine aspects of human psychology. Its *complexity and confusion, or as we called it above, its curse, lie in the fact that while a particular approach to interpreting human behavior may be chosen, any choice will be limited, incomplete, and not convincing enough to explain why a person acted one way and not another.* In his book *The Paradox of Choice*, the remarkable American sociologist and social psychologist Barry Schwartz, analyzing different aspects of human choice, also pointed out this paradox: "The fact that the possibility of choice is good," *he wrote*, "doesn't necessarily mean that more choice is even better" (Schwartz, 2004, p. 265). In his opinion, an abundant variety of goods and services greatly limits our freedom of choice. And the process also has an adverse effect on a person's general psychological condition by creating tension, emotional instability, irritation, and stress. The psychological paradox of choice

---

[5] *Psychological relativism* is the absolutization of the relativity and arbitrariness of psychological knowledge, phenomena, and processes. Without assuming the existence of any one source of creation, moral standards, values, and moral foundations, relativism in its extreme form leads to agnosticism.

indicates the ambiguity of all psychology, its self-sufficiency, and at the same time its incompleteness, its presence and absence, its manifestation where people pay no attention to it, and its "disappearance" when it forces us to pay attention to it. This is similar to Ludimar Hermann's illusion, which he discovered back in the 19th century, whose paradox lies in the appearance of bright gray spots between photographs when we view them, and the spots' rapid disappearance as soon as we shift our gaze from the photographs to the spots themselves (see Figure 1.1).[6]

The same thing occurs at the sociopolitical level, when any events and their sociopsychological roots become a very attractive topic of discussion. But when people start studying them in depth, economic, political, legal, cultural, and other factors come to the fore and "erase" the original psychological roots of social phenomena. The recent events in Georgia, which focused the attention of the entire world community on the Caucasus, provide a clear example of this. The war between Georgia and Russia that broke out in early August 2008 elicited a lively discussion of the personality traits of the leaders of Georgia and Russia; but psychology faded to the background when a geopolitical analysis of the situation came to the fore. And while in the initial phases of the conflict the psychological characteristics of the Georgian leaders were the most interesting subject for the world's top media outlets, subsequent events caused this interest to "disappear." The same happened with the leaders of Russia, when an analysis of their decisions gave way to a discussion of Russia's geopolitical and economic interests in the region.

---

[6] When you look at these photographs, you see gray spots on the white spaces between them. As soon as you focus your gaze on one of the gray spots, it immediately disappears and only reappears as soon as you shift your gaze back to the photographs. The appearance and disappearance of the spots may be attributed to the operation and interaction of central and peripheral vision. This visual illusion was named in honor of the 19th-century psychologist Ludimar Hermann, who first discovered and described it. (The person in the photos is irrelevant to the visual effect.) Psychobox. A box of psychological games (Card 36). UK, 2004.

Figure 1.1

Hermann's Gray Spots Illusion

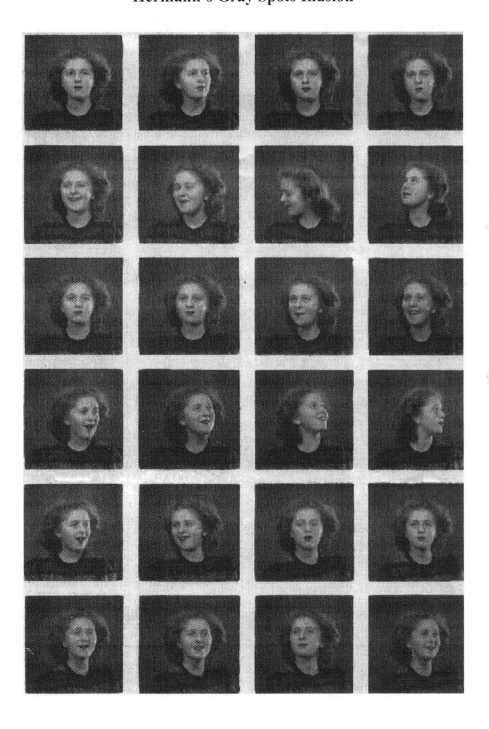

But the dominance of "non-psychological factors" does not last long. For example, if we take another look at the Georgia-Russia conflict, we can see that now that its active phase is over, the psychological traits of the participants in the conflict, the abilities of the leaders to manipulate the situation and "capture" the global media, etc., are coming back to the limelight. As we can see, the psychological parameters of a particular event still have primacy, even if other factors later come to the fore.

The relationship between psychology and sociopolitical processes is another remarkable feature of this science. Human psychology, while it is determined by social processes, itself determines the development of society, thus becoming a "determined determinant." May my readers forgive me for the tautology, but by embodying both cause and effect, psychology becomes a factor in the development of and at the same time a systematizing element of society.

Human psychology is a vast, mysterious world which we perceive, feel, and understand, but at the same time is infinitely remote from us. Albert Einstein, who changed our notions of reality, evidently did not suspect that the relativistic world he described was directly related to the human psyche and psychology. As a product of a three-dimensional world, the human brain constitutes the basis for the multi-dimensional psyche, and while it is limited in space and time, the human psyche does not just overcome space and time, but alters them; and while dependent on biochemical and physical processes, the human psyche rises to the "supraphysical" level, by escaping the bounds of the "material" and contacting the divine.

These and many other surprising aspects of the psyche once again clearly demonstrate all of the paradoxes and contradictoriness of human psychology, her "infathomability," mystery, and "virginity" even when she fully "gives herself" to the researcher by revealing her "intimate" aspects. No one will ever fully "master" her and no one has the right to speak to her condescendingly or treat her rudely. Such approaches lead their authors down the road of vulgar mechanism, which has nothing in common with real psychology.

Only people who are cautious in their judgments but are not afraid of paradoxes, contradictions, "curses," and taboos, people for whom there are no absolutes, but for whom there are also no "pure" ideas, people who are willing to explore their own inner worlds in order to understand the worlds of others, are worthy of the honor of touching the very delicate fabric of the psyche.

CHAPTER I

THE HISTORY OF THE STUDY OF

CREATIVITY IN PSYCHOLOGY

1. In Support of an Historical Analysis of the Problems of Creative Psychology

*W*e have accomplished a great deal, we have learned a great deal, but quite often what was discovered or said quite recently is a reflection of the distant past. Any field of knowledge in the modern world, no matter how highly developed it may be, refers back to its own history and seeks confirmation or refutation of a particular theory, hypothesis, or point of view. Why? Is it really impossible to avoid a study of the history of an issue? Apparently the answer will be negative, because it is impossible to call oneself a scientist and be uninformed of the history of one's subject. At the same time, we should always remember that the social mission of a genuine scientist is to generate new ideas, to be creative, and to create something new, something that was never known before. And as M. G. Yaroshevsky rightly put it, this imposes a "taboo on repetition" with respect to a scientist's behavior (Yaroshevsky, 1985, p. 4).

In order to discover the new, you have to know what your predecessors did. Of course we can imagine a situation where a particular scientist made a discovery without caring whether other people had ever done something similar. But the probability of such an event is negligible, because everyone, not just scientists, but ordinary people, makes discoveries – but only in the sense that these discoveries were unknown to them, although known to other people. Consequently the generation of new ideas and genuine creativity is only possible when a scientist is well informed of advances in his field of expertise, and not just in his own era, but in the historical past. This statement is consistent with the ideas of the outstanding American student of creativity Mihaly Csikszentmihalyi,[7] who, in his bestselling book *Creativity: The Flow and*

---

[7] *Mihaly Csikszentmihalyi* (b. 1934) is currently the best-known and most-cited researcher in the field of the psychology of creativity. A Hungarian born in Italy, he immigrated to the United States at the age of 22, where, after starting his studies of psychology, he managed to become one of the world's leading researchers in the field of

Psychology of Discoveries and Inventions, clearly demonstrated the error of notions that inventions and discoveries are the result of accidents, coincidences, insights, epiphanies, revelations, and so forth. In his view, all of these "unexpected sources" of creativity are preceded by not just the hard daily work of scholarly activity, but a profound knowledge of the subject in question (Csikszentmihalyi, 1996).

The Need for Wisdom

A scientist's quest to study the history of an issue must not be a matter of compulsion, a mandatory attribute of research, or a tribute to conformity. Such research is generally unoriginal and full of desiccated theories and concepts. The historical reflections of a scientist will only bear fruit when they are determined by the need for "wisdom." Figuratively speaking, the history of a subject acquires the image of a "wise man" in the mind of the scientist, a "wise man" the scientist can go to for advice, with great respect and admiration. The scientist can compare his ideas with the "wise man" and seek the solution to his puzzles. It is the "wise man" who serves as a kind of critic and reviewer of a scientist's research. And the need for this is no coincidence; there are several factors that explain why it is a necessary condition for gaining knowledge from the treasure troves of the history of science.

The first reason lies in the availability of the necessary knowledge and experience in the researcher's field of interest. A scientist must be well-versed in his field of study; this does not mean knowing everything, but the scientist's general knowledge of the subject must be quite substantial.

The second reason for the need for "wisdom" is the scientist's understanding of the impossibility of a complete, comprehensive, and exhaustive knowledge of a subject, and, conversely, a desire to study it as widely and deeply as possible. This is a singular ability to see the limitations of one's own intellectual capabilities and time constraints, on the one hand, and the infinity, albeit relative, of historical experience, on the other.

---

creativity. His concept of "flow," as an optimal state of inner motivation towards creativity, is rightly considered an outstanding contribution to the modern psychology of creative human activity.

And finally, ***the third reason*** is the desire to ask *anyone* for advice and assistance when it is otherwise unavailable. All of the aforementioned reasons are behind the need for "wisdom," which in turn is one of the necessary conditions for the historical reflections of a scientist.

Self-Improvement and the Study of History

The study of history helps us know ourselves better. A scientist's historical reflections are a kind of introspection, whereby the scientist tries to find the most concealed and thus most important and crucial moments in history, those which changed existing ideas. The American psychologist David Krantz maintains that the historian of science can play a kind of psychotherapeutic role for the modern scientist, if he motivates the scientist to recognize the tacit premises behind his own views, passions, and mindset. In our view, even greater "psychotherapeutic" possibilities will open up for a scientist if he starts studying his subject from a social and historical point of view, because any scientific work has its social and historical determinants as well as its personal attributes. Recognizing why a particular subject is of interest to a researcher and identifying the source of his motivation to move in a particular direction becomes much easier if you analyze not just your own inner world and the inner world of your peers, but the value orientations, mindsets, level of intellectual development, and outlook of your predecessors. From this vantage point, we can see a logical relationship between the level of understanding of the social and historical roots of the field, and a scientist's critical attitude towards himself, his scientific ideas, hypotheses, and achievements. In other words, the deeper a scientist delves into the secrets of history, the better he will be able to look at himself, both his mistakes, miscalculations, and illusions, and his correct judgments, conclusions, etc. A scientist will get to know himself, and self-knowledge is the beginning of self-improvement; thus the study of history means not just improving one's knowledge, but also improving one's self.

Historical Analysis and the Success of Research

Study of the history of a subject is also a necessary condition for successful research. This hypothesis can be indirectly confirmed by an analysis of the categories of "continuity and discreteness," which are studied in many fields of knowledge. Historians speak of the continuity of historical development, while experts in probability theory and mathematical statistics speak of continuous random variables and continuous functions; developmental psychologists speak of the continuity of human development, and so forth. But all of these branches of science analyze the concepts of *segment, interval, period,* or *finiteness* – i.e., discreteness together with and inseparable from the concept of continuity. A study of the continuity of any phenomenon or process could hardly ignore an analysis of the discreteness of its manifestations. It is well known that consideration of the unity of continuity/discreteness is a general strategy for analyzing the temporal and spatial characteristics of phenomena, processes, and events. To illustrate this, we will use an example of two sciences: probability theory and developmental psychology.

A continuous random variable considered in *probability theory* and *mathematical statistics* is in practice always quantized (i.e., divided into arbitrary components) and expressed as a discrete random variable (Sukhodolsky, 1972, p. 238). In other words, in order for a random variable with the properties of continuity not to change over the time in which it is being studied, it is divided into arbitrary components that reflect its position at each specific moment in time. In describing the characteristics of a random variable (such as a *mode*), mathematicians use at least three quantization intervals: the interval of the most interest to them, the interval preceding it, and the interval following it. This allows them to improve the probability of predicting the "behavior" of a random variable.

Developmental psychologists proceed in a similar manner. In this case, age, which also possesses the property of continuity, serves as the random variable. For research purposes, psychologists divide age into components, periods, and stages.[8] For example, Barbara Newman and Phillip Newman of Ohio State University use the following age periodization:

1. *prenatal* – from conception to birth;

2. infant – from birth to 2 years;

3. toddlerhood – from 2 to 3 years;

4. early school age – from 4 to 6 years;

---

[8] *Age periodization* is a basic topic of both the psychology of age and educational psychology. By analyzing the different age changes that take place in a person over the course of his life, scientists have concluded that most people not only have age periods in common, but have similar issues in certain periods of their lives. For example, what is most important to an infant is belief, in toddlerhood it is *will*, in early school age it is the *goal*, in middle school age it is *competition*, in adolescence and youth it is *affection*, in early adulthood it is *love*, in middle adulthood it is *care*, in late adulthood it is *wisdom*, and in old age it is *trust*. E. H. Erikson (1978). Reflection on Dr. Borg's life cycle (Erikson, 1963a).

5. middle school age – from 6 to 12 years;

6. early adolescence and youth – from 12 to 18 years;

7. late youth – from 18 to 22 years;

8. early adulthood – from 22 to 34 years;

9. middle adulthood – from 34 to 60 years;

10. late adulthood – from 60 to 75 years;

11. old age – 75 years to death (Newman & Newman, 1998, p. 37).

As in the case of probability theory and mathematical statistics, the characteristics of each age period cannot be described without studying the preceding period and predicting the future behavior and development of the child.

On the basis of the above, we can say that an analysis of the historical development of a particular subject conforms to the same patterns. The success of research can be ensured by demarcating the periods of development of a subject and studying at least three of these in detail: *the current status of the subject, its past, and its future development.* I would once again like to stress the importance of the constantly changing factor of time. Only if, in looking at the past, we try to find the most basic characteristics and features of human psychology in general and creative psychology in particular, and complement this data with current research results, will we have a better chance of predicting future human behavior.

Historical analysis helps us systematize our knowledge. After all, only systematized knowledge can serve as the basis for rising to the top. "Philosophizing without a system," wrote Hegel (1929, p. 31), "cannot be scientific in any way. Any content acquires validation only as part of a whole." Hegel's statement is applicable to all scientific knowledge, but we have cited it for the purpose of emphasizing its importance for history. History is systematic like no other science. Like no other science, it allows us to understand one phenomenon after making sense of another. This is its power, and not using it to understand and resolve the problems facing us is exactly like not using a lever when our arms by themselves are not strong enough.

The Creativity of History and the History of Creativity

The basic purpose of this research is to study the psychology of human creativity. In this context we can see a logical relationship between the psychology of creativity and the history of science. If we analyze the history of any field of human endeavor, we are mainly looking at any manifestation of unconventional thinking and original behavior and decision-making. We are most interested in discoveries and achievements as manifestations of creativity, outstanding individuals and leaders as creators, and so forth. But we cannot deny that any achievement, discovery, or innovation would be impossible without its social and historical, economic, political, and in certain cases even military determinants. In other words, what is important to us is not just an analysis of the individual and his role in the creative process – i.e., what this individual created and accomplished. An analysis of the conditions under which the individual lived and worked and the social system in which he lived, with its upheavals and achievements, wars, territorial divisions, the rise and fall of nations, cities, and so forth is also extremely important. Thus, in analyzing the history of science as a reflection of the history of human development, we are analyzing the history of the extraordinary, the unconventional, the innovative. If we take this line of thinking to its logical conclusion, we can be so bold as to say that the history of science is, on the one hand, the history of human creativity, and, on the other, the history of creative change. But if it is true that history has creative potential and if we study creative psychology without an historical analysis, this means that we are studying the effects without knowing the causes that gave rise to them.

2   The Subject of Human Creativity in the History of Indian, Chinese, and Classical Philosophy

There are amazing coincidences in the histories of peoples. One very striking coincidence was the simultaneous emergence of philosophical thought in the three greatest ancient civilizations: the Indian, Chinese, and Greek.

A comparison of these three philosophies is important not just as a comparative study of societies that developed at the same time and experienced basically similar social and economic processes, but as an analysis of a certain phase in the history of the development of human thought in the broadest sense of the word.

Ancient Indian Philosophy

Let us begin with an analysis of ancient Indian philosophy, which is most clearly reflected in the philosophical teaching of the Vedas (2000-1000 BC). What is a Veda? The Sanskrit word root *veda* can be interpreted in different ways, but ultimately it has just one meaning: *Veda* means knowledge, and "Teaching of the Vedas is the original meaning" (*Shri Ishopanishad*, 1991, p. 7). In examining the basic literature on the teaching of the Vedas, including the Puranas, Mahabharatas, the four Vedas (Rigveda, Samaveda, Atharvaveda, and Yajurveda), and the Upanishads, we will focus particular attention on the Upanishads. The Upanishads, which came after the other works and include 108 philosophical treatises, best reflect the topics that are of the greatest interest to us. But there is one treatise that reflects the essence of Vedic knowledge and is the most important Upanishad: the Bhagavad Gita. There are a huge number of commentaries on the Bhagavad Gita, each of which sheds light in one way or another on this great handiwork of mankind. We consider A. H. Bhaktivedanta's (1986) commentary the one that most accurately reflects the very essence of the Bhagavad Gita.

A distinctive feature of this work is the fact that while it discusses the Supreme Intelligence and the nature of the divine, it focuses most of its attention on the nature of man himself. This is no accident, because the study of human behavior and its requirements is mainly directed at the formation of his essence and the emergence of his identity. That is why this work focuses special attention on the "deficiencies" of the human soul:

- People invariably make mistakes.

- People are constantly under the influence of illusions.

- People are inclined to deceive others.

- People are limited by imperfect feelings.

The book also examines phases in the development of the spiritual life of the Shards, Visas, Kshatriyas, and Brahmins, the concept of *activity* (*karma*), the concept of *consciousness*, the concept of faith, and a lot more. We must point out that the philosophy of the Bhagavad Gita does not directly dwell on human creativity, because activity, especially creative activity, is typical of the Supreme Lord alone. "Material consciousness has two mental properties: The first is that a person thinks that he is creating and the second is that he thinks that he is enjoying himself. But in reality, the Supreme Lord creates and enjoys himself, while a living being, who is just an inseparable part of the Almighty Lord, does not create or enjoy himself, but merely cooperates. He is created and he is enjoyed" (Bhaktivedanta, 1986, p. 26). Notwithstanding, the Bhagavad Gita contains a very large number of personal, intellectual, and other characteristics that set the creative person apart. But why? From our vantage point, the answer lies in the assessment of the role of human creativity in the teaching of the Vedas. For example, while from today's vantage point the creation of what is new, what has never existed before, and what has social value is the highest social good, according to the Vedas "any human activity should be considered meaningless if a person does not ask the question of the nature of the Absolute" (Bhaktivedanta, 1986, p. 20). If we follow this logic, recognition of the Absolute in the philosophy of the Bhagavad Gita is the highest good, in today's terminology. In other words, recognition of the Absolute is creativity – not active creativity, but "passive" creativity. We put the word "passive" in quotation marks in order to imply that creativity in the philosophy of the Bhagavad Gita is self-creation, self-awareness, self-perfection, and attaching oneself to the highest knowledge: the Absolute.

So what, according to the teaching of the Vedas, are the characteristics of a person who can attach himself to the Highest Knowledge? By focusing a great deal of attention on a person's inner world, the teaching emphasizes three basic points:

- personal traits;
- cognitive processes;
- social environment.

In defining the personal qualities of a refined wise man, the Bhagavad Gita notes that "dispassion, cleansing one's being, developing one's spiritual life, charity, self-possession, sacrifice, studying the Vedas, asceticism, simplicity, non-violence, uprightness, freedom from anger, self-denial, calm, unwillingness to find fault in others, empathy for all living beings, freedom from greed, kindness, humility, resolve, energy, the willingness to forgive, strength of spirit, cleanliness, freedom from envy and from glory seeking ... are transcendent qualities inherent in righteous people imbued with the divine spirit" (Bhaktivedanta, 1986, p. 700). As a matter of fact, we have a profile of a human personality. We should point out that this profile performs two functions:

1. These traits allow a person to rise to the level of knowledge of the Absolute.

2. The combination of these qualities serves as a standard to which everyone who wants to know the truth should aspire.

Such a detailed analysis of personal traits makes it possible to resolve the issue of the interdependence of personality traits and cognitive characteristics. In other words, the presence of these personality traits is an essential condition and premise for the aspiration towards knowledge. In addition to qualities worthy of refined people, we also find in the Upanishads an analysis of personal traits that have the worst effects on personal self-realization. These include *excessive pride and arrogance, vanity, anger, rudeness, and ignorance.*

An analysis of human cognitive characteristics in the teaching of the Vedas is limited to the level of self-awareness. We should not understand this as the denial of awareness in general; the logic is that a human being, as a particle of the divine, is endowed with the qualities of the Lord, and by knowing himself and his essence, he can come closer to knowledge of the reality around him and of the Absolute. For example, the Bhagavad Gita (Bhaktivedanta, 1986) makes special mention of the following cognitive processes:

- the capacity for "inner vision" (p. 60), which means the capacity for self-analysis, exploring one's inner world, finding the determinants of one's behavior, and so forth;

- mental "equilibrium" (p. 149) as the ability to go through the stage of mental analysis of a problem and arrive at a good decision and conclusions that do not imply fear of the consequences;

- the idea that "A person's most important trait … is his ability to speak, because speech is the most important human quality" (p. 147);

- the ability to listen, which is the foundation of understanding (p. 247);

- the ability to accept the views of others – not just anybody, but only a person who commands real respect (p. 237);

- the integrity of the perception of reality and the ability to find the relationships between phenomena which at first glance seem opposite and contradictory (p. 272);

- the ability to see a topic from one point of origin to different outcomes and the ability to conceive of the same topic from different points of view (p. 284);

- the ability to rise above one's own mind (pp. 302-303), i.e., to see illusions – not illusions of perception, but rather false conclusions. This is the ability to make the right decisions when what seems to be a lie is actually the truth.

Isn't it amazing that people in 2000-1000 BC were able to describe actual characteristics of human creativity, and even with an accuracy that is characteristic of only the experimental psychology of creativity of our century?

In discussing the role of the *social environment* in the development of the personality and in the process of self-perfection, the teaching of the Vedas mainly emphasizes the nature of its effect on people. According to the philosophy of the Bhagavad Gita, a self-perfecting person must be able to rise above his social environment and be so purposeful that no outside influences will be able to make him stray from his chosen path. According to Vedic philosophy, the ability to resist environmental influences and to stay strong in victory and defeat are the basic traits of a "perfect man who is aware of the Absolute" (Bhaktivedanta, 1986, p. 242).

Thus human creativity in Indian philosophy was primarily considered an issue of **self-perfection**. The careful analysis of the entire gamut of human personal, cognitive, and sociopsychological characteristics served this purpose. Creativity was understood as the "creation" of a new self, a new "I," free of all material desires and capable of changing one's activity and ignoring the influence of the social environment. Assuming that a person's inner world is boundless, a person's creativity could only extend to this inner world, and that is where it was manifested in all its glory. The material world, with all of its shortcomings and temptations, only performs an accessory function which often complicates this process.

Chinese Philosophy

Another no less interesting conception of the nature of human creativity activity is characteristic of Chinese philosophy. Among the philosophical schools that emerged by the middle of the first millennium BC, the teachings of Laozi and Confucius enjoyed the greatest influence and popularity. But while Laozi required his followers to follow the path (*Dao*) of the world process, Confucius thought more about man himself and of customs and mores and their effect on man's behavior. That is why I am planning to dwell in greater detail on the Confucian analysis of creativity.

Confucius's thoughts are not presented systematically in a strict logical sequence; there are only records of his sayings on a certain subject or case in connection with a specific event. Nevertheless they contain a wealth of material that sheds light on the nature of human creative behavior. In this respect his sayings on the nature of cognition are very important to us. He stressed that the process of cognition is not just the acquisition, possession, assimilation, or understanding of something, but changing oneself and what happens around oneself. For example, Confucius wrote: "Anyone who loves the truth is better than someone who simply knows it, and anyone who finds his highest value in the truth is better than someone who simply loves it. Only a man who possesses the truth can understand the essence of the law of his life. Anyone who can understand the essence of his life can understand the essence of the law of the life of others. And after understanding the essence of the laws of his life and the life of others, he will be able to understand the essence of the laws of physical nature. Anyone who can understand the essence of the laws of nature will be able to act on the creative forces of the universe. And anyone who can act on the creative forces of the universe can join the forces of the universe" (Boulanger, 1991, p. 12).

As we can see, Confucianism made a very significant step forward in contrast to the teachings of the Vedas. It does not limit itself to self-awareness, because according to Confucius, self-analysis is just one step necessary for human creativity. We might say that the subject of human creativity, which Vedic philosophy views as self-perfection, moves in the direction of creativity affecting the reality around a person, but creative acts are possible only by means of profound and comprehensive self-analysis and self-actualization.

We should mention another relatively important aspect of the Confucian concept of creativity. For the first time, creative activity is associated with a person's emotional and moral world. Confucius believed that by loving oneself, by loving one's near and dear ones, and by loving the truth a person could "gather the forces of the universe" and create and thus qualitatively "change the very universe."

Considering that human mental traits are a gift from God and are innate, Confucius could not ignore the subject of human **talent**. It serves as one of the necessary conditions for creativity. In the ancient Confucian Analects the *Lun Yu*, the basic categories are the categories of the Path (*Dao*) and Talent (*De*). Scholars have calculated that the term "talent" is encountered in the *Lun Yu* 36 times (Delyusin, 1982, p. 13). For example, we can cite the following quotes: "In striving for the Path, take hold of Talent, rely on Humanity, and explore the arts" or "If a person has Talent without breadth and believes in the Path without conviction, he won't be where he is supposed to be." Talents are interpreted as a good gift from heaven: "Heaven gave birth to Talents in me." The opposites of Talents and the characteristics that impede them are:

- *administration* as a restriction on the freedom of thought, action, and choice;
- *rancor* as a biased view of an object or event, solely from a single negative point of view;
- *force* as the lack of desire to achieve a goal by using one's mental capabilities and exclusive reliance on physical capabilities;
- *outward attractiveness* as emphasizing one's "I," however not the inner genuine "I" but just the outer fleeting "I."

According to the *Lun Yu*, Talents can be "refined," "enhanced," "valued," "made permanent," and so forth, but at the same time they may be "wasted," "ruined," or "disorganized." Talents "may also decline." Thus, while asserting the divine nature of Talents, Confucianism placed special emphasis on the dependence of their manifestations on the person himself. Without a constant effort to improve and enhance the value and importance of what a person has received from God, these Talents can never show themselves. They will not serve their basic purpose as the preconditions for human creativity.

In contrast to the philosophy of Confucianism, which, as we showed above, has a large number of ideas concerning the nature of individual creativity, the philosophy of neo-Confucianism was inclined to construct a basic concept of the individual differences between people in general and creative and non-creative people in particular. In the language of the ancients, the neo-Confucianists tried to find the differences between people who are "wise," "perfect," "creative," and "marked by heavenly principles" on the one hand, and people who are "stupid," "backward," "dark," and "weak" on the other. For example, Zhu Xi (1130-1200), a representative of the Song school of philosophy, was the first to develop a complete and stylized concept of individual differences. We will dwell on the aspects of this concept that are of the greatest interest to us.

Using the concepts of **Li** and **Qi**, Zhu Xi classified people on the basis of their manifestations of these concepts. *Li* means all-encompassing order, universal law, and the principle of creation, while **Qi** means that which is physical, abundant, transient and variable, unequal in different respects, and which creates physical matter and is destructible; it is the mechanism and raw material for creation and creativity, and includes both good and evil. "Those who have pure and bright **Qi**," *Zhu Xi claimed,* "are perfection itself. These are wise and worthy people who get **Qi** in all of its fullness. Those who have clear and bright **Qi** are intelligent and upright. Those who have strong and substantial **Qi** are mild and tender. Those who have pure and lofty **Qi** are noble. Those who have abundant and lavish *Qi* are wealthy. Those who have lasting and extended **Qi** are long-lived. Those who have weak and dark **Qi** are stupid, backward, poor, and ignoble" (Boulanger, 1991, p. 140).

Thus Zhu Xi made an attempt (which was quite important for the history of the psychology of creativity) to distinguish between "wise" and "perfect" people – or in modern language, creative people – and all other people (intelligent, stupid, and so forth), on the basis of their special organization, manifestation, and quality of **Qi**, the physical element.

Eight hundred years before M. Wallach's and N. Kogan's experimental studies (1972, p. 234) proved that creative "abilities and intelligence are not strictly related, and that highly creative people can have a relatively low level of intelligence and vice versa," Zhu Xi distinguished the concepts of "intelligence" and "creativity" on the basis of their non-equivalence from the standpoint of **Qi**, the element that creates physical matter. A creative

28

individual is a manifestation of genuine **Qi** in its perfection, while an intellectual, an intelligent person, is a manifestation of bright and distinct **Qi** – *Qi* that exists within a certain framework.

Ancient Greek Philosophy

Ancient Greek philosophy focused no less attention on the subject of human creativity. What the two great Greeks Plato and Aristotle accomplished, the entire subsequent history of the psychology of creativity could not ignore. Their works set the general directions of research in the field for centuries to come (Aristotle, 1976, p. 103).

Plato touched on the phenomenon of human creativity in most of his works, but explored this subject in greatest depth in the *Phaedrus* dialogue. "The third kind is the madness of those who are possessed by the Muses; which taking hold of a delicate and virgin soul, and there inspiring frenzy, awakens lyrical and all other numbers; with these adorning the myriad actions of ancient heroes for the instruction of posterity. But he who, having no touch of the Muses' madness in his soul, comes to the door and thinks that he will get into the temple by the help of art – he, I say, and his poetry are not admitted; the sane man disappears and is nowhere when he enters into rivalry with the madman" (Plato, 1989, p. 24). This quote from the *Phaedrus* dialogue is extremely valuable material, which makes it possible to appreciate the full depth of Plato's speculations on human creativity. His analysis allows us to identify several extremely important factors for understanding the phenomenon of creativity.

- *First* of all, according to Plato, creativity is associated with "madness" and "frenzy," which on one hand constitute an entire combination of qualities, including personality, will, and character, and on the other hand are a certain set of mental processes and psychological states. In short, the creative process is the unity of mental and personal activity.

- *Secondly*, Plato asserted, and the subsequent history of the psychology of creativity confirmed (Luk, 1985; Yaroshevsky, 1985), that creativity will be more likely manifested in a sensitive person with fine feelings, who grasps the nuances of a subject and can see that which other people cannot see. In our view, this meaning was contained in his concept of a "delicate and virgin soul."

- *Thirdly*, according to Plato, the creative process is closely associated with human emotions: "It awakens the expression of Bacchic ecstasy."

- *Fourthly*, Plato emphasizes the social importance of human creativity, by means of which "the actions of ancient heroes are adorned" and "posterity is educated."

- *Fifthly*, Plato expresses the brilliant hypothesis of the decisive role of gifts and talents in the creative process: "But he who … comes to the door and thinks that he will get into the temple by the help of art alone – he, I say, and his poetry are not admitted" (Plato, 1989, p. 25).

- And finally, *sixthly,* Plato clearly specifies that sanity – i.e., the reliance of human activity on reality and rationality – cannot serve as the foundation of creativity. In his view, creativity bears the mark of frenzy, "the mark of the divine," and irrationality: "The sane man disappears and is nowhere when he enters into rivalry with the madman." Plato divides madness, as a manifestation of "divine power," into two specific kinds: "And of madness there were two kinds; one produced by human infirmity, the other a divine release of the soul from the yoke of custom and convention" (Plato, 1989, p. 50).

For the first time in the history of the psychology of creativity, Plato expressed the idea of recording and defining creativity as a deviation from the norm, as "abnormality." But this "abnormality" is not "abnormality" with a minus sign; it is not an infirmity, but "abnormality" with a plus sign in its social importance and value.

The social value of "divine madness" may be expressed in four forms: *inspired prophecy*, which was ascribed to the god Apollo; *devotion to the mysteries*, which was directly attributed to Dionysus; the *creative madness* associated with the Muses; and the *erotic madness* attributed to Aphrodite and Eros (Plato, 1989, p. 51). Divine madness "is given by the gods for our greatest happiness" and "should not be feared," *Plato wrote*, "and may it not torment us and let us not be confused by anyone who says that we should befriend persons of sound mind instead of persons in the grip of inspiration" (Plato, 1989, p. 51). In general, even at the level of interpersonal communications, Plato believes that creativity plays an enormous role.

Aristotle, as Plato's student for a long time, could not help but adopt much of his thinking, but had his own approach to the interpretation of the phenomena of human psychology. In discussing the need for sensory perception, he distinguished two types of cognition: cognition of that which exists – "is determined individually in a natural manner" – and cognition as the creation of something by human art, i.e., by means of skill. In other words, Aristotle spoke of creativity from the standpoint of its product. He elaborated this idea in greater detail in his tract *On the Soul* (Aristotle, 1976, p. 50): "Since in every class of things, as in nature as a whole, we find two factors involved, (1) a matter which is potentially all the particulars included in the class, (2) a cause which is productive in the sense that it makes them all (the latter standing to the former, as, e.g., an art to its material), these distinct elements must likewise be found within the soul. And in fact mind, as we have described, it is what it is by virtue of becoming all things, while there is another which is what it is by virtue of making all things.... [T]his alone is immortal and eternal" (Aristotle, 1976, p. 436).

According to Aristotle, philosophers did not always make this distinction properly, because they ignored the "experience and meaning of nature" that is common to all people. He thought that particular attention must be paid to the experience of scientific cognition, which has a very complex organization, because it, relying on the sensory "essence of things," makes it possible to explore the "element of the naturally existent." "Experience" includes not just the elements of sensory perception, but imagination and a powerful memory. In Aristotle's conception, all of these components constitute the capabilities of the soul, which in combination make it possible to reveal the general definitions of things and thus identify the genus/species order of natural being – that is, to make it possible to create. From the standpoint of revealing the components of the creative process (experience, sensory perception, imagination, powerful memory, etc.), Aristotle definitely ascended to the highest level of ancient philosophy and laid the foundations for the scientific psychology of creativity.

In analyzing the ideas, pronouncements, and works on human creativity in Indian, Chinese, and ancient philosophies, we have identified a large number of extremely valuable patterns which have not only not lost their relevance, but conversely, still help us to appropriately understand and study the phenomenon of creativity today. Of course our analysis does not even pretend to be complete and comprehensive – it is practically impossible and moreover unnecessary to do this in a single book. But, on one hand we have managed to identify what we consider important factors in human creativity that are often mistakenly left unconsidered, forgotten, and even in certain cases simply ignored, while we also note avenues of investigation of this phenomenon which subsequently proved to be dead ends.

An analysis of approaches to the interpretation of creativity has made it possible to identify the basic avenues of development of this topic in the history of ancient philosophy. For example, creativity in Indian philosophy was presented as a problem of self-perfection, the "creation" of a new self, free from everything material and terrestrial. The problem of self-actualization as a manifestation of creativity in Confucianism began to move in the direction of creative behavior that "qualitatively changes the universe itself" (Sheynman-Topishan, 1978, p. 198). Human creativity is no longer just self-perfection (although that is not ruled out), but has become creative behavior on the basis of self-perfection. According to Confucius, the social aspect of human creativity is an integral part of it. As for ancient Greek philosophy, this was the first time in history that philosophers studied human creativity as an independent subject of analysis. The analysis of creativity as a mental process crystallized and a transition occurred from the description of creativity to its scientific interpretation.

Each one of these trends reflected real aspects and integral components of human creativity:

- the impossibility of creativity without self-perfection;
- the impossibility of creativity without a corresponding type and manner of social behavior;
- the impossibility of creativity without knowledge of the patterns of its mental organization.

3. Human Creativity as One of the Basic Attributes of Medieval Arabic Philosophy

Arabic philosophy is the combination of the philosophical teachings that were developed in the Middle Ages by the Eastern thinkers who adopted the Moslem faith and wrote in Arabic (Frolov, 1980, p. 21). It turns out that "Arab philosophy" is an arbitrary concept: The medieval Arab culture that developed after the Arab conquests was not exclusively Arab; its creators also included Iranians, Azerbaijanis, Caucasian Persians, Jews, Tajiks, and Uzbeks – in short, all the peoples of the Arab Caliphate. But most important, in our view, is the fact that despite all the diversity of the teachings, Arabic philosophy was able to assimilate all the best that mankind had accumulated before it, to combine, creatively modify it, make its own contribution, and advance original philosophical concepts.

The perception of creativity in Arabic philosophy can serve as evidence of this. By adopting the ideas of self-perfection from Indian philosophy, creative behavior from Confucianism, and the study of creativity as an independent phenomenon from ancient Greek philosophy, it attained significant heights in the study of this human phenomenon. And while the influence of ancient Greek philosophy on the analysis of creativity was most vividly embodied in the teachings of Abu Ibn Sina (Avicenna), Ibn Rushd (Averroes), and Abulgasan Marzuban Ogly Bakhmaniar, it seems to us that Indian and Chinese philosophical ideas on creativity were most completely reflected in the philosophy of Sufism, which, starting in the ninth century, became extensively developed and widespread in the Near and Middle East.

As we begin our analysis of Arabic philosophy, I would like to note first of all that the influence of the three great civilizations on Arabic philosophy did not mean that it was bereft of its own social and historical basis of development. Hellenic culture, Iranian culture, and the culture of the peoples of the Trans-Caucasus and Central Asia, accumulated over many centuries vast spiritual and material treasures which became fertile soil for new ideas.

33

Eastern Peripateticism

The outstanding representative of Eastern peripateticism was **Abu Ibn Sina** (Avicenna, 980–1037). He, along with Galen, was the most important teacher of psychophysical functions. His scientific approach to intense emotions is considered completely innovative: The physician determines the cause of a spiritual or emotional trauma by pronouncing several significant words and observing the patient's reaction to them. The name of Ibn Sina is associated with the first experiments of direct relevance to emotional psychology. He was also a founder of the psychophysiology of age, and he studied changes in human psychology that accompany the physical development of the body.

We consider it totally unfair that psychologists have ignored his concept of creativity. Of course, under the influence of the Aristotelian school, he did not develop his own concept in studying this phenomenon, but his analysis of the process of imagination, one component of the creative process, made a significant contribution to the psychology of creativity. Of all Ibn Sina's treatises that make it possible to clarify his conception of human creativity, his allegorical tale *The Living Son of the Watchful* is the most valuable. It is a small tract, just three pages long, and contains an allegorical tale of a "powerful intelligence" (Ternovsky, 1969, p. 188). "With respect to your closest companion [the imagination], it brings you information where truth is mixed with lies," wrote Ibn Sina, "and you will strive to separate … truth from falsehood and accuracy from error; but despite all this you need it [the imagination]…" (Ternovsky, 1969, p. 51). This is how Ibn Sina described the phenomenal ability of the imagination to conceive of a result and a truth until the result or the truth is actually obtained. To Ibn Sina, the truth and the conception of the truth are completely different things. And quite often ideas of the truth and the final result are false, which cannot be said of the truth itself, because it always is what it is.

By asserting this apparently "negative" aspect of the imagination, Ibn Sina stressed that nevertheless, "you need it." The great philosopher was fully aware that the ability to anticipate and foresee events and the results of an action is a necessary condition for human activity and human creativity in particular. While calling the imagination prevaricating and capricious, and warning people not to trust it, he nevertheless claimed that it "is what brings you the truth and you should never refuse its help" (Ternovsky, 1969, p. 52). Ibn Sina considered the capacity for abstract thinking, or as he calls it, "the power of reason," to be a "reliable guarantee of this assistance from the imagination" in the process of "creating the arts and sciences."

This scholar attached a great deal of importance to the concept of the "evolution of power," which progresses from a lower "nutritive power" to a "sensory power," and from there to the "power of the imagination" and then to the "power of reason." Only by a combination of these powers, but to a greater extent by virtue of the amazing talent to control the imagination with the power of reason and to guide it in the necessary direction – a talent which, as Ibn Sina asserted, not everyone has – can a person "create art and science," i.e., find actual truth.

Another outstanding representative of Arab philosophy was **Abul Walid Ibn Rushd** (1126-1198). His teaching about man's highest cognitive power, namely reason, was also an outgrowth of Aristotle's theory of psychology. In examining the creative process as a process of finding the truth, he represented it as a "difficult ascent from what a person is given in his perceptions, to a place which can be reached only by reason; from a place closer to him to a place closer to reality" (Grigoryan, 1961, p. 174). According to Ibn Rushd, a seeker of the truth cannot bypass any of the steps of cognition and could "stumble on any of them."

As we can see, Ibn Rushd's and Ibn Sina's notions of creativity basically agree. For both of them, finding the truth, understanding the genus/species order of things, and activity directed towards this purpose constitute the essence of creativity.

The ideas of the remarkable Azerbaijani philosopher **Abulgasan Marzuban Ogly Bakhmaniar** are consonant with the views of these philosophers. As a student and philosophical heir of Ibu Sina and a popularizer of the ideas of Aristotle, he approached their development from the standpoint of logic. He believed that logic was a necessary condition for discerning vice and error, recognizing the truth, and creating something new (Geyushev, 1966, p. 34).

Sufism and Creativity

Perhaps no philosophical school has examined the subject of the psychology of creativity, creative acts, and creation as thoroughly or placed it at the head of the table more often than the philosophy of Sufism. This was made possible by the very essence of this philosophical teaching, which deified man and as a result attributed to him a fundamental divine capacity: the ability to create. "Sufism claimed that everyone can achieve personal contact with the divinity. Sufism saw the way to this destination in the form of non-materialism, self-denial, and a prolonged meditative and ascetic life under the supervision of a mentor, an 'elder.' The Sufis even considered it possible to achieve a complete fusion with the divinity. *Fana* (the Arabic for 'disappearance'), or total self-denial of one's personality and its 'dissolution' in the divine, was considered a necessary condition for this" (Pigulevskaya, Yakobovich et al., 1958, p. 157).

Despite the fact that one of the conditions for fusion with the divinity is the "dissolution" of the individual in the divine, Sufism, like most philosophical currents of the day (Hurufism, Naqshbandism, Nuqtawism, Beqtashism, etc.), had very clear views on the nature of human self-perfection. This process was divided into certain stages or steps. Most of the representatives of the four schools posited the existence of four steps: *Shariat, Tariqat, Maarifat,* and *Haghigat.* They believed that a person must begin his self-perfection by cultivating feelings of honor, dignity, justice, loyalty, benevolence, and so forth. After acting in accordance with *Shariat* at the beginning, he must then continue his development through *Tariqat.* "The path … of perfection in *Tariqat* lies in self-knowledge and self-perfection, which helps a man gradually and finally to separate himself from everything bad and achieve complete moral purity from vices – lying, hypocrisy, envy, greed, lechery, and hatred – he comes closer to God and becomes a bearer of the divine essence or one with God, the very God. At this stage of perfection, a man from the heights of his position recognizes the relativity of all moral standards and values and their unity and realizes that both good and evil come from God and that everything is in God" (Quluzade, 1983, p. 148). The highest step of self-perfection, *Haghigat,* is characterized by genuine human greatness and man's capacity to be all-powerful, Godlike, and God. "At this stage – in unity and unison with the One – lies true happiness. At this stage a man is divine and is God, to whose word and will everything **is** obedient; he is a demiurge of the universe and the world must be obedient to his reason and will" (Quluzade, 1983, p. 149).

A completely new statement of the subject of human perfection and creativity crystallized in Arabic philosophy from this description of the stages.

In Indian philosophy, where the subject was investigated with particular thoroughness, the recognition of the All-Powerful, the Absolute, the God Krishna was the highest limit towards which man must strive. Recognition of the Absolute, according to the teachings of the Vedas, implied an understanding of and closeness and obedience to God, but not becoming God. Thus human creativity was a means of reaching the Absolute. In other words, man, according to Indian philosophy, manifests creativity by perfecting himself, and, by manifesting creativity, perfects himself.

In contrast to these notions, Sufi philosophy posited not just recognition of the Absolute and "dissolution" in It, but becoming It. And the entire process of human self-perfection must be directed towards this goal. Thus self-perfection is an active process of getting close to the truth, but this becomes creative only after *Haghigat*, or true communion with God, has been achieved. In our view, it is especially important that Arabic philosophy was the first to represent man as a being that has a creative element and is capable of creating, building, re-creating, guiding, and organizing. As Prof. Ali Bayramov (1989, p. 35) rightly noted: "The consideration of oneself as a creator in Arabic philosophy was completely unknown in the Middle Ages or even in antiquity." After all, it is one thing when a man understands the truth but cannot create anything new; but it is completely different when a man, having understood the truth, starts to create, because he himself then acquires the quality of the Creator. This understanding of the nature of man was, in our opinion, one of the basic philosophical and psychological premises of the great creations of Nizami, Haghani, Maraghei, Shabustari, Nasimi, and Fizuli, and many other geniuses of Islamic philosophy in general and Azerbaijani philosophy in particular.

In analyzing the problem of creativity, we must also consider so-called mystical ecstasy, "in which a person ceases to feel his body and existence separately from the divine, which is **achieved** in a variety of ways, from silent meditation and self-perfection to loud cries and agitated body movements" (Bartold, 1966, p. 115). According to the Sufis, this kind of ecstasy makes it possible to achieve two great goals:

- Fusion with the divine;
- Becoming the divine and creating the new and Godlike.

The association of a creative act with mystical ecstasy and certain movements, postures, rhythms, and music is no coincidence. In the understanding of the Sufis, simple, spontaneous creativity is impossible. Even though quite often it may seem to be a spontaneous process, this does not mean that it has no predetermination. According to the Sufis, at least two conditions are required in order to create:

- by perfecting oneself, going from the stage of *Shariat to Tariqat*, then to *Maarifat*, and through them to *Haghigat*. In other words, recognizing the divine, becoming the divine, and acquiring a basic divine capacity – the capacity to create;

- using mystical ecstasy in order to incarnate this creative capacity in a product of creativity.

Thus the history of the psychology of creativity took another great step forward in its development. Arabic philosophy was the first to pose the question of not just the determination of a creative act, but of stimulating creativity. From this time onward, this topic began to excite the minds of scientists and researchers, who are still trying to resolve it to this day. It was demonstrated that it was both legitimate and possible to stimulate human creativity, and this was done, along with everything else, by the most common form of philosophy in Arabic culture, namely "philosophical poetry..., which used almost all of the poetic genres, starting with the Rubais and ending with theoretical tracts written in the form of Mesnevis" (Quluzade, 1989, p. 26). Nizami, Shabustari, Nasimi, Fizuli, and many other geniuses of the Islamic Renaissance were, to one degree or another, subject to the influence of the Sufi doctrine of the stimulation of creativity. And even if we deny the value of their philosophical and psychological views (which would be completely unacceptable to do), it is impossible to deny the value of their poetic creativity and the extremely powerful development of their literary genius.

In summation, I would like to point out again the most important concepts that were developed in Arabic philosophy:

- The further development of ideas of creativity as a mental process; an analysis of perceptions, imagination, and thinking as immediate components of the creative process;
- The idea of man as an active, not passive, being, who has a creative element and can create (like God) arts, sciences, and crafts, and change the world;
- The origination and development of the concept of the stimulation of human creativity.

4. *The Understanding of Human Creativity in the History of the Major Western Schools and Trends of Psychology*

Sigmund Freud's conception is still one of the best-known and most controversial ideas about human creativity. The study of myths and mythmaking, a basic knowledge of history, the study of the psychology of superstitions, totems, and taboos, the psychology of jokes, the analysis of certain literary works, the analysis of the personalities of great artists (Leonardo da Vinci), writers (Fyodor Dostoyevsky), poets (William Shakespeare), and politicians (Woodrow Wilson) from the standpoint of his theories of psychoanalysis, the unconscious, the "Oedipus complex," dreams, and so forth, allowed Freud to interpret the creative process and its stimuli and motives in a very unique, productive, and interesting way.

We are deliberately making a great historical leap from 12th-century Sufi philosophy to psychoanalysis, which emerged in the late 19th and early 20th centuries. **First** of all, medieval Europe, while it experienced the very powerful influence of all Eastern and ancient philosophy, was nevertheless bound by the dictates of religion,[9] so the search for psychological ideas there about human creativity (which of course did exist) would require a painstaking separate study. **Secondly**, psychoanalysis was one of the first schools of thought in recent history to treat creativity as a separate topic. And **thirdly**, we have found a striking similarity between certain basic principles of Sufism and psychoanalysis. Before we proceed to a direct analysis of Freud's conception of creativity, I would like to briefly dwell on these quite interesting similarities between the Sufi and Freudian interpretations of the psychological roots of human behavior.

---

[9] "Scholastics" (the Greek *scholasticos*) dominated the life of the mind of Europe in the Middle Ages. This special type of philosophy ("school philosophy"), which dominated from the 11th century to the 16th century, was characterized by a rational attempt that used logical techniques to justify Christian doctrine (http://www.gumer.info/bibliotek_Buks/Psihol/Jaroschev/03.php).

Sufism and Psychoanalysis

In Sufi philosophy, the identity of man and God is rooted in love: It is by glorifying and worshipping love that man comes closer to God. Sufism places special emphasis on love as man's driving force. In Sufism, love is mystical and Platonic. But Sufism was not a homogeneous current, and a vast number of schools and trends fundamentally distinguished one kind of love from another; quite often in certain schools, "love distracted and remote from the life of the flesh ultimately turned into its opposite" (Bertels, 1962, p. 258). Non-material, divine love was often represented in the most attractive fleshly and erotic images of beauty. This distinctive feature was most vividly manifested in the Azerbaijani, Iranian (Persian), and Central Asian varieties of Sufism, and in Asia Minor. As Prof. V. A. Drozdov (2005, p. 130) rightly noted, "Persian mystics often made no distinction between divine and human love, i.e., a person in love could consider his earthly beauty, i.e., the object of his love, to be God. The worship of a beautiful terrestrial being was an essential component of divine love and was in no way considered sacrilege." This trend was evident in the works of Haghani, Nizami, Fizuli, and other geniuses of Azerbaijani poetry, where the manifestations of love have not just a mystical side, but an earthly, carnal side. "There is no one in the world today who is not inspired by a book of passion," *Nizami stressed* in his evaluation of his poem "Hosrow and Shirin," in which love scenes have a significant emotional impact. The same applies to Fizuli. In almost all of his *qasidas*, he writes of a strong attraction to a being of incredible beauty, and of sufferings on the way to unity with the object of his love. On this subject, Prof. Ye. E. Bertels (1962, p. 511) wrote, "The poet is in the grip of a mad passion…. Love is his only goal in this world, a world which he deeply despises. He is faithful to his beautiful woman (or man) and bears all of the misfortunes that pile up on his head submissively; moreover, he is even prepared to meet them halfway and to take delight in these endless trials and tribulations."

Now let us turn to psychoanalysis as Sigmund Freud understood it. He noted: "We begin with the axiom that in the psychic life of man, from birth, a force is active which we call libido and define as the energy of the Eros" (Freud & Bullitt, 1967, p. 36). This is sexual energy – the motive force whose energy a person uses to establish his relationship with the real world around him, and with himself. We certainly understand that sexual energy according to Freud is the total opposite of the mystical love of the Sufis. There is no doubt that asceticism, the liberation from one's own "I," and communion with the divine "I," dissolution in the divine "I," and becoming the divine "I" are characteristics of Sufi mystical love, not carnal love. But as we have already mentioned, the mystification and worship of love and its transformation into the Absolute according to the Sufis came from a profound sensory self-analysis. Lofty love described in colors of human feelings acquired a natural, profoundly erotic hue, especially in Azerbaijan. The mysticism of love often gave way to sensuous, carnal love for another object.

In exactly the opposite way, Freud's carnal, erotic love, which carried a huge charge of sexual energy and which he elevated to an Absolute, began to acquire mystical traits. It is no coincidence that Freud so carefully studied the traditions, culture, and history of various peoples, in an attempt to find evidence of the correctness of his work. His brilliant student and heir Carl Jung was more successful in this regard. His mystification of love as universal vital energy came closest to the Sufi understanding of this phenomenon. The mysticism of Jungian psychoanalysis was essentially the first attempt to "Europeanize" Sufism, in particular its branch in Azerbaijan and Asia Minor.

Let us also turn to a basic category of psychoanalysis, the "Oedipus complex." According to Freud, all males use the same method of resolving the dilemma of the Oedipus complex, namely identification with the father. This is an all-powerful, all-knowing father who possesses all virtues and becomes, starting in childhood, as a result of introjection by the child, "the inner psychic force" called the superego. "In many cases this exaggeration is so excessive that the father with whom the little boy identifies himself, whose image becomes his superego, expands into the Almighty Father Himself: God. No matter what the ego may achieve in life, the superego is never satisfied with the achievement. It admonishes incessantly: You must make the impossible possible! You can accomplish the impossible! You are the Beloved Son of the Father! You yourself are the Father! You are God! ... Psychoanalysis can confirm that identification of the father with God is a normal if not a common occurrence in the psychic life. When a son identifies with his father and identifies his father with God and erects that father as his superego, he feels that he has God within him and that he himself will become God. Everything that he does must be right because God Himself is doing it" (Freud & Bullitt, 1967, pp. 41–42).

We find this with Freud, but if we rephrase these words in Sufi terminology, we get the Sufi's view of the process of becoming divine, described in the third section. We will make a brief attempt to demonstrate this. All Sufis must identify with a wise old man, a teacher and spiritual father under whose supervision one must perfect oneself. This almighty, omniscient "father" becomes part of a Sufi and gives him the inner strength for self-perfection. This image turns into God for the Sufi. For example, Nasimi (*The manuscript couch*, p. 58) wrote that Fazullah Naimi was his spiritual father and God at the same time, to whose level he always wanted to rise and whom he felt in himself. Hence, by identifying themselves with "fathers" and by identifying their fathers with God, the Sufis and Hurufis felt that God was inside them and that they themselves were God.

Of course, the relationship between psychoanalysis and the Sufi and Hurufi doctrines requires additional proof. Here we have merely stated a hypothesis, which nevertheless has substantial support, because Freud himself and his students, especially Jung, not only specifically studied the history of myths, religion, and culture, but, as they repeatedly said, they looked for confirmation of their own concepts there.[10]

Psychoanalysis and Creativity

As we turn to the concept of creativity in psychoanalysis, we must point out that it quite consciously absolutizes the sexual stimuli of creativity, not in and of themselves, but their interaction with real human life. The interaction of two forces and basic principles of human behavior (the principle of satisfaction and the principle of reality) becomes decisive in the creative process. For example, Freud, in his book *Basic Psychological Theories in Psychoanalysis,* (1923, p. 88), wrote that "Art achieves a unique reconciliation of these two principles. An artist is first and foremost a man who has turned away from reality, because he is incapable of reconciling himself with the denial of the satisfaction of his urges demanded of him: He opens up space for his egotistical and ambitious plans in the realm of fantasy. But from this world of fantasy he finds his way back to the world of reality, by transforming his fantasies into a new form of reality by virtue of his talents. Humanity perceives his new form of reality as a

---

[10] In almost every volume of Jung's complete works one can find an article devoted to Eastern philosophy and psychology. He also wrote a large number of commentaries on books about the East or translated original texts of Eastern philosophers, thinkers, scholars, and teachers. In 2008, Routledge Classics of London-New York published the most recent special collection of Jung's works, entitled *Psychology and the East*, which is a compilation of his most important works on Eastern philosophy, culture, traditions, history, religion, etc.

valuable image of reality. Thus, he becomes the hero, the king, the creator, and the beloved he wanted to become, while avoiding the need to make real change in the outside world."

In analyzing the role of sexual energy, psychoanalysis did not neglect the analysis of psychopathological symptoms in the stimulation of creativity. Freud analyzed situations capable of producing psychic trauma and situations which, in and of themselves, seemingly exclude a person from the circle of normal, generally accepted, and legitimate forms of relations and relationships. It is no accident that most of the great people whom Freud was interested in as a psychoanalyst (Hannibal, Leonardo da Vinci, Cromwell, Shakespeare, Napoleon, Dostoyevsky, Woodrow Wilson, et al.) could attract attention to themselves not just by their recognized status as "great," "talented," "brilliant," "strong-willed," and "hard-working" people, but also by the unusual facts of their biographies. Marked by "trauma," the subjects of Freudian analysis gave him the opportunity to deal with such states as "fear," "grief," "a reaction of spiritual pain," and "tragic premonition." To Freud, analysis of the lives and creations of artists basically lay in the realm of negative emotional states. These typical trends are clearly evident in his work *Leonardo da Vinci and a Memory of His Childhood* (Freud, 1912, p. 145). In studying the biography of the great artist, Freud focused on the fact that Leonardo never knew his mother and never saw her face. The artist lived a long life but never married and never had a family. On this basis, according to Freud, Leonardo's creativity was stimulated by grief for his mother. The women's portraits he created were a search for the artistic incarnation of his mother's imaginary face. Freud was inclined to believe that Leonardo's atypical life had a positive effect on his creativity, because the artist's "sexual instincts," which possessed an inexhaustible power, were directed not towards the satisfaction of purely physical desires, but were embodied in his creativity.

Freud used Dostoyevsky's personality to demonstrate the importance of psychopathological features and their role in stimulating creativity, believing that an inclination towards hysteria and impulsiveness put the writer in a state of heightened affectivity and neurosis, which stimulated his creative talents.

Freud believed that another source for the stimulation of an individual's creativity was rooted in the Oedipus complex. Above we observed that the Oedipus complex (the desire to get rid of the father and the desire to obey him completely) and the superego (identification with and dissolution in the father) constantly require making the impossible possible, accomplishing great feats, and creating (Freud & Bullitt, 1967, pp. 41–42). In other words, they act as a determinant of human creativity. He tested this approach in his analysis of the personality of Thomas Woodrow Wilson, the 28th President of the United States (Freud & Bullitt, 1967).

Thus, Freud's theory of creativity awarded the laurel of supremacy in stimulating creativity to sexual energy, the libido. But its manifestations were expressed in a variety of forms, the most important of which were:

- The impossibility of the direct natural satisfaction of sexual needs for one reason or the other and the embodiment of their power in creativity;

- The psychopathological symptoms of "grief," "fear," and "trauma," which by themselves stimulate creative talents;

- The pressure of the superego, which demands that the ego achieve more, accomplish something outstanding (surpass the father), and create.

Alfred Adler and the Individual Psychology of Creativity

Alfred Adler, one of the most brilliant representatives of the psychodynamic school of psychology, created a theory which can be rightly called an anthem to the human aspiration to perfection. It is no coincidence that the subject of personal creativity plays a special role in his views. According to his theory, man, as an integral being, is constantly striving for perfection, change, growth, and development.[11] A person's special creative force allows him to make his drives and aspirations a reality. The realization of his dreams, those which he considers the most valuable, becomes possible, according to Adler, by virtue of man's innate creative potential. He was one of the first psychologists in the 20th century to give man credit for his unique creative energy, as manifested in life's activities. Adler's advancement and reasoned proof of the presence of this power in man, his analysis of how it affects the development of the personality, and his study of the mechanisms for the actualization of personal potential make it possible for us to add Adler's theory to the list of outstanding conceptions of human creativity in psychology.

---

[11] *Alfred Adler* (1870-1937) was an outstanding psychologist and first President of the Vienna Psychoanalysis Society founded by Sigmund Freud. His views at the beginning of his career were consonant with the basic principles of Freudian psychoanalysis, but over time they gradually changed and led to a complete break with Freud. Focusing on the study of man as an integral whole "individual," he created a theory that he called "individual psychology." The basic principles of his theory were categories such as the inferiority complex, lifestyle, compensation, the striving for superiority, the "Creative Self," fictional finalism, etc.

His concept of the Creative Self had a special impact on the subsequent development of the psychology of creativity. According to most historians of psychology, this concept "is the main construct of Adlerian theory" (Hjelle & Ziegler, 2006, p. 177). In essence the Creative Self is an individualized system that makes it possible to change the direction of personal development "by interpreting a man's life experience and giving it different meanings" (Yaroslavsky, 2004). By possessing the freedom of action and determining our own destiny, Adler believed that we use creativity to compensate for our shortcomings and not only acquire meaning for our own lives, but become responsible for them. A feeling of inferiority, as the desire to overcome our shortcomings and stand out among other people, merely actualizes our creative talents (Yaroshevsky, 1985, p. 385). Our own destinies are in our hands, Adler claimed; we are the creators of our own world, and no one but us can make full use of what nature has given us and what has emerged in the process of our social development. These ideas were subsequently used not just by the adherents of Adler's individual psychology, but by the proponents of the humanist psychology that emerged in the late 1950s in the United States.

The Analytical Psychology of Carl Gustav Jung

Carl Jung was an outstanding 20th-century thinker whose ideas, hypotheses, research, books, and life had and continue to have a huge impact on the intellectual thought, cultural life, and social activity of modern man. It would be difficult to find a field of psychology that does not reflect Jung's ideas: the personality, individual differences, psychotherapy, psychological diagnostics, ethnic psychology, cultural psychology, and so forth. Creativity is no exception. And in contrast to Freud and Adler, to whom creativity was critical, but only part of their overall conceptions, to Jung creativity was everything! This especially applies to the comparison between him and Freud, whose pansexualism Jung rejected. Jung represented the libido as the sum total of creative vital energy which encompasses man's entire being. "Here lies the divide between Freud and Jung; pansexualism is rejected in Jung's analytical psychology – the libido is not sexuality, but spiritual energy in general, in all of its diverse manifestations and metamorphoses"[12] (Jung, 1994, p. 12). In this spiritual energy, a special, key, and decisive role is assigned to fantasy, imagination, myth, and symbolic images. "I believe that fantasy," wrote Jung, "is the most vivid expression of the specific activity of our psyche … it is the mother of all possibilities … and creative fantasy plays a dominant role in any creativity. Everything great started out as a fantasy…. Fantasy is a direct expression of psychic energy (Jung, 1994, p. 14). It becomes clear why Jung devoted so much of his research to symbols, myths, mystical phenomena, and so forth. They, it seemed to him, directly reflect the creative vital energy of man and his libido. Their study will make it possible to understand the intricacies of man's mental life and thus his creativity.

In this monograph I will have many occasions to return to Jung's creativity. The collective unconscious discovered in our psyches by the Swiss psychologist and psychiatrist, the different archetypes described in his works, and his studies of psychic transcendence as a specific mechanism for uniting different and conflicting mental tendencies into a single whole are extensively used in this work. And the author does not just accept and use the ideas of the great Jung, but is trying to develop them, because the manner and style of statement of the problems that Jung studied embody the potential for their subsequent development.

Gestalt Psychology and Creativity

Gestalt psychology is another major trend in psychology that broaches topics of human creativity. Max Wertheimer, Wolfgang Köhler, and Kurt Koffka, who constituted the nucleus of this scientific school, studied a variety of topics, but proceeded from a consistent theoretical concept of integrity. Among the geniuses of Gestalt psychology, Max Wertheimer was the most prolific student of human creativity. He systematically presented his views and those of the Gestalt psychologists in his summarizing and at the same time programmatic book *Productive Thinking*, published in New York in 1945. In analyzing the results of his own experiments and the observations and the discoveries of Galileo and Einstein, Wertheimer stressed that in the process of thinking, man looks at and becomes aware of the specific features and requirements of a problematic situation, which he uses to change the situation for the better. "This allows a

---

[12] This quote is taken from the foreword to Jung's book *The Libido, Its Metamorphoses and Symbols,* published in St. Petersburg in 1994. The author of the foreword, Emil Karlovich Medtner, was a close associate, friend, disciple, and publisher of Jung's works.

person to regroup, identify structural centers, and make sense of the role and importance of mental operations" (Wertheimer, 1945, p. 191).

His ideas that the reorganization of material and rearrangement of a system of knowledge constitute a necessary condition for achieving a necessary result are of value, not just because they reveal genuine aspects of mental work, but also because these mechanisms are directly involved in human creativity. According to the Gestalt psychologists, the movement from a situation distinguished by structural tension to a situation of structural harmony is a law of the perceptual field. And creativity, in the meaning that the Gestalt psychologists gave it, is a special case of the laws of the perceptual field. Thus creativity is a process of self-regulation. This idea proved to be quite fruitful. Hence the understanding of creativity as the achievement of harmony, and creativity as a process of regulating the relationship between man and his environment (a "field" in the terminology of Gestalt psychology) and between man and himself (the inner field) made it possible to remove the psychological barrier of "elitism" from creativity and thus make it a vitally necessary and inherent tool of personal development for everyone.

The Würzburg School of Psychology

Another trend that would be wrong to ignore in analyzing this subject was extremely important from the standpoint of the history of the psychology of creativity. What I have in mind is the Würzburg school of psychology (Külpe, Ach, Bühler, Messer, and Watt), which, while not placing special emphasis on the study of human creativity, nevertheless, by its very nature, had a significant impact on how the subject was examined in several other currents of psychology. By focusing its research not on the effects of the behavior of a test subject, but on the actions he took, the members of this school advanced explanatory concepts of mental activity such as "attitudes," "objectives," and "determinative tendencies." The predominant concept was the "objective," which was conceived as a guiding, organizing tendency which subordinated to itself the movement of associative goals. In turn the objective gave rise to attitudes in a test subject that were understood as an inner readiness that controlled the process of choice.

The new variables introduced by the Würzburg school played a huge role in subsequent studies of creative activity. By laying the foundation for the study of the concepts it put forth (objectives, attitudes, determinative tendencies), it created the basis for a completely novel approach to the analysis of creative processes. The Würzburg school's approach was developed by other researchers who did not belong to the school. Quite a bit of time would pass before scientists established close correlations between the nature of objectives and human creativity, between attitudes and creativity, but the preconditions for finding these correlations were discovered by the Würzburg school.

Abraham Maslow's Humanist Psychology

Humanist psychology, whose most outstanding representative was Abraham Maslow, is a relatively new trend, which considers the priorities to be the development and self-perfection of the individual and the discovery of his creative potential. By adopting the idea of man's positive nature as their foundation, the researchers made a huge contribution to the study of psychological categories such as happiness, success, self-realization, self-actualization, and creativity. And the understanding of creativity as a means of self-actualization of the personality, and self-actualization as a creative process, allowed the humanists to discover a new level for the study of individual creativity. Maslow was the key figure who set the tone for this kind of research.

In most of his works, Maslow studied creativity in tandem with the process of self-actualization. In his last book, *The Farther Reaches of Human Nature* (1975, p. 423), he hypothesized, "My feeling is that the concept of creativeness and the concept of the healthy, self-actualizing, fully human person are coming closer and closer together and may perhaps turn out to be the same thing."

From this point of view, he insisted on separating primary and secondary manifestations of creativity. "The primary creativeness," Maslow (1975, p. 59) wrote, "or the inspirational phase must be separated from the working out and development of the inspiration. This is because the latter phase stresses not only creativeness, but also relies very much on just plain hard work, on the discipline of the artist who may spend half a lifetime learning his tools, his skills, and his materials, until he becomes finally ready for a full expression of what he sees." True creativity, which embodies both inspiration and hard persistent work to transform the original idea into a product of creativity, is manifested in certain conditions, of which Maslow particularly emphasized the following:

- the ability to "become lost in the present" and "become timeless, selfless, outside of space, of society, of history";

- the ability to give up the past, to avoid the pressure of past experience and existing approaches and views;

- the ability to give up the future, i.e., to avoid using the present to prepare for the future; the ability to "forget" the future, not be apprehensive about it, and live in the present;

- innocence as a quality that distinguishes highly creative people. This category has no prior expectations and its vocabulary does not know the words "should," "ought," and so forth. These people are willing to perceive the new without surprise, shock, indignation, or denial.

- the narrowing of consciousness in the sense of reducing the burden of conscious experience, and the ability to be more natural and not overly dependent on others;

- "loss" of the ego: self-forgetfulness, the loss of self-consciousness. In explaining this aspect of the creative process, Maslow (1975, p. 65) wrote, "This means dropping masks, dropping our efforts to influence, to impress, to please, to be lovable, to win applause. It could be said so: If we have no audience to play to, we cease to be actors."

- the ability to maintain an optimal level of influence of consciousness (especially self-consciousness) as a factor that carries doubts, conflicts, and fears that generally adversely affect creativeness;

- the removal or reduction of the defense and inhibiting mechanisms that block human creativity;

- strength and courage, understood as the ability to think independently, self-sufficiency, strength of character, etc.;

- acceptance: positive behavioral attitudes and a reduction in the general critical attitude towards events and phenomena inside and outside oneself;

- trust in oneself and the world that allows one to be more passionate and persistent in the process of creativity;

- a Daoist*13* receptivity to the world, which implies the priority of categories such as "let it be" and "let it happen" in the process of life;

- integration of the B-cognizer,*14* which implies tendencies (which usually come with experience) toward the behavior of the person as an integrated and whole personality;

- the ability to immerse oneself in primary processes as the ability to sense one's unconsciousness, preconsciousness, the mystical, archaic, etc.;

- an aesthetic perception of the world and the ability to obtain satisfaction, to do what is pleasant, to be concerned, etc.;

- fullest spontaneity as the possibility of the free, voluntary exhibition of all our talents, without limitation in the process of creativity;

- fullest expressiveness as pride, naturalness, honesty, lack of guile, uniqueness, etc.;

- fusion of the person with the world around him, the ability to feel and be part of it.

Maslow's concept of creativity, as we can see from the characteristics cited above, is integral and does not imply the differentiation of creative manifestations. In his view, a person's path in life, which he takes in the desire to actualize himself, is accompanied by creativity and, figuratively speaking, more precisely constitutes a process of self-creation. In the history of psychology it has often been the case that particular researchers and even schools which did not set themselves the task of studying a particular topic did much more for its understanding and development than those who formally declared their allegiance to a specific subject. That was the case in humanist psychology, in which Maslow's "positive person" was transformed into a creative, self-actualizing individual, the study of whom made it possible to make new discoveries in the field of human creativity.

In emphasizing Freudianism, Adler's theory, Jung's concept, Gestalt psychology, the Würzburg school, and Maslow's theory, we have consciously attempted to avoid straying into other theories of human creativity. Our purpose is to show not so much the trends in the

---

[13] *Daoism* is the traditional Chinese teaching of the achievement of the *Dao*—the path of things, which developed by the middle of the first millennium BC. Its founder, Laozi, called on people to follow nature and live a natural life. In the section on Chinese philosophy, we touched on the philosophy of Laozi, while obviously emphasizing Confucianism.

[14] *B-cognizer* (from B-Being: being, life) is a concept introduced by Maslow to interpret the behavior of people who have reached the peak of self-perfection, which is accompanied by joy, enlightenment, and depth of understanding.

psychology of creativity in foreign psychology, but to reflect the atmosphere in which the subject of human creativity developed in the early and mid 20th century.

5. *The Issues of Individual Creativity in the History of*

Russian Psychology

*T*he early 20th century in Russia was characterized by conflicting and divergent views of the nature of the psyche. Russian psychology naturally experienced the influence of European psychology and often followed the ideas of leading Western psychologists in interpreting particular psychological topics. But "the development of Russian psychology was significantly different from the development of psychological thought in the West" (Petrovsky, 1967, p. 111). The basic and most important difference in Russian psychology was its materialistic elements, which "were rooted in the psychological views of Lomonosov, Radishchev, Herzen, Belinsky, Dobrolyubov, and Chernyshevsky, were continued in the works of Sechenov, and determined the main direction of development of this science in both the 19th and 20th centuries" (Petrovsky, 1967, p. 11).

In this era, "the activity of the conscious and the personality became one of the central issues whose solution determined … the understanding of the structure of the psyche in relation to the object of reflection and the position of the individual in relation to society" (Petrovsky, 1966, p. 170).

Vladimir Bekhterev, the founder and creator of reflexology in psychology, assigned a great deal of importance to the subject of individual activity and creativity, interpreting this topic in an original way. Considering the psyche as a product of the intensity of energy or nervous current in particular regions of the cerebral cortex, while other regions are inhibited, he claimed (Bekhterev, 1926, p. 65) that "creativity is a complex act of a progressive nature, like any search for the truth that requires an uncommon expenditure of effort and time." Reflexology considers this act as a "complex chain of associative or higher reflexes designed to accomplish something new and to excite an upsurge of energy by means of analysis (the differentiation of stimuli) or synthesis (selective generalization), under the positive impact of the act itself and the results in the mimic-somatic sphere" (Bekhterev, 1926, p. 71). If creativity is a "complex chain of the associative forces of the higher reflexes," then what is the stimulant of these reflexes? Bekhterev answered this question in the following way: "[T]he direct *stimulant of creativity* [emphasis added], in my understanding, is always a particular problem or goal, which, as the main stimulant, may occur as a quite definite culmination of any kind of work, as it happens in a systematic study of a particular subject. In this case a problem is a working hypothesis, subsequently tested by analysis and synthesis. Otherwise associative activity causes a person to suddenly dwell on a thought as an externally unidentified reflex that becomes the basis of a problem. The problem is the stimulant, and creativity is a reaction to it, and the product of creativity is a result of the culmination of this reaction, which is a combination of reflexes" (Bekhterev, 1926, p. 77).

V. M. Bekhterev could not limit himself to associative-reflexive activity stimulated by a problem in explaining human creativity and could not ignore the social determination of this process. "Any creativity," he wrote, "is an act intended for a social environment, and the key *impulses towards creativity* [emphasis added], given all we have inherited from our ancestors, i.e., the biological preconditions for it, are taken from the physical-cosmic and social environment of a creator of science, technology, or art. That is why the direction of creative activity proceeds from the conditions of the time in which the creator lives and the conditions of his upbringing and social environment, which guide the creator's associative-reflexive activity in one direction instead of another" (Bekhterev, 1926, p. 78). Bekhterev's perspective on creativity made it possible to analyze it and reveal its complexity, integral nature, importance, and problematic nature, but most importantly allowed the researcher to grasp the social, or more precisely sociopsychological, determination of the process.

A different, no less interesting, point of view on the nature of individual creativity and its sources and stimuli was presented by A. F. Lazursky. By comparing the "process of mental growth" in different people, he concluded that the "highest, maximum boundaries of this growth, … which determine what we call a person's mental level, differ markedly among different people" (Lazursky, 1924, p. 57). This variability depends on an individual's "degree of talent," i.e., the richness and intensity of his natural abilities, and on the effects of external conditions (mainly upbringing and education), which either promote or, conversely, impede the development of natural talents (Lazursky, 1924, p. 60).

Lazursky used these data to develop a system for classifying personalities based on the principles of "open adaptation to the environment," where the extent of a person's overall activity is commensurate with the amount of neuropsychic energy. By distinguishing the endopsyche (basic neuropsychic organization) and exopsyche (the psyche in its relationship to the environment), Lazursky identified three human mental levels:

The first level, the lowest, which is characterized by poverty and primitiveness of the psyche, is expressed "on the one hand, in the monotony and barrenness ... of its manifestations (both external and internal) and, on the other hand, in the dominance of lower, more basic, mental processes over higher, more complex, processes" (Lazursky, 1924, p. 121).

The second level is characterized by greater development of the higher mental functions than the lowest level. "Here we no longer have a passive and helpless submission to external conditions.... While dealing with and adapting to environmental conditions, a person nevertheless guides the adaptation process so that it is compatible with his own goals and desires" (Lazursky, 1924, p. 30).

The most interesting level for us is the *third level* and highest mental level. According to Lazursky (1924, p. 137), at this level the supply of psychic energy reaches a peak, which entails an extraordinary richness of personality and the diversity of its manifestations. In his opinion, persons on the highest mental level are, with respect to their environment, not only adapted but adapting, and usually endeavor to remake the reality around them in accordance with their own internal desires, needs, and ideals; in other words, they always exhibit to a greater or lesser extent the **"capacity for creativity"** (emphasis added) and the ability to blaze new trails along which everyone else follows them.

While considering creativity a distinctive feature of individuals of the third-highest mental level, Lazursky claimed that it is not reducible to any particular mental function. In these individuals, creativity itself is just one variety of the mutual adaptation that takes place between talent and its stimulant, with talent playing the dominant role. According to Lazursky, at the highest mental level, man does not adapt to his environment and instead adapts it to his own needs and requirements. The greater the effort to adapt the environment, the more intense the act of creativity.

In Lazursky's conception, we can identify very valuable factors for understanding creativity. *First*, there is the hypothesis of the mutual influence and mutual adaptation of stimulated talents and external conditions (upbringing in a certain social milieu, the level and type of education, and so forth), which either promote or inhibit the manifestation of personal creativity. *Second* is the hypothesis of the relationship between the intensity of and engagement in activity, and the likelihood of the manifestation of creativity in a specific individual (the more a person is engaged in an activity, the greater the probability of the manifestation of creativity). *Third*, there is the hypothesis that a person with high creative potential does not adapt to his environment and instead adapts the environment to his own requirements and needs.

A no less original interpretation of personal creativity can be found in the theory of S. O. Gruzemberg. This scientist did not just do his own personal research, but collected and analyzed discourses, ideas, and works on the creative process and its incentives and the motives of the outstanding personages of his time, and concluded that "by its nature, an artist's creative process is the same as an act of aesthetic perception on the part of a reader, listener, or spectator" (Gruzemberg, 1924, p. 93). According to Gruzemberg, the perception of an artist's ideas, images, and emotions is a dynamic process of reflexive reproduction of the artist's creative emotion in an individual's psyche. In this sense, aesthetic perception can be defined as a true act of creative processing and of evoking the artist's emotions in the psyche of a reader, listener, or spectator, as a desired mental innovation. "A reader, listener, or spectator not only experiences aesthetic perception, but at the same time 're-creates' images of the artist's fantasies," *wrote Gruzemberg*. But the manifestation of creativity by an individual in perceiving highly artistic works still does not answer the question of what leads to the creativity of the artists themselves. What "impels" them to be creative? The perception of the works alone or something else?

In an attempt to answer these questions, Gruzemberg tried to find a psychological impulse towards creativity in impressions of the persons, pictures, and events of early childhood that took root in the artist's consciousness and emerged in maturity, cross-breeding with the observations of later years and forming "generic images" or "generalized schemes of summary observations" in the artist's memory.

In Gruzemberg's view, they give an affective coloration to a particular artistic work. The identification of the "generic images" themselves may be attributed to the so-called "affective dominant," which shows the artist where to go and what to do to "re-create images in his consciousness." The introduction of the concept of the "affective dominant" in creativity, as the notion of a special locus of stimulation that suppresses all others and uses the power of the latter for its own purposes, was formulated by Gruzemberg under the influence of Alexei Ukhtomsky's research.

Our analysis allows us to point out two significant aspects of the analysis of the topic of creativity in Russian psychology:

- Treating the social environment as a key source of creativity; understanding creativity as a socially significant act (Bekhterev) and an act that alters the environment (Lazursky);

- The correlation of creative processes and physiological reflexes, the dominant, etc., with processes in the cerebrum.

These features had a significant impact on all of the subsequent development of the topic of creativity in Russian and then Soviet psychology, by confining it to a certain framework, but at the same time giving basic research in the field a firm foundation.

> ## 6. *Soviet Psychology and Studies of the Psychology of Creativity in Azerbaijan*

Marxism-Leninism and Psychology

Now that the Soviet Union is history, a sufficiently objective view of our past makes it plain just how politicized the science of that time was. The lack of any opportunity to conduct truly politically independent research in the field of psychology basically led to its degradation. Psychology was so ideological that calling it a science, in the true meaning of the word, was simply false. It would be more accurate to say that psychology met the requirements of a pseudoscience that played the role of pretty "humanized" wrapping paper for the ideology of Marxism-Leninism. As Prof. V. V. Nikandrov rightly noted, "There was a ridiculous situation when former Soviet science (and the associated science of the former socialist countries) was artificially set in opposition to backward 'bourgeois' science. This self-isolation had an extremely detrimental impact on world science as a whole" (Nikandrov, 2005, p. 739). In reality, the opposition of ideologies led to the opposition of ideologized Soviet psychological research to Western research, especially that in the United States.

Freudianism and Marxism

By the way, it did not start out all that badly. At the time of its emergence, Soviet psychology started to look for suitable theories and viewpoints in the West. For example, in the 1920s practically all of Sigmund Freud's most important works were translated into Russian. Bolshevik ideologists believed that Freud's scientific revolution, which absolutized the importance and role of human needs (in this case sexual needs) and which "realized" man's irrational psychic tendencies, most accurately reflected materialist ideology, which expressed the attitudes of the working class as the driving force of progress. The names of Karl Marx and

Sigmund Freud were often spoken in the same breath, and research to identify "common" methodological principles of their theories began. The world revolution in human consciousness that Freud hypothesized became just as important for the ideologists of the new regime as the world proletarian revolution. We know that in several speeches and articles, even Leon Trotsky said that Freudianism was totally acceptable to Marxism. A. B. Zalkind (1924), one of the best-known ideologists of Soviet Russia in the 1920s, wrote about this. But it did not take long for people to realize that Marxism, or more precisely, Leninism, had no intention of sharing the honored pedestal of the "scientific" foundation of human behavior in the new society with anyone. In 1925 the very same Zalkind publicly renounced his ideas as false, just a year after his articles on the relationship between Freudianism and Marxism were published. Lenin's interpretation of Marxism, with his own philosophical ideas concerning the nature of man and the essence of worldly events, proved to be quite adequate for the goals that the creators of the new world order set for themselves. Step by step, decision by decision, and resolution by resolution they isolated the "new" Soviet science from the "pernicious" influence of everything foreign, "bourgeois," and anti-Soviet.

The Image of the Soviet Scientist

But doing this was not as easy as it seemed, because scientific relationships, the continuity of scientific ideas, and the mutual influence of the scientists and researchers of the new Russia and the outside world proved to be much stronger than ordinary human relations. Every means possible was used to accomplish the urgent "national" objective, ranging from the physical elimination of inconvenient, incorrigible scientists, to the creation of "special" conditions for world-renowned scientists and researchers. While shooting and destroying thousands of inconvenient intellectuals, scientists, and researchers, the government also created the necessary conditions for the emergence of new, conformist scientists who bowed to its "standards" and ideas. The image of the Soviet scientist who was free of "bourgeois" heresy, was armed with the ideas of Marxism-Leninism, met "high moral standards" of behavior, and was ready to sacrifice himself for the sake of the "high" ideals of science and progress was carefully crafted, drawn, and propagandized by all kinds of media. There was less and less room for real science.

Psychology in the National Republics

Under these conditions, the development of genuine science and education free of ideological dogmas became increasingly more difficult in the national republics than it was in the Soviet heartland. The uprooting of the indigenous national intelligentsia was carried out by barbaric, fiendish methods which almost led to the total destruction of the best scientists.[15] Scientists from Russia proper or ideologically sound locals were appointed and dispatched to take their place. There was never any thought of mentioning the possibility of free creativity. Azerbaijan was no exception to the rule and was subjected to a very thorough purge and "disinfection" to rid it of everything anti-Soviet, traditionally ethnic, Turkic, and Moslem. For many years these very terms were prohibited and subject to condemnation, and were thus considered anti-Soviet. In a split second, the historical experience of an entire people became prohibited and was "reinterpreted" from the standpoint of the new realities. Those historical events, personages, and currents that could be squeezed into the new ideological framework or used for propaganda purposes acquired the right to exist. Everything else was mercilessly destroyed and banned. It is strange but true: Nizami's works, which in the new interpretation acquired the veneer of Communist ideology, were made available to the mass reader, while the philosophy of Sufism, which was one of the inspirations for his brilliant works, was basically banned. The same applied to the works of Haghani, Fizuli, Nasimi, and many other geniuses of Azerbaijani poetry. Another example is related to the history of the national liberation movement in Azerbaijan, in which Babek's fight against the Arab invasion was mentioned, while the heroic resistance of Ganja, led by Javad khan against the Russian army of occupation headed by General Tsitsianov was essentially erased from history.[16]

---

[15] There were persecutions in Azerbaijan in the '20s and the '40s, but because of their magnitude, the persecutions of the 1930s, especially 1937, have remained indelibly in the popular memory. It was in 1937 that Husein Javid, Mikail Mushfig, Ahmed Javad, and Seid Husein were taken away from the people of Azerbaijan. Now everyone knows that Stalin used the Commissariat of Internal Affairs to protect his personal power and to destroy thousands of people who enjoyed a great deal of respect among the people. They included members of the intelligentsia, workers, collective farmers, and prominent party officials and statesmen. According to the People's Commissariat of Internal Affairs' figures, 27,458 people in Azerbaijan alone were executed in the five years from 1934 to 1939. (Documents from the museum of the Ministry of National Security of the Republic of Azerbaijan, http://www.mns.gov.az/museum2 ru.html)

[16] *P. D. Tsitsianov* (1754-1806) was a Russian general who became the commander in chief in the Caucasus in February 1803. Under his command, battalions of the Russian Army attacked and captured Ganja, killing 1,500 and taking 17,222 prisoners. The Battle of Ganja, which was a battle of national defense, was basically erased from the

Centers of Psychological Research in the USSR

Under the conditions of rigid ideological control, conducting scientific research without permission or guidance from the top was not just impossible, but life-threatening. "Authorized" science came to rule the roost and promote the "construction" of a new society and new life. It is no coincidence that people once again became interested in psychology as a science armed with tools for manipulating human consciousness, tools that the authorities so desperately needed. Aware of the importance of research in this field, and at the same time fearful of the consequences and possible outcome of scientific developments, the central Soviet government always kept psychology under tight control and surveillance. Consequently there were no major psychology centers or institutes on the periphery. Moscow, Leningrad, and Tbilisi were the authorized centers of psychological research in the Soviet Union. While Moscow and Leningrad made this list because they were capitals, Tbilisi was there because of the special attention given to everything Georgian[17] in the Soviet Union and the undoubted talent of D. N. Uznadze, who succeeded in transforming the Georgian school of psychology into one of the leading schools in the USSR.[18] Even though practically every city and educational institution had psychology departments, research there conformed to work programs and plans prepared by the aforementioned centers. In this vast country there were only two psychology faculties – at Moscow State University and Leningrad State University – several psychology departments at various higher educational institutions, and two or three psychology research institutes, with the flagship institute at the Soviet Academy of Sciences. However, classified research was obviously conducted under contracts with various ministries and agencies. The Ministry of Defense and KGB were especially active in this respect and awarded contracts for classified psychological research. Hence there is not much to say about basic psychological research in the national republics during the Soviet era.

---

history books of the Soviet era, because it did not fit the propaganda that Azerbaijan had joined the Soviet Union voluntarily (Aliyarly, 2008, p. 558).

[17] Because Stalin was a Georgian—editor's note.

[18] This in no way means that there were no outstanding psychologists in Moscow and Leningrad. Quite the contrary, Leningrad State University, of which I have the honor of calling myself an alumnus, was able to gather the flower of Soviet psychology: V. G. Ananyev, B. F. Lomov, V. N. Myasishchev, A. L. Bodalev, Ye. S. Kuzmin, N. V. Kuzmina, A. I. Nuftulyev, A. A. Krylov, L. M. Vekker, V K. Gaida, V. P. Trusov, and others. No less illustrious names were at Moscow State University: L. S. Vygotsky, A. R. Luria, A. N. Leontyev, S. L. Rubinshteyn, B. M. Teploye, K. K. Platonov, B. V. Zeygarnik, V. P. Zinchenko, and others.

Phases of Development of the Psychology of Creativity in Azerbaijan

As the Soviet government took root, approaches to the study of different social science topics in Azerbaijan and other parts of the Soviet Union gradually began to converge. The single Marxist-Leninist ideology imposed by the Bolsheviks (later known as the Communists) made it practically impossible to study philosophical or psychological subjects from a viewpoint other than Communist ideology.

And the subject of creativity, as the most "dangerous" from the standpoint of Bolshevik theorists, was no exception. They saw creativity, more than other human phenomena, as bearing the stigma of idealistic philosophy, the psychology of intuitivism, irrationality, which could not in any way be compatible with the ideals of Marxism-Leninism. It is true that in spite of all these dangers and difficulties, researchers in Azerbaijan not only studied problems of creativity, but also designed original approaches to its interpretation. One of the distinctive features of the Azerbaijani approach to the subject of personal creativity was the influence of the original philosophical and psychological perception of it that had already taken root by the time Soviet power was established in Azerbaijan. These points of view were based on the extremely rich philosophical legacy of the East. Thus, the study of human creativity in Azerbaijan passed through several **phases**.

The *first phase* may be described as one of the dissemination of the assessments of the study of creative processes that had already emerged in Russia. This phase began in 1920, when the distinguished Russian poet Vyacheslav Ivanov arrived in Baku and became a professor at Baku University. The lectures on topics of artistic creativity and poetics that he gave for three years were basically a reflection of the most promising views of this topic in Russian philosophy and psychology, but the Russian poet and scholar in no way ignored the traditional ideas about it that already existed in Azerbaijan.

A distinctive feature of the *second phase* of research on creativity was the application of Soviet psychological approaches to the analysis of Azerbaijani philosophy and psychology. This phase began with the work of Prof. Aleksandr Osipovich Makovelsky at Baku University.

The *third phase* is closely associated with the name of the prominent Azerbaijani psychiatrist and psychologist Fuad Ahmed Ogly Ibrahimbekov. By laying the foundations for experimental psychology in the Republic, he was the first person to turn to experimental studies of intellectual and creative processes. His approach, which was distinguished by its originality and which relied on profound knowledge in the fields of psychiatry and psychology, did not fit within the official ideological framework of Soviet psychology. That is why the researcher's professional career was cut off at its very peak by the persecutions of 1936-1938.

The resolution "Concerning Pedagogic Distortions in the System of the People's Commissariat of Education," adopted by Stalin's regime in 1936, marked the beginning of the *fourth* and darkest phase in the history of psychology in Azerbaijan. This phase may be briefly described as a new "expansion" of Marxism-Leninism. By cutting off the most original ideas and by physically destroying progressive scientists, the proponents of Communist ideology basically transformed the history of the psychology of creativity into a handmaiden of their own ideas.

The "thaw" that replaced Stalin's regime quickly had an effect on research in psychology. A new generation of Azerbaijani psychologists took up the topic of human creativity anew, and research on creative thinking, artistic creativity, intelligence, and critical thinking picked up speed. The scholarly work of Bayramov, Itelson, Mustafayev, Seyidov, Alizade, and others marked the beginning of a new phase in the development of the psychology of creativity. Of course, they were also under the watchful eye of ideological doctrine, but a new day had come. Even under the existing regime, psychologists created original, "working" concepts of human creativity that received high praise, not just in the Soviet Union, but far beyond its borders.

The collapse of the Soviet Union and Azerbaijan's independence were momentous events that had a huge impact on Azerbaijani psychology. A new phase in the development of the psychology of creativity began to emerge in 1990, containing basically two elements. The first is related to a return to our roots and requires free access, and most importantly, free interpretation of the very rich philosophical and literary heritage of Azerbaijan, while the second is the possibility of utilizing and analyzing all of the contemporary international expertise on the psychology of creativity to the greatest possible advantage and benefit. Under these conditions, psychologists of a completely new type are emerging, who are free of ideology, patriotic, and focused on specific pragmatic research results. "It is impossible to approach the study of creativity uncreatively" is an approach that has become a distinctive feature of the new phase and is propounded by psychologists such as B. Aliyev, R. Ibrahimbekov, S. Mejidova, Ch. Gajiyev,

K. Aliyev, R. Karakozov, R. Kadyrov, and many others (I would like to see this work on the phenomenology of creativity added to the list).

The Ideas of Russian Symbolism in Azerbaijan

The most brilliant representative of the first phase of development of the problem of creativity in Azerbaijan was the outstanding Russian poet Vyacheslav Ivanov.[19] Setting aside a direct analysis of his poems, let us consider the lectures on ethics and literary creativity that he delivered over the course of three years at Baku University. Ye. L. Belkind found a 175-page manuscript of his lectures in the archives of Prof. V. A. Manuylov (Blagaya, 1980, p. 209). Ivanov, who was quite familiar with A. A. Potebin's theory of philology, proceeded from his approach to language as creativity. In the 1920s this idea was analyzed and developed with special care, because a large number of studies on the psychology of creativity elicited a fierce methodological debate. "The subject of poetic talent," Ivanov said, "is the power of language. The marriage of poetic talent and the power of language gives birth to a poetic work" (Blagaya, 1980, p. 210). In analyzing Ivanov's conception of artistic creativity, we should mention that in his view, visual thinking plays a huge role in the creative process, in addition to language and symbols. It is in visual thinking, *he claimed*, that we must look for the "key to major achievements in artistic creativity." Ye. L. Belkind, in analyzing a synopsis of Ivanov's lecture, described his understanding of the process of artistic creativity: "from an analysis of poetry from the standpoint of the image, to examining poetry from the standpoint of thinking" and then "from the concept of 'meditation' to a conscious presentation of the product of creativity" (Blagaya, 1980, p. 212).

In examining the role of symbols, language, and images in the creative process, Ivanov tried to find confirmation of his ideas in antiquity and the European Middle Ages. Working in Baku, he defended his doctoral dissertation in 1921, and in 1923 he used it as the basis for publishing a monograph entitled *Dionysus and Predionysianism*; but strange as it may seem, he

---

[19] *Vyacheslav Ivanovich Ivanov* (1866-1949) was a Russian poet, philosopher, philologist, and translator, and one of the greatest Russian symbolist poets. In 1924, after three years of work in Azerbaijan, he went abroad with the help of Soviet People's Commissar of Education Anatoli Lunacharsky and met E. Medtner, the publisher of Jung's Russian translations. Their association, according to Ivanov's daughter Lydia, helped the poet find a similarity between analytical psychology and his former mystical visions (Etkind, 1994, p. 9).

totally ignored the "symbolic" approach to creativity that had existed in the history of Azerbaijani philosophy. His talent for languages and his fluency in ancient Greek, Latin, and several European languages did not, however, engender any desire to study the history of Azerbaijani philosophy, which was quite disappointing, considering his talent. The history of Hurufism in Azerbaijan, whose greatest representatives were such geniuses of the Islamic Renaissance as Fazrullah Naimi and Imadedin Nasimi, who proceeded from the concept of the influence of symbols (*hurufis*) on man and his creative process, could have yielded many answers to the questions that Ivanov raised in his works. This fact vividly demonstrates the basic characteristic of the first phase of research on the psychology of creativity, namely the importation of concepts that had already emerged in Russia into Azerbaijan, with no consideration of the specific character of Azerbaijani philosophy and psychology. As a Russian symbolist, Ivanov basically became the disseminator of these ideas in Azerbaijan. After performing his role as a "missionary," he left Baku University, but his ideas concerning the psychology of artistic creativity remained in the consciousness of Azerbaijani intellectuals as the ideas of a Russian symbolist, an "outsider."

A. O. Makovelsky and Azerbaijani Psychology

Prof. Aleksandr Osipovich Makovelsky, Academician of the Academy of Sciences of the Azerbaijan Soviet Socialist Republic, Corresponding Member of the Academy of Sciences of the USSR, and a prominent Soviet scholar and philosopher, took a completely different approach to understanding the psychology of creativity. He spent 44 of the 60 years of his career as a researcher and teacher in Azerbaijan. From 1920 to 1930, Makovelsky's research was mainly focused on the philosophical legacy of the ancient Greek materialists, but subsequently he concentrated on the history of philosophical thought in Azerbaijan. This encyclopedically educated scholar realized that these topics had been basically ignored and that the failure to consider the influence of the very rich philosophical heritage of the East on modern civilization was totally wrong-headed. Makovelsky started studying Sufism, Ismailism, and other currents. He was especially interested in the legacy of the great Azerbaijani poet Nizami Ganjevi and devoted some 20 articles to different aspects of his world view. One of them was devoted specifically to the subject of creativity, "Nizami's Thoughts on the Power of the Word and the Tasks of Artistic Creativity," which was published in the collection *Nizami Ganjevi* by the

Azerbaijan Soviet Socialist Republic Academy of Sciences Press in 1947. Its writing was a logical product of the scholar's research, because in studying the philosophical and literary heritage of the Azerbaijani people, Makovelsky was impressed not only by the theoretical, philosophical, psychological, pedagogical, aesthetic, and other concepts of the ancients, but by the brilliant creative talents of the figures of the Islamic Renaissance, the power of their words, the beauty of their phrases, and the harmony of their works. All of this impelled the scholar to study topics of creativity, which he undertook using Nizami's works as an example.

His analysis was based on a careful and comprehensive study of Nizami's ideas of the power of poetic work and the interpretation of these ideas from the standpoint of contemporary knowledge of the psychology of the creative process. "Thus," he wrote, "Nizami demanded the following qualities from artistic works: 1) a focus on ideas, 2) a faithful reflection of reality, 3) sincerity on the part of the author, 4) a profound knowledge of the subject, 5) originality of creativity, 6) mastery of form, and 7) effectiveness (the power to win the readers' hearts and minds)" (Makovelsky, 1947, p. 34). There is no doubt that in characterizing the creative process as it was represented by Nizami, Makovelsky interpreted it from the standpoint of his own ideas. As a result, we understand that he has presented not so much the concept of creativity according to Nizami, but his own conception, which he "found" that the great poet had confirmed. Unfortunately, the professor basically ignored facts of the creative process that Nizami had observed, such as the exaltation of the emotional state, intuition, the unconscious operation of the brain, and much more. The ideological stereotypes at the time did not allow Makovelsky to go further than was allowed. Nevertheless, even his attempt to portray Nizami as a "forefather" of the Soviet (Communist) theory of creativity does not diminish the value of Professor Makovelsky's work, as he was one of the first scholars in the Soviet Union to start broaching and analyzing the role of originality, effectiveness, and so forth in the creative process.

F. A. Ibrahimbekov: The Founder of
the Experimental Psychology of Creativity in Azerbaijan

The name of F. A. Ibrahimbekov[20] is associated with a new phase in the development of the psychology of creativity in Azerbaijan. Of particular importance to us is the fact that his study of intelligence and his design of national tests marked the beginning of the experimental psychology of creativity in our country.

Of course we should keep in mind that his perception of the concept of intelligence was greatly influenced by the work of the Würzburg school of psychologists and the research of the Gestalt psychologists. Their ideas concerning the determinative tendencies in cognitive activity, and the problem as a mechanism and method to study human intellectual activity, were creatively modified and used in Ibrahimbekov's studies. For example, he observed, "We can hardly doubt that the basic, characteristic feature of intellectual activity is the solution of all possible problems with the greatest possible economy" (Verdiyeva et al., 1992, p. 7). This distinguished psychologist understood quite well, and we completely agree with him on this point, that a problem is a kind of lever that can be manipulated to produce a particular characteristic of man's intellectual activity. He stressed that "human actions involving the intelligence are characterized by a number of features, the most important of which are:

1. The transfer of experience from one field to another;

2. The existence of a latent period of a process until activity is manifested outwardly;

3. A problem solved with the participation of the intelligence can later be solved much more easily and quickly" (Verdiyeva et al., 1992, p. 7).

---

[20] *F. A. Ibrahimbekov* (1901-1985) was an outstanding Azerbaijani scientist, psychiatrist, psychologist, and educator. The founder of Azerbaijani experimental psychology, Ibrahimbekov left works whose importance is still greatly appreciated by experts today. Of particular importance to us are his ideas on the creative activity of the individual and the testing of creative talents, which preceded Guilford's well-known studies of divergent and convergent thinking, which were popular in the scientific literature of the 1960s.

While the second and third characteristics of intellectual activity identified by Ibrahimbekov are directly relevant to human intelligence, the first (the transfer of experience from one field to another) is more a characteristic of the creative process. Much later, the research of the leading American psychologists Ellis Torrance, Teresa Amabile, and others would experimentally prove the role of this characteristic in the occurrence of creativity. This means that Ibrahimbekov's studies using the method of wordless study of intellectual functions can quite rightly be considered not just studies of intelligence, but of creative talents.

Moreover, the methodologies he used are remarkably similar to the American psychologist J. P. Guilford's creativity tests, developed much later. For example, the "figure identification," "structure mapping," and "figure combination" tests he developed were designed to produce the concrete from the abstract. Only 20 years later, in the 1950s, Guilford (1967a, 1967b) identified a methodology to study the creation of the concrete from the abstract, by means of tests of "convergent thinking," which, along with his concept of "divergent thinking," plays a special role in the creative process.

Ibrahimbekov also played a major role in the study of the personality aspect of human creative activity. It required genuine scientific and simply human courage for this scientist to speak of the role of intuitive creativity under the reigning ideology of the time. Ibrahimbekov stressed that "intuition is spontaneous and is always an act of cognition; intuition is associated with physical and spiritual stress … intuition is an expression of cognition in forms produced by human culture … many human advances are associated with intuition, and intuition is the future" (Verdiyeva et al., 1992, p. 49). Thus, according to Ibrahimbekov, intuition converges with intelligence and is useful in the creation of works of science and art and in creativity.

F. A. Ibrahimbekov's work was a major step forward in the development of our country's psychology of creativity, but the new era of obscurantism associated with the Stalinist persecutions of 1937-1947 greatly hindered its progress.[21]

---

[21] Ibrahimbekov was also persecuted and exiled to Siberia, where, according to his grandson E. Mamedyarov (the Minister of Foreign Affairs of Azerbaijan), he stayed alive solely by virtue of his profession. In fact, the commandant of the camp where Ibrahimbekov served his time was in urgent need of the assistance of a psychiatrist. After going over the list of prisoners, he found the name of just one man whose personnel file contained the word "psychiatrist." The doctor turned out to be Ibrahimbekov, and this ultimately saved his life.

Growth of Psychological Research in the 1960s

The growth of psychological research in Azerbaijan in the 1960s is associated with the names of psychologists such as A. Bayramov, I. Seyidov, A. Hamzayev, A. Alizade, and many others. They did not neglect the subject of creativity. Bayramov's research on artistic creativity, Itelson's research on educational psychology, Alizade's studies of childhood creativity, and so forth enabled significant advances in the understanding of personal creativity in Azerbaijan.

Professor Bayramov's studies of critical thinking occupied a special place in this research. According to him, "criticism, as an important aspect of thinking, is an individual's mental capacity to find the best way of solving a problem…. The critical approach is manifested in a constant effort to find errors and deficiencies in the objects of cognition, and most importantly, to determine or discover ways of correcting them. It is critical thinking that allows a person to select the most effective, quickest, and most rational method of action in every respect" (Bayramov, 1989, pp. 143–144). If we compare these characteristics and those observed by scientists in their study of creative processes, we can see an interesting trend: Many of the cognitive characteristics of a creative individual (the ability to find order in chaos, the importance of asking "why?", alertness to innovation) can be combined under the common name of "a critical approach to the reflection of the real world." In short, critical thinking, if we consider it not just as a mental capacity but as a personality trait, can act as an integrating factor that truly reflects the specific aspects of an individual's creative activity.

Professor Bayramov (1989) identified three levels of critical thinking:

1. *"Nascent" criticism*: A subject observes that errors and inconsistencies have been made in the representation of an object of cognition, but is incapable of making sense of them and explaining them and cannot find their source.

2. *Diagnostic criticism*: Test subjects ordinarily recognize absurdities and errors in the substance of an object of cognition, but by no means do they always go deeper towards understanding their essence, and they often make no effort to discover their source and describe ways of correcting them.

3. *"Corrective" criticism*: Test subjects not only perceive the parts and details of an object of cognition in their interrelatedness and interdependence, but also identify the

errors and absurdities in them, discover their causes, and, most importantly, describe ways of correcting them.

According to Bayramov, these levels can transition to other levels by complementing each other. Their interaction allows an individual to move forward in recognizing the objects and phenomena of reality. In other words, references to levels of criticism are cyclical, but each new reference acquires a higher level in reflecting objective reality. Bayramov maintains that this process serves as a "psychological mechanism of human creativity." At first glance, it is hard not to agree with this, because creativity is inseparable from intellectual thinking activity, one of the basic characteristics of which is critical thinking. But if we turn to the "Paradox of Logic" discussed in Chapter II of this book, we can see that creativity is not reducible to thinking, let alone to one aspect of thinking, no matter how important this aspect may be (in this case, critical thinking). This is the first point; and secondly, from our point of view, critical thinking is more likely to be manifested not where "errors are discovered" or their causes are identified, but where attempts to recognize ways of correcting them are unsuccessful. In examining the levels of critical thinking from this standpoint, we can say that the manifestation of creativity, strange though it may seem, is more likely at the level of "diagnostic" criticism than at the level of "corrective" criticism. Recognizing the impossibility of solving a problem takes place at the level of "diagnostic" criticism, and if we have the motivations of the "desirability" and "necessity" of finding a solution, plus the requisite talents, the creation of a new solution occurs – i.e., creativity. All of the above in no way denigrates the importance of "corrective criticism," which in our opinion is more closely related to the convergent thinking that constitutes the intellectual basis of creative thinking.

The views of L. B. Itelson, who worked in Azerbaijan for a long time on the topics of creative thinking, are no less interesting. In his studies of non-conceptual and alogical kinds of thinking, he focuses particular attention on visual thinking. This occurs where an individual still does not possess the necessary concepts or where the concepts are still "performing poorly," at a time when a person needs to recognize reality. If, in Itelson's view, a person still does not know the necessary concepts or the terminology needed to describe them and has no way to solve a problem, the person comes up with a creative solution, which allows him to identify "incomprehensible" relationships and solve "insolvable" problems. From this follows the immense importance of teaching critical thinking. This "requires subjecting all learnable concepts and methods to severe criticism and evaluation. It must teach us how to see the limitation of any learnable concepts and methods and their sketchiness and incompleteness *vis-à-vis* reality itself and the problems it poses. It must teach a person to see the difference between reality and conceptions of reality. It must help a person break through the confines of 'understanding' created by words, to the 'vision' created by interacting with objects and phenomena themselves. It must teach boldness in going beyond the habitual and obvious notions, views, and patterns of thinking legitimated by 'common sense' or by the authorities. And at the same time it must teach extreme caution, self-denial, and criticism in assessing one's new creations. It must teach a person not to search for faith, but for evidence; not for confirmation, but for truth; not for contentment, but for eternal agitation; and not for the end of the road, but always its beginning. In short, it must teach a person always, everywhere, and in every respect not to fit facts to his preconceptions, but to test these conceptions against the facts, not to conjure up an artificial world convenient for understanding, but to create an understanding suitable for the real world" (Itelson, 1972, p. 257). The importance that Itelson assigned to creative thinking is reflected in our research. For example, his description of creative thinking as a process in which a problem is not understood but has to be solved, has been experimentally confirmed by the phenomenon of "the recognition of unrecognizability" which we discovered, and which has a significant impact on human creativity.

Another prominent Azerbaijani psychologist, Prof. Abdul Alizade, devoted most of his research to the psychological issues of creativity. In his view, creative activity, like other kinds of activity, is cognitive in nature. Before commencing creative activity, a person determines the goal and the means of achieving it. On the basis of his observations and empirical research, Alizade identified three phases in childhood creativity. The problem of awakening the cognitive activity of pupils also played a leading role in the professor's research. In a world of scientific and technological advances, Alizade believed that a school curriculum could only be learned by creative thinking, not by memorization, as was the case in the traditional educational system. In other words, we need a transition from the school of memory – "rote learning" – to the school of thought, feelings, and creativity (Alizade, 2005, p. 352).

Searches for a New Paradigm

Searches for a new paradigm to explain the creative process were undertaken in Azerbaijan starting in the late '80s and are continuing to this day. The freedom of creativity which is so essential to studying creative processes became a reality with the change in the Republic's sociopolitical situation. This gave rise to public interest in and "demand" for research on the psychology of individual creativity. The various civic associations for the study and development of human creative potential that emerged in the early '90s in the Republic provide additional proof of this. Unfortunately, many of these initiatives never came to fruition, but one non-governmental organization is worthy of special note. This is the Istedad Association, which was founded by a group of young, energetic, and promising scientists for the purpose of identifying, supporting, and developing gifted and talented children and youth in Azerbaijan. Equipped with modern methods of psychological diagnostics and having the opportunity to conduct a variety of psychological studies in complete freedom, they have turned a new page in the history of Azerbaijani psychology. It is quite symbolic that the first director of the Association, which set itself the task of revealing and developing that which had been persecuted and banned in Azerbaijan for many years, was the daughter of a scientist who had been persecuted for free thinking, Rena Fuad kyzy Ibrahimbekova. A highly educated scientist, a splendid psychologist, and a member of one of Azerbaijan's leading intellectual families, she embodied all those qualities that had been uprooted from my people for many years, but which my people had managed not only to preserve, but to find the inner courage and strength to develop. In addition to Rena Ibrahimbekova, the Association was joined by M. Abbaszade, Z. Beisova, V. Mamedova, R. Guseinov, S. Seyidov, R. Mahmudzade, and many other young scientists who were assigned to a certain field of research and specific tasks.

Thanks to the efforts of the Association, the necessary methodological and technical framework was constructed for identifying gifted children and youth; long-term plans were made to set up special educational centers for gifted children; the foundations were laid for mass aptitude testing; the latest methods of instruction from Europe and the United States were adapted, and much else was done in a short period of time in the Republic. It is no coincidence that, over time, most of the participants in the Istedad project became heads of various institutions for the development of individuals and their creative potential. For example, Rena

Ibrahimbekova headed a department of the country's Cabinet of Ministers and a department at Baku State University; M. Abbaszade was appointed Director of the National Student Admissions Committee; Z. Beisova became the principal of the European Lycée, one of the most prestigious schools in the Republic; V. Mamedova took over another no less prestigious and advanced school, the 20th Century School; R. Guseinov was appointed principal of the Heidar Aliyev School; Samad Seyidov was appointed Rector of the Azerbaijan Languages University; and R. Mahmudzade became Director of Information Technology and Computer Programs in the Ministry of Education.

At present there are substantial efforts underway to identify, study, develop, and guide gifted children and youth in Azerbaijan under the auspices of the Ministry of Education. A large number of studies of childhood talent, the establishment of special schools for talented members of the new generation, and a variety of competitions, programs, and Olympiads for the most talented students have allowed the Ministry of Education to design a special national program in this field. But the development of the rising generation's creative potential is also a priority for all government agencies, civic organizations, and the family. I am overjoyed that this understanding is evident at the level of the country's top leadership. One proud occasion was President Ilham Aliyev's 2006 signing of a decree establishing a National Program for the Development of the Creative Potential of Gifted Children (Youths) for 2006-2010. This decree instructed the Ministry of Education, National Academy of Sciences, Ministry of Youth and Sports, Ministry of Economic Development, Ministry of Social Security, Ministry of Finance, and local governments to take specific actions in this field.[22]

Another of President Ilham Aliyev's decrees on the development of the creative, intellectual, and especially the vocational talents of the youth of Azerbaijan should be considered historic: his 2007 signing of a decree adopting a National Azerbaijani Youth Study Abroad Program for 2007-2015. This program appropriates special funds from the Azerbaijan Petroleum Fund to allow 5,000 of the best representatives of Azerbaijani youth to study at leading institutions of higher learning around the world. I am certain that this direct investment in creativity and the younger generation will not only be written in gold letters in the history of

---

[22] One practical result of the adoption of this program was intensified research in the field of gifted children in Azerbaijan. For example, a series of books concerning child giftedness and talents was published under the auspices of the Ministry of Education. Among these books, E. Beylerov's study (2008) might be the most interesting.

Azerbaijan, but will play a key role in transforming our country into one of the world's leaders in economic, cultural, civil, and democratic development (Mardanov, 2009, p. 513).

The research of the Azerbaijani scientist Ch. M. Gajiyev is distinguished by a new approach to the sociopsychological study of creativity. "In our view," he wrote, "the topic of the organization of creative communications is a priority in the strategy for comprehensive study of creativity." Gajiyev believes that the topic has not been studied adequately and is still at the stage of abstract knowledge; consequently it needs to make the transition to the stage of applied abstract knowledge. He believes that this transition can occur by means of a comprehensive approach to creativity and utilization of the "law of transformation of the phases of development of the phenomenon into the structural levels of its organization" (developed by Ya. A. Ponomarev). Gajiyev has identified five phases of creative communications:

First phase – mainly pure communications involving the conveyance of information.

Second phase – communications where information is used for a specified purpose. Unclear and meaningless information is not accepted.

Third phase – communications are more creative in nature. Information is used for both a specified purpose and as a "prompt."

Fourth phase – communications become creatively communicative. The transmission of information as such is secondary.

The fifth phase can be called purely creative. Practical methods of organizing creative communications suitable for this phase have yet to appear, according to Gajiyev (Ponomarev & Gajiyev, 1990, p. 98).

A no less interesting approach to the study of creative processes may be found in the research of the prominent and remarkable Azerbaijani psychologist Svetlana Mejidova. As a student of typology, individual psychological differences between people, and psychological intervention and rehabilitation, S. Mejidova could not ignore topics of personal creativity. In her approach we can clearly discern ideas of the utilization of creative potential for the purpose of personal growth and self-improvement. On the basis of contemporary research in differential psychology and the use of the extremely rich experience of Eastern schools of philosophy, Mejidova (2001) has developed practical techniques for resolving management, creative, and other problems.

In recent years, the transition from classical education to modern education has revealed global problems in the educational system. It has become obvious that the success of education is primarily dependent on the personal involvement of the student. It is not surprising that now a great deal of attention is being focused on the development of the students' personalities and their self-realization and self-actualization. It was in this context that Prof. B. Aliyev wrote the book entitled *The Problem of the Personality in Education* (2008). The author writes of the need to choose forms and contents of education that will stimulate students to think, know themselves, and be creative.

Equally interesting conclusions are found in the works of Doctor of Psychology K. Aliyeva. After becoming interested in the subject of individual creative potential, Dr. Aliyeva conducted an original study that identified new aspects of this complex topic. For example, she has identified the psychological conditions that promote the realization of an individual's creative potential. In her view, these conditions may be classified as *general, external*, and *internal*.

General conditions include stimulating interest in independent creative study, individual-oriented education, the use of integrated teaching techniques, and the optimization of education. *External conditions* include an atmosphere of success, collective creativity, the nature of interpersonal relationships, and the creation of a productive educational environment. *Internal conditions* include a positive attitude towards creativity, the ability to reflect and evaluate oneself, inner freedom, self-development, and self-realization.

According to Dr. Aliyeva, creative activity is a special predisposition of a person, which essentially involves the ease of transitions from purely reproductive to creative methods of solving a wide range of problems. The author also believes that the necessary conditions for the manifestation of creativity are unity of the manifestations of creativity, the creative process, and a creative environment in the system of professional education (Aliyeva, 2008).

The author of this monograph also decided to take a new approach to the study of the psychology of creativity (see Seyidov, 2009d, 2009c, 2009a, 2008; Seyidov & Hamzayev, 2008; Seyidov, 2000, 1997).

First of all, we should admit that practically all manifestations of creativity are paradoxical. This applies not just to the creative process, but to the personality of the creator.

Secondly, the paradoxical nature of creativity, in contrast to the paradoxical nature of the logical or mathematical, has its own solution, manifested in the personality of the individual and his communications and the product of his activity.

Thirdly, creativity, as a factor of personal development, is simultaneously a protective mechanism against disintegration, degeneration, depression, etc.

Fourthly, with respect to society, creativity plays the same role: As a driving force of social progress, it is a necessary condition for preventing social degeneration and an indicator of a society's free development.

Fifthly, creativity possesses the property of transcendence, which allows it to integrate diverse structural elements of a personality in an individual without loss of the integrity of each element.

And finally, ***sixthly***, the transcendence of creativity is one of the basic conditions for shaping personality types.

In making such pronouncements, we are aware of the responsibility we are taking in describing the phenomena of creativity and are accordingly making an effort to cite quite convincing arguments in favor of our position. This task is made easier, strange as it may seem, by the complexity of an individual's creative activity, by both the logicality and alogicality of the creative process, by the high morality and amorality of an individual's creative manifestations, by the conscious and also unconscious nature of creativity, by the purposefulness and aimlessness of searches for creative ideas, and much, much more (which will be described in Chapter II).

In summation, we must say that research on creativity in Azerbaijan is still just beginning (Seyidov, 1999). I am confident that by utilizing the products of international psychology, especially Western and Russian research on creativity, and by relying on the inexhaustible treasure trove of Eastern philosophy and literature, Azerbaijani scientists are on the threshold of creating their own original concepts. The rich legacy and unique style of analyzing and studying problems characteristic of Azerbaijani researchers will allow them to make real progress in studying the amazing human phenomenon of creativity.

7. *Avenues of Development of the Subject of Personal Creativity*

*I*n analyzing the historical development of the subject of personal creativity, we have managed to trace the general paths of its progress. As far back as ancient Indian philosophy, we have found a wealth of ideas that are directly relevant to creativity. We have identified the essence of Indian philosophy's understanding of creativity as activity designed for the self-perfection of the individual. This was the first concept in history that explained creativity in terms of the individual himself, his personality traits, and the structure, mechanisms, and phases of personal development.

Ancient Chinese philosophy considered the subject of creativity from a somewhat different point of view. To the ancient Chinese, creativity meant creative activity and creative behavior. In addition to man's self-perfection, the Chinese emphasized the products of his activity and behavior. These constituted the basis for the many studies of the role of the human environment and man's ethical and moral principles, the differences among individual people, and the nature of actions that determine creative activity.

The emergence of the psychology of creativity as a separate field of study is directly related to the philosophy of antiquity. It revealed completely new and heretofore unknown aspects of the subject; laid the foundations for understanding the creative act as a process; analyzed its components (perception, thought, imagination, etc.); and developed concepts concerning the role, place, and mechanisms of creativity and methods of affecting it.

The Indian, Chinese, and ancient Greek philosophies had a major impact on Arabic philosophy. The effect of these three great civilizations was manifested in two avenues of the development of Arabic philosophy: The *first* involved the adoption of a particular pre-existing concept and its further development (so-called "Eastern peripateticism"), while the *second* involved the creation of uniquely Arabic concepts of creativity (Sufism, Hurufism, etc.). While, for example, the peripatetics analyzed and supplemented knowledge of the processes of perception, imagination, and so forth, the Sufis, Hurufis, and other representatives of Arabic philosophy created highly original concepts that were quite different from the generally accepted concepts of human creativity. They introduced the phenomena of "identification" for the purpose of dissolution in the object of delight, *Fana*, for the first time in the psychology of creativity (it seems to us that Sigmund Freud subsequently used these concepts to interpret "identification with the father" in the "Oedipus complex"); they were the first to invest man with the divine ability to create and change the world, and endow him with a creative element; and they were the first to develop the concepts of not just creativity, but the stimulation of creativity, i.e., certain "techniques" for stimulating creative processes, and so forth.

We found that the subject of creative activity was further developed in the Western psychology of the late 19th and early 20th centuries:

- in *psychoanalysis*, which opened the doors to the world of man's unconscious desires and which claimed that sexual energy, the libido, had an effect on human creativity;

- in *Adler's individual psychology*, which demonstrated the role of the inferiority complex and a person's "Creative Self";

- in *Jung's analytical psychology*, which rebelled against Freud's pansexualism and endowed man with creative energy;

- in *Gestalt psychology*, which looked for the key to the mystery of creativity in the individual's establishment of harmony with his environment and with himself;

- in the *Würzburg school*, which emphasized the nature of problems as the determinative trend in intellectual activity;

- in *humanist psychology*, which considered self-actualization and creativity to be the meaning of human life, etc.

Russian psychology, which largely adopted Western concepts of creativity, made its own valuable addition to its understanding. Its contribution was consideration of the role of factors in the social environment in the determination of creativity, and at the same time basic research on cerebral physiological processes, for the purpose of explaining creative acts (see Figure 1.2).

Figure 1.2

General Avenues of the Development of the Topic of Personal Creative Activity

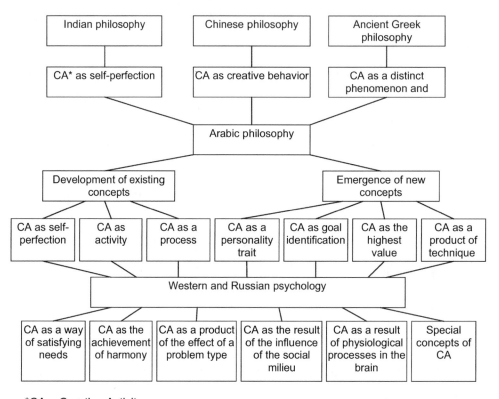

*CA – Creative Activity

Communist ideology, which became the ruling ideology after the 1917 Revolution, changed approaches to the understanding of human creativity not just in Russia, but in the national republics. Under the conditions of total ideological control, it was practically impossible to present a concept that actually "worked." Nevertheless even under these conditions in the Soviet Union, quite original approaches to the interpretation of human creativity emerged in the Soviet national republics and in Azerbaijan in particular.

CHAPTER II

THE PHENOMENOLOGY OF

THE CREATIVE PERSONALITY

1. *The Paradoxes of Creativity*

hile psychology is the most complex and contradictory field in the humanities, there is nothing more complex and contradictory in psychology itself than creativity. And the problem is not just that the subject of creativity, despite the enormous number of works, concepts, and theories, is still extremely under-investigated, but that human creativity knows no bounds and is just as unlimited as the universe in which we live. We are moving forward, gaining a great deal of new knowledge, discovering the laws of existence, applying them in practice, and achieving splendid results, but we are also just as far from complete knowledge as we were at the very beginning of our journey. This in no way means that the study of creativity is pointless, just because perfect knowledge of it is impossible. After all, there is no any astronomer or physicist in the world who is thinking of quitting the study of the universe just because it is boundless. We also can and need to study human creativity, because knowledge in this field will not just help us understand human knowledge, but will also allow us to get closer to an understanding of the "creation" of the world around us.

But *studies of the psychology of creativity encounter difficulties that are not always encountered in analyzing other human phenomena.* These difficulties trouble everyone who is earnestly engaged in the subject of creativity, by leaving a unique legacy of research in the field. No one has specifically analyzed this legacy, which has a very strong impact on our understanding of the subject itself, and no one has tried to identify its components. Scientists were always repulsed by the main distinctive feature of the subject, namely its paradoxical nature, i.e., its insolvability from a formal logical point of view. But insolvability from a formal logical point of view does not mean that it is impossible to "eliminate" the problem, as we shall see.

The legacy of man's thought on creativity, which is paradoxical by nature, consists of specific paradoxes, whose number is apparently just as infinite as creativity itself. But we believe that it is quite possible and expedient to analyze the basic paradoxes that manifest themselves in research on the phenomenon of creativity.

The Paradox of Logic

It is difficult to imagine any true scientific research with no logical structure. Dialectic, formal, symbolic, and other branches of logic contribute to an adequate perception of the truth. And by studying the forms of thought (the concept, judgment, inference, and proof) and the patterns of the objective world's reflection in thinking, we not only get close to the truth, but also penetrate the mysteries of thought as a mental process. Jean Piaget (1968, p. 90; in English, 2001) pointed this out when he wrote, "There is no doubt that logical schemes, if skillfully constructed, always help psychologists in their analysis; a good example of this is the psychology of thinking."

Thinking, in turn, is directly relevant to the subject of our research, human creativity, because it is impossible to separate one from the other. This relationship was observed by the ancients and has been confirmed by a multitude of contemporary studies (Bogoyavlenskaya, 1983; Dunchev, 1985). Thus logical schemas which help us get closer to an understanding of human thought processes can in turn use the latter to help us rise to the level of creativity by establishing a logic–thinking–creation axis.

At the same time, the experimentally confirmed fact that there is no clear correlation between creation and thought is indisputable. It is impossible to understand creativity by knowing the patterns of thought processes (albeit quite significant ones). But if creativity is not reducible to thinking, it is also not reducible to logic. *Consequently creativity is alogical, and when we try to logically explain an alogical process, we do not suspect that we are under the sway of the amazing paradox of creativity.*

Is there a way out of this impasse? It can be found quite easily if we ask ourselves whether alogicality is the "logic" of creativity. This statement of the question requires an unconventional and original approach to the understanding of creativity – an approach that considers both the rational and irrational elements of creative activity.

The Paradox of Morality[23]

This paradox is closely associated with the preceding one and follows directly from the conclusions cited above. "Logic is the axiomatics of reason," observed Jean Piaget (1968, p. 86; in English, 2001, p. 30), understanding axiomatics as a "schema" of reality whose elements have become firmly embedded in our consciousness in the form of axioms that do not require proof and which "reduces to a minimum appeals to experience (it even aims to eliminate them entirely...." (Piaget, 1968; in English, 2001, p. 30). On the other hand, human morality also contains axiomatic elements. If axiomatics is a "schema" of reality, *morality is a "schema" of the acceptance of reality*. The requirements of morality also take the form of axioms that program and guide human behavior. "Morality seems to be constantly in 'a condition of combat readiness,' going into action every time the appropriate situation arises. From this follows the universality and 'impersonality' of moral standards, because they are designed not for a specific individual, but for all men and every man..." (Vichev, 1978, p. 92). For example, proceeding from the assumption that logic is the axiomatics of reason and morality possesses elements of an axiomatic character, we can say that *logic is the morality* of reason.

If we compare our conclusion with the conclusion cited above under *The Paradox of Logic*, we will arrive at one more paradox of creativity that is important from the standpoint of our approach to research. *Logic, as stated above, is the morality of reason. In "The Paradox of Logic," we concluded that creativity is alogical. If we compare these two assertions, we will arrive at a third conclusion: that creativity is amoral.*

"The highest social value" – the quality attributed to creative activity – becomes amoral, i.e., a phenomenon subject to condemnation. This is indeed a paradox or contradiction, but how? We can probably boldly assert that creativity is amoral, but only in the sense that it denies existing morality and creates a new morality. Wasn't the heliocentric system of the world created by Nicholas Copernicus in opposition to Ptolemy's geocentric system amoral? After all, the Church condemned Copernicus's discoveries not only as false, but as amoral in the true sense of

---

[23] The paradox of logic and the paradox of morality are subjects to which the outstanding scientist *Arkadi Ilyich Naftulyev* paid special attention. At the Psychology Faculty of Leningrad State University his lectures were (and I hope still are) the embodiment of living creativity for many people. His paradoxical ideas and unlikely inferences transformed every listener into a participant in the amazing creative process known as the "Naftulyev lectures." It was in his classes that the author of this book became familiar with the idea of the paradoxicality of creativity.

the word, and waged a fierce war against them. But Copernicus's "amorality" gave way to the higher social value of his truth. Wasn't Einstein's theory of relativity the creation of a new "schema" for the perception of reality, which revealed the limitations of the notions of absolute space and time in classical physics?

There are a large number of such examples, and all of them once again confirm the view that creativity cannot and must not be limited to the bounds of the reality in which it originated. Allowing creativity to escape the bounds of the "reasonable" and accepting it for what it is means creating the conditions for individual creativity.

The Paradox of Quantity

The modern world around us can be called a world of problems. A multitude of problems oppresses humanity with its heavy weight and requires solutions. And people try to surmount problems to the extent of their strengths and capabilities, by harnessing their intelligence and physical abilities and relying on their experience and knowledge. This requires an enormous amount of creative energy. Creative activity needs creative energy like the body needs air, but no matter how much creative energy there is, it is always in short supply.

Everything in this world can cause a surfeit. Even life itself, the highest value a person has, can cause repulsion. Only creativity does not cause a surfeit, because there is never enough of it. *Not only do we perceive a shortage of creativity, but the shortage of and need for creativity becomes greater, the more creative activity a person demonstrates.* And I will cite still another paradox of creativity.

Its occurrence may be attributed not so much to the nature of creativity itself but to its effect on the reality around us. By using creativity to solve any problem, internally or externally, a person creates something that is qualitatively new, which in turn leads to other, previously unknown, problems, which also require a solution. One example could be the discovery of the secret of the atomic nucleus, which helped mankind make a huge leap forward in its development. But this discovery created a huge number of new problems that require solutions. These are problems related to the safe use of nuclear power (Chernobyl, etc.), environmental disasters, the storage of nuclear weapons, the disposal of nuclear wastes, and so forth. There is also an entirely new class of problems related to radiation-induced genetic mutations in humans, animals, and plants. In essence, we are speaking of changes not just in the world around us, but in man himself, as a result of the consequences of his discoveries. The problems have led to the closure of nuclear power plants, the adoption of international treaties banning the proliferation of nuclear weapons and manufacturing technologies, appeals for nuclear disarmament and the destruction of nuclear weapons, etc. All of this activity has required enormous expenditures of creative energy. Mankind has started a frantic search for solutions and is expending manpower and resources far greater than those spent on the discovery itself.

There is not a single mental process or personality trait other than human creativity that has had such distinctive results. Even intelligence, which plays an essential role in creative activity and in solving any problem, does not have the "consequences" described above.

Having begun to "counteract the consequences" of creativity, we cannot prohibit creation just because it results in new problems. *Man is a creator by nature and any restriction of his creativity is in essence a restriction of his freedom.* The only way to "counteract" the consequences of creativity is by creativity itself, like the discovery of new problems and new horizons, whose solution will reveal to us even more problems and horizons. This is the essence of the paradox of the quantity of creativity, the impossibility of too much creativity, and at the same time the ever-present shortage of creativity.

The Paradox of Universal Access

The scientific and technological revolution expects of us not just more creativity, but also requires us to make it universally accessible. The huge number of problems burdening mankind today lie like a heavy weight on the shoulders of not just the people directly engaged in creative work, but of "ordinary" people: blue-collar workers, white-collar workers, doctors, soldiers, and so forth. In this situation everyone must maximize the use of his intellectual and physical powers and creativity. In order to realize this social value, we need to give everyone the opportunity to access it. This understanding has guided and continues to guide the many theoretical and applied studies of the psychology of creativity (Walbeg, 1988).

But the same studies have posited another fact characteristic of creativity, namely that it is a profoundly internal process, which bears the mark of the inner world of everyone who exhibits it (Barron, 1958). That is how we will approach the statement of another paradox of creativity, namely the Paradox of Universal Access: *In our desire to make creativity generally accessible and popular, we lose the "living" tissue of creativity, because creativity is a mystery of an individual's inner world.*

The fact that this paradox cannot be resolved from a formal logical point of view does not render it insignificant. It is this paradox that allows us to focus our efforts properly on achieving the goal that modern society has assigned us, namely maximizing the scope for application of creativity as a "tool" for solving the urgent problems of life, because if we cannot make creativity itself generally available due to its individualized character, we can make the desire to create universal. By focusing our efforts on making creativity desired, valued, and important, on the one hand we can encourage everyone to manifest it; and on the other hand, we will not violate the principle of the subjectivity and intimacy of personal creativity.

The Paradox of Desirability

This paradox is closely related to the preceding paradox and has a special effect on the perception of the subject of creativity. As a powerful means of individual self-affirmation, creativity becomes a desired goal whose "possession" enables not just the solution of many human problems, but most importantly, allows an individual to rise above other people and nature itself. Under these conditions, people exhibit in abundance all kinds of activity – creative, social, and intellectual (Bogoyavlenskaya, 1983a, p. 172). In the process, when people understand creativity as the highest value, they start to portray any kind of activity as creative. Researchers have erased the boundaries between intellectual and creative activity (Bogoyavlenskaya, 1983b, pp. 182–195) and between social and creative activity (Nadirashvili, 1987, p. 168), in their desire to ascribe greater significance to intellectual and social activity.

In this regard two questions arise: Can we clearly distinguish creativity from intellectual and social activity? What are the criteria for individual creative activity?

In order to answer the first question, we need to define the concepts of *social* and *intellectual* activity. Most researchers are inclined to believe that there are three basic forms of social activity: **work, sociopolitical activity,** and **cognitive creative activity**. In discussing intellectual activity, for the most part they also single out three basic forms: *conventionally productive, heuristic,* and *creative.* Thus at the highest, most desirable level, both social and intellectual activity are manifested as creative activity, in the opinion of most researchers. If this is the case, then *first of all,* representing social or intellectual activity as creative activity is not so

85

difficult, and *secondly*, is often done in everyday life. This conclusion allows us to formulate the first part of the paradox of desirability: *Creative activity is desirable, and quite often what is not really creative is portrayed as creative.*

No less paradoxical is the question of the criteria for evaluating creative activity, which has still not been finally resolved to this day. Most of the criteria that investigators consider the most acceptable in evaluating creativity are mutually exclusive and contradictory. In human history and the history of science we encounter many facts that have confirmed the bankruptcy of criteria that were originally used to evaluate individual creativity. For example, the tower that Eiffel built in 1889 was perceived by Parisians as a pile of scrap metal that disfigured their beautiful city. The architect was criticized not just by ordinary people but by experts, who proposed expelling Eiffel from the society of learned men. Only a short while later the tower was "transformed" into a great creation of human hands and a symbol of not just Paris, but all of France. The criteria for evaluating creation changed and also changed attitudes towards it. Another example of the contradictory nature of the criteria for creative activity is J. P. Guilford's evaluation criteria for divergent thinking of (1965, pp. 433–456). According to his conceptions, productivity (as the greatest number of responses to a stimulus), flexibility (as the ability to go from one class of objects to another), and originality (as the uniqueness of a given response among the total number of responses to a stimulus) are the most relevant criteria for human creativity. Researchers picked up these criteria, which they considered closely associated with creativity, and the criteria have become quite well known (Guilford, 1967a, p. 402; Guilford, 1967b, p. 419). But even in this case, the large number of ideas, their diversity and originality, still cannot serve as exclusive criteria for evaluating individual creativity.

There are many examples of this kind, and all of them confirm the above statement concerning the imperfection of the criteria for creativity. Even the concept of "criterion" itself is in conflict with the concept of "creativity." In the *Dictionary of Foreign Words* (1990, p. 268), this word is defined as an attribute used as the basis for an evaluation, while in mathematical statistics it is a rule that makes it possible to accept a true hypothesis and reject a false hypothesis (Sukhodolsky, 1972, p. 238). This means that we can say that *a criterion is an attribute that becomes a rule.* But how can we apply rules to human creativity, when creativity rejects rules (see *The Paradox of Logic*)? This statement of the question allows us to formulate the second part of the paradox of desirability: *We cannot distinguish creative activity from "uncreative" activity, because the evaluation criteria are variable and imperfect.*

After combining the two questions raised above, we will formulate the paradox of the desirability of creativity in this way: *Because creativity is desirable and that which is not really creativity is often portrayed as such, we cannot distinguish creativity from "uncreative" activity, since the criteria used are variable and imperfect.* But what might be surprising is the fact that despite all the pessimism of the paradox of desirability, scientists have quite successfully not just "diagnosed" creativity, but are also developing and identifying its criteria.

The Paradox of Searching

It is hard to imagine psychologists working on nuclear physics or higher mathematics. But we observe a very interesting picture when physicists, chemists, musicians, or artists take up an issue of psychology, namely the issue of human creativity. Creativity has become a subject of research in all fields of science, with the only difference being that each science makes its own "mark" on the problem. No one is surprised in the least by a book on mathematical creativity written by a mathematician or a study of artistic creativity written by a novelist. We are not just used to this, but read these books with a great deal of interest, and most importantly, benefit from the reading.

Thus we come face to face with another paradox of the psychology of creativity: *The general patterns of human creativity studied by psychologists have become a subject of study for other scientists not directly engaged in psychology.* This actual approach to the study of creativity compels us to consider this not so much an issue of psychology (as we said above), but more of a psychological issue. This is not just a play on words – there is a major difference in the approaches. If we consider creativity to be an exclusive issue of psychology, then for those in other fields of knowledge to study it will prove to be meaningless. If we consider it a psychological issue, then it is both an issue of psychology and an issue of any other field of knowledge that involves the creations of human intelligence.

The Paradox of the Model

Most psychological research culminates in the construction of a model or structure of the studied phenomenon. This is aided by the analytical approach, which involves the study of not just the phenomenon itself, but a structural analysis of its organization. But an analytical approach that can be quite successfully applied to most psychological phenomena (feelings, perception, memory, the personality, and so forth) encounters certain difficulties when it is applied to creativity (Bratko, 1969, p. 22). In order to explain this view, we will resort to Kurt Gödel's theorem (Smullyan, 1981, p. 238).

In 1931 Kurt Gödel[24] made a striking discovery. He found that mathematical truth in a certain sense cannot be completely formalized. *Gödel proved that a mathematical system belonging to a broad class of systems will always have an assertion that cannot be proved (i.e., deduced from the system's axioms), in spite of its truth!* Consequently no axiomatic system, no matter how cleverly it is constructed, is sufficient to prove all mathematical truths. Gödel first proved his theorem for Whitehead and Russell's *Principia Mathematica* system,[25] but it had an impact on many other scientific systems, including the system of knowledge of human creativity, which, in our opinion, can also not be formalized completely. It will always have a principle which, even though it may be completely obvious, cannot be explained on the basis of prior analysis. It becomes necessary to draw on other knowledge from another seemingly unrelated field of science and practice (see *The Paradox of Searching*). For example, it is impossible to understand the creations of Leonardo da Vinci solely from the standpoint of the psychology of creativity without conducting, along with everything else, a social-historical analysis of the Renaissance. It is impossible to explain the phenomenon of insight solely on the basis of

[24] *Kurt Gödel* (1906-1978) was an Austrian and then American mathematician. In his one brief article published in the *Vienna Journal*, he turned the world of mathematical logic upside down. The theorem that acquired his name is still splendid proof that complex phenomena are always contradictory and paradoxical.

[25] Alfred North Whitehead and Bertrand Russell's three-volume monograph occupies a unique place in the world's mathematical literature. Its first English edition saw the light in 1910-1913 and was almost 2,000 pages long. *Principia Mathematica* is rightly considered one of the most brilliant compositions on the fundamentals of mathematics and, in the broad meaning of the word, an outstanding contribution to the intellectual life of the past century. Whitehead and Russell started their joint work on the fundamentals of mathematics in 1903 for the purpose of deriving all mathematical knowledge from a small number of clearly stated axioms by means of the logical rules of deduction. The cornerstone of their work is a logical concept which asserts that mathematics is fundamentally reducible to formal logic. Their concept includes two basic principles: (1) all mathematical truths can be formulated in terms of a certain symbolic language and recognized as logical truths; (2) all mathematical proofs can be restated as symbolic chains of logical deduction (Yarovoy & Radayev, 2004).

knowledge of the psychology of the process. Unfortunately, certain researchers, in constructing models of creativity, have failed to consider or recognize this truth and have attempted to prove that there is no need for proof, namely that their models are the most complete and perfect (Ponomarev, 1976, p. 213). *We should understand that the modeling of creativity cannot presuppose the construction of a closed, completed structure. Any model of individual creativity (if such a thing is at all possible) must be dynamic, open to new elements, and flexible and incomplete. Otherwise we will create a model of activity that ignores the fine fabric of creativity.* And this is the Paradox of the Model.

The Paradox of the Narrowing of the Domain of the Unconscious

Any research on the problems of human creativity will inevitably encounter the "conscious/unconscious" dilemma. On the one hand, scientists analyze the role of the conscious in the creative process; on the other, they look for the determinants of creativity in the unconscious manifestations of the human psyche. For example, starting with Hegel's *Philosophy of Mind*, the examination of unconscious acts of the mind was equivalent to shedding light on the dark "hiding place of the unconscious," where "a world of infinitely many symbols and conceptions that are not present in the conscious is preserved" (Hegel, 1956, p. 256). In the process, the great philosopher did not try to penetrate the unconscious itself, claiming that the images and conceptions sleeping in the depths of the human being are included in the creations of his hands and thoughts when they rise to the surface of the conscious. Friedrich Nietzsche (1919, p. 189) expressed similar ideas when he wrote that "the unconscious is a necessary condition for any perfection." But scientists who recognized the role of the unconscious in human creativity proceeded to study it specifically.

Obviously the Freudian interpretation was one of the most interesting attempts to explain this phenomenon. The basic factors that determine a person's creative orientation and activity were identified in the unconscious from the vantage point of psychoanalysis. In this case all of the paradoxicality of the situation lay in the fact that by studying the unconscious as one of the critical sources of creative activity, Freud, in contrast to his predecessors, tried to make it conscious. This scientist was the first to go where no one had gone before. He identified the structure, mechanism of operation, phases of development, and general "constitution" of the unconscious. The "Oedipus complex," "Electra complex," and much, much more that he discovered and described made the unconscious a part of our conscious, by revealing all of the riches of its world and thus narrowing the possibilities of the unconscious as a determinant of creative activity.

Thus, *the attempt to make the unconscious the property of the conscious results in the devaluation of the unconscious for creative activity.* Every researcher who identifies the importance of unconscious processes in creativity becomes hostage to this paradox. But it makes it possible to maintain a balance between the unconscious and conscious in creative activity by "reining in" those who completely deny the role of conscious factors, as well as those who try to ignore the unconscious.

The Paradox of Determinants

Perhaps the most surprising aspect of creativity is what "impels" a person to manifest it. Over the entire history of the psychology of creativity, researchers have never stopped looking for the causes and sources of creative activity. Especially numerous are the works on the motivations for creative activity and the identification of particular needs, motives, attitudes, value orientations, and so forth. And this is no coincidence, because the very founders of the science recognized the priority of motivational factors long ago. "It is not his special intellectual talents that distinguish a researcher from other people," *Ramón y Cajal*[26] stressed, "but his motivation…. [I]t is he who gives common reason the high intensity that leads to a discovery."

In reasoning this way, psychologists have identified a large number of specific motives, values, and attitudes that stimulate creativity. Among them we can cite: unconscious tendencies, love for the truth, glory-seeking, the desire for achievement, the desire to have the "correct attitude" towards the reality around one, sexual needs, spiritual questions, self-realization, self-affirmation, a propensity for risk-taking, fear, freedom, love for people, narcissism, skepticism,

---

[26] *Santiago Felipe Ramón y Cajal* (1852-1934) was an outstanding Spanish neurohistologist who was awarded the Nobel Prize for Physiology and Medicine in 1906 (along with Camillo Golgi) for his study of the structure of the nervous system. He was the discoverer of dendrites (branches of the nerve cells) and founded the science of neurons as structural units of the nervous system. Ramón y Cajal not only studied histology and medicine, but also published a collection of aphorisms entitled *Conversations at the Café* in the last years of his life.

the desire to resolve conflicts, etc. Even on this short list of the motives for creativity we can find motives that are directly contradictory to each other; and yet all of them have been experimentally proven. Consequently, *while it may determine the creative activity of an individual, no particular motive can serve as a determinant of creativity in general.*

This is just one side of the paradox in studies of the motivation for creativity, which significantly reduces the value of a search for the specific motives that stimulated a person to engage in creative activity. *Another side of the paradoxicality of specific "stimulants" of creative activity is that they cease to be stimulants after the creative activity starts to occur.* In other words, the manifestation of creative activity dialectically negates the causes that give rise to it. This well-known philosophical principle is most clearly evident in the study of creativity.

The Paradox of the Product

The ultimate goal of creative activity is the creation of a new product, work, theory, idea, type of relations, and so forth. The product of individual creative activity is so valued, elegant, beautiful, necessary, and useful that it ceases to be the "property" of its creator and becomes impersonal, common property. Suffice it to recall the fates of folk songs, legends, and tales, whose authors have either been forgotten or were never known. The same applies to scientific and technological advances that have become so deeply embedded in our lives that we do not even think about their creators, the individual scientists and inventors. *A product of creativity that possesses the attributes of high value, beauty, simplicity, general availability, and desirability becomes so firmly part of our lives that it times at "destroys" the very personality of its creator, by leveling and dissolving into itself the entire inner world of he who created it.*

There is another side of the paradox of the product. It applies to works whose authors are well known. In this case, *the product of creativity "detaches" its creator from his immediate environment, elevates him, and "destroys" the crowd, dissolving all of the crowd's hopes, desires, and goals into the person of the creator, who then expresses the ideas and hopes of others.* This aspect is most evident in talented politicians who acquire the authority to speak for the people. From the standpoint of this aspect of the paradox of the "product," in a certain sense the power to control and guide people towards certain actions, up to and including war, can be effective only if a leader has creative talents and is creatively active.

The Paradoxes of the Creative Personality

We have only looked at 10 paradoxes of creativity. This list could be expanded, but the paradoxes listed above are sufficient to convince us of the paradoxicality of the creative process as a whole. But if this is the case, a person manifesting creative activity should also possess paradoxical, contradictory personality traits. It is impossible for the creative process to be paradoxical and the person who manifests creative activity not to be paradoxical. This proposition is contrary to the generally accepted notion of the creative individual as a harmonious, integrated, and stable personality. And in fact it is difficult to imagine an integral personality torn apart by contradictions and conflicts. The situation becomes even more problematic when we look at the literature. The varying descriptions of the personality traits of a creative individual leave absolutely no chance of arriving at a common denominator. Among investigators of the psychology of creativity, as we mentioned above, Mihaly Csikszentmihalyi focused particular attention on this discrepancy. In his book *Creativity: Flow and the Psychology of Discovery and Invention* (1996, p. 56), he wrote: "The reason I hesitate to write about the deep personality of creative individuals is that I am not sure that there is much to write about, since creativity is the property of a complex system, and none of its components alone can explain it."

Personality traits are not just diverse, but are mostly opposite to each other. This allows psychologists to construct certain personality profiles and diagnose the presence or absence of certain qualities and personality traits in an individual. It is rare for one and the same person to exhibit opposite qualities at the same time, but it does occur. Carl Jung made an attempt to explain this surprising phenomenon, concluding that every clearly manifest trait of our personalities has a suppressed shadow side which we refuse to recognize. "The very orderly person may long to be spontaneous, the submissive person wishes to be dominant. As long as we disown these shadows, we can never be whole or satisfied. Yet that is what we usually do, and so we keep on struggling against ourselves, trying to live up to an image that distorts our true being" (Csikszentmihalyi, 1996, p. 57).

So the incarnation and manifestation of directly opposite personality traits in an individual should not be considered inappropriate or abnormal. The exact opposite is true, because the ability to combine mutually exclusive characteristics distinguishes extraordinary, unconventional, and creative people. In support of this point of view we shall briefly describe

Mihaly Csikszentmihalyi's 10 paradoxes that demonstrate the paradoxicality of the creative personality.[27]

1. Creative people, who are extraordinarily energetic, are at the same time quite often calm and relaxed. They can work for hours, concentrate, and look fresh and energetic. This doesn't mean that they are hyperactive, always "engaged," and constantly agitated. In fact they rest frequently and sleep for a long time. What's important is that their energy is not under the control of the calendar, the clock, or any outside schedule, but under their own control. Another manifestation of the energy of creative people is their sexuality. Creative people are also paradoxical in this regard. While they have quite strong erotic or general libido energy, which in certain cases is expressed directly in sexuality, they can adhere to Spartan chastity, which, by becoming part of their image, leads to outstanding achievements.

2. Creative people are distinguished by their minds (high intelligence) and aptitude, but at the same time they are quite naïve. It is true that how intelligent they are is an open question. We know that the "g factor" that lies at the basis of general intelligence is highest among those who have creative accomplishments.[28] While realizing that limited intelligence affects creative accomplishments, we should remember that you can be a splendid intellectual and at the same time do harm to creativity.

3. The third paradox of a creative personality is its cotemporaneous combination of playfulness and rigor, responsibility and irresponsibility. There is no doubt that

---

[27] I don't know how it could happen that both Mihaly Csikszentmihalyi and I identified exactly 10 paradoxes. While in my description of the creative process I selected what I considered the 10 most vivid and illustrative paradoxes from the standpoint of the creative process, Dr. Csikszentmihalyi identified 10 paradoxes of the creative personality. Of course these are different paradoxes: Mine are directly related to the creative process, while his are related to the creative personality. But in 1994, in my description of the paradoxes of creativity in my book *The Social Psychology of Creativity,* I could not have imagined that on another continent, at approximately the same time (Dr. Csikszentmihalyi's book was published in the United States in 1996), another scientist was studying the paradoxes of the creative personality.

[28] The *"g factor"* is a mathematical variable that reflects the basic capacity on which the activity of accomplishing a variety of intellectual tasks is based. Quite often the "g factor" is formulated as a capacity with which all other primary particular factors of intelligence correlate (Corsini, 1999, p. 407).

playfulness and jocularity are clearly pronounced attitudes typical of creative personalities. But the manifestation of these qualities does not eliminate their opposites in a creative individual, such as stubbornness, steadfastness, and persistence. These qualities start to dominate when a creative individual needs to do a colossal amount of hard work to overcome the difficulties he inevitably encounters in bringing a new idea to fruition.

4. Imagination and fantasy are constantly alternating with a firm grasp of reality in a creative individual. A creative individual needs this disposition to overcome the bounds of reality without losing his connection to the past.

5. A creative personality is a storehouse of such conflicting traits as extroversion and introversion. Normally each of us is predisposed to one of these characteristics, preferring to be either at the center of the crowd (extroversion) or sitting on the sidelines and observing events (introversion). Modern psychological studies have identified extroversion and introversion as the most stable personality traits that make it possible to quite clearly distinguish certain people from others. But the creative personality "refutes" these studies by possessing both traits at the same time.

6. Creative people are distinguished by astonishing simplicity and at the same time arrogant pride. And we often encounter the opposite case, when prominent people we consider haughty and conceited are in reality self-effacing and shy.

7. In most cultures, if not all, a man tries to demonstrate his manhood and carefree nature and to suppress the sides of his temperament and character that have traditionally been considered feminine. A similar type of behavior is characteristic of women, who, by exhibiting the generally accepted forms of female behavior, try to avoid masculine standards of communication. But creative individuals in a certain sense avoid such rigid stereotypes imposed by gender roles. For example, a *masculinity/femininity* test administered to young people revealed that creatively gifted girls are more dominant and tough with other girls than their more ordinary girlfriends, while creatively gifted boys are more sensitive and less aggressive than their peers. This trait is clearly exhibited by creatively gifted youth from a

94

sexual point of view. In this case we are dealing with a specific psychological androgyny, which in the broad meaning of the word is related to an individual's ability to be both aggressive and cultured, sensitive and rigid, dominant and subservient, and disengaged and familiar at the same time. The psychological androgyny of the creative individual ultimately doubles his repertoire of responses and allows him to interact with the world by means of a broad and diverse range of possibilities. It is no surprise that creative individuals embody the strength of not just their own sex, but of the opposite sex also.

8. Creative people are usually portrayed as independent rebels who reject all the social and cultural principles of society. At the same time, it is impossible to manifest creativity without familiarity with these very same cultural roots. A creative individual must believe in the importance of these aspects of the culture and assimilate its rules; consequently, a creative individual must be a traditionalist to a certain extent. Thus, a creative individual, while exhibiting traditional and conservative behavior, is at the same time a rebel who rejects authority.

9. Most creative people are extremely passionate and subjective about work in general and about their work in particular, but at the same time they may be extremely objective in evaluating themselves and the results of their activity.

10. Finally, the openness and sensitivity of a creative individual often result in severe physical suffering and spiritual pain in the process of creation, but this suffering and pain, strange though this may seem, may give him indescribable pleasure.

These are the conflicting personality traits that most often characterize creative individuals. Of course this list is arbitrary in a certain sense. We may have ignored certain important personality traits. But it is more important not to forget that the opposing traits described above (or any others) are difficult to find in the same person. For example, without the ability to look at an idea from the opposite viewpoint, the idea cannot be identified; and without the ability to look at it directly, the idea cannot be brought to the point of acceptance. Thus creativity is a person's ability to deal with both sides of the contradictions that exist inside and outside him. This is precisely the type of individual whom we call "creative" (Csikszentmihalyi, 1996, pp. 55-76).

---

2. *Creativity as a Psychic Protective Mechanism*

So what does impel a person towards creativity? What lies at the roots of creative activity as a specific need? What motivates and conditions human creative activity? The aforementioned paradoxes, especially the *Paradox of Determinants*, do not permit an unambiguous answer. Maybe we should change the statement of the question? Perhaps we should first formulate and answer the questions that are most often asked of the researchers of creativity? After all, as soon as a conversation turns to the topic of creativity, these are the questions that are asked. These traditional questions were stated better than anyone else by the outstanding American student of creativity Frank Barron.[29] In his last book, *Creators on Creating*, written in collaboration with a group of authors in 1997, he tried to answer eight of what he considered the most important questions directly related to creativity. Below is an excerpt from his book (answers are summarized), in which Dr. Barron states his questions on creativity.

1. ***Question***: "Is a high IQ[30] essential in creativity?"

Answer: The relationship between creativity and IQs is quite relative, and if IQ is greater than 115 or 120, this relationship is extremely rare.

---

[29] *Frank Barron* (1922-2002) was one of the most prominent modern researchers of creativity. He taught and worked at the University of California at Santa Cruz. His research is considered classic and serves as a practical guide for students of the psychology of creativity. Two works from his psychological legacy are especially important: *Creativity and Psychological Health,* published in 1963, and *Creativity and Personal Freedom,* published in 1969. Both publications have become part of the treasure trove of 20th-century psychological literature.

[30] IQ (the intelligence quotient) is determined by the ratio of so-called mental age to the true chronological age of an individual, by the formula

$$\frac{MA}{CA \times 100\%} = IQ.$$

Mental age is determined by psychological tests designed so that the results are described by a normal distribution with a mean IQ equal to 100 points and with a dispersion so that 50% of people have an IQ between 90 and 110 and 25% have IQs below 90 and above 110, respectively. An IQ above 115 is considered an indicator of high intelligence and an IQ above 135 is considered an indicator of very high intelligence. Certain researchers classify an IQ below 70 as signifying mental retardation. Recently, in addition to greater interest in IQ, a large number of other intelligence tests have appeared, whose results, being sometimes directly opposite, have greatly reduced the informational value of the IQ.

2. **Question**: "Are there some motives, as well as personality traits, found more often in people known for their creativity?"

Answer: Yes, there is a certain motivational pattern found in creativity. It is the desire to create! With respect to the personality, in this case the following characteristics are most often cited: non-conformism, resistance to authority and the *status quo*, intuition, originality, mental imbalance, introversion, and the willingness to take risks.

3. **Question**: "Is creativity inherited?"

Answer: Studies of twins and a variety of other experimental studies have allowed us to answer this question in the negative. My personal experience tells me that I should ignore genetic differences and focus on the role and importance of the environment.

4. **Question**: "Are creative people more unstable mentally?"

Answer: If you are not in an extreme manic state and you are not in a state of deep depression, then certain symptoms of the aforementioned states are more likely helpful than destructive for creativity.

5. **Question**: "Are there gender differences in creativity?"

Answer: The psychological studies clearly show that creative potential (in the sense of creative talents) is absolutely the same for men and women.

6. **Question**: "Is creativity related to age?"

Answer: The most likely answer seems to be that creative people exhibit creativity throughout their lives.

7. **Question**: "Why does creative potential sometimes seem to go to waste, or to go unused for many years?"

Answer: If the society in which we live establishes too many "proper" modes of behavior and life, the attractiveness of experimenting and the desire to create dry up and are lost. Being original and productive in solving important problems often requires a person to be brave enough to be different from the other people around him.

8. **Question**: "Is an unhappy environment more likely to produce a creative person than a happy one?"

Answer: Let's hope not! But remember that it is not always easy to determine how favorable or unfavorable an environment is. Your unhappiness may be my happiness and vice versa (Barron et al., 1997, pp. 11–20).

As we can see, Barron's eight questions and answers about creativity are ambiguous and elicit at least as many questions, even though we can agree with certain approaches formulated in the first and seventh questions and partly in the eighth. These approaches reflect the fact that creativity contradicts the obvious. For practically every researcher, creativity is characterized by terms that start with the prefix "un" (unconventional, unusual, untraditional) or the sense of "anti" (contradictory, opposite), etc. Of course there are other aspects of creativity, such as originality, productivity, beauty, and feasibility, but to one degree or another, all of them reject the obvious. This presupposes certain traits in an individual, but it is mainly a psychological state that a person enters into. In other words, a search for the sources of personal creativity should be aimed not at differentiating specific stimulants of creativity (which might be anything imaginable) or personality traits (which, as was shown above, are contradictory in a creative person), but at identifying the psychological state that predisposes a person to creativity.

But an individual's psychological states, in contrast to his psychological traits, are not stable and invariant. They emerge as a result of a variety of factors, conditions, and situations, and are subject to change. Recording them and determining their uniqueness is just as painstaking a task as identifying the different "stimulants" of creativity. If we approach the study of psychological states from the standpoint of the relationship between man and his environment, it becomes possible to identify the primary source of psychological states. This fundamental source of certain psychological states is an imbalance in the relationship between man and his environment (in our case, when man rejects the obvious).

Since the mid 20th century, psychologists have focused special attention on the role of the man-environment relationship and its balance. This is not surprising, because an introspective approach to the study of psychological phenomena, as well as attempts to explain all of the diversity of man's inner world in terms of external stimulants alone, had come to an impasse. By combining man and the reality around him into a single dialectical whole, scientists have discovered completely new strata of psychological phenomena. They have used them as the basis for constructing splendid theories that explain man's relationship to the environment and are still important to this day. These theories include Fritz Heider's *theory of cognitive balance*, Leon Festinger's *theory of cognitive dissonance*, Charles Osgood and Percy Tannenbaum's *theory of congruence*, Theodore Newcomb's *theory of communicative acts*, and many other theories that have become treasures of 20th-century psychological thought. The basic idea of all these theories of cognitive consistency lies in the fact that a person's cognitive structure cannot be unbalanced or disharmonious; and if an imbalance occurs, there is a tendency to restore the internal consonance of the cognitive system. Practically all human mental processes, traits, and states have been subjected to careful study and analysis from this standpoint. The intellect and creativity have been studied in particular detail. It is no coincidence that Howard Gardner (1993, pp. 19–45), in identifying different approaches to creativity, mentioned the cognitive approach[31] first, emphasizing the contribution that the cognitivists made to the study of this amazing phenomenon.

Nevertheless, in focusing attention on the solution of problems, almost none of the representatives of the cognitive school have analyzed situations where the restoration of balance and internal consonance was impossible. In order to fill this "gap," the author of this monograph has adopted a new approach to analyzing the psychological state that predisposes a person to creativity. *Our efforts were focused not on a search for methods of achieving the harmony, consonance, congruence, or balance of the human cognitive structure, but on an analysis of a human state in which it is impossible to achieve harmony or to solve a problem.*

When a person encounters a problem in life, the first thing he does is to restrain his "impulsive" behavior and then, by comparing the problem with his internal references, evaluate it, and only at the end develops an attitude towards it. The "final" phase of developing an attitude is essentially the beginning of the choice of a way of relating to a problem. In our view, there are three possible ways of relating:

1. Act as if the problem does not exist and simply ignore it.

2. Accept and recognize its existence, but postpone or fake a solution.

3. Try to solve the problem.

We need to accept and understand the exceptional importance of all three ways of "relating": Their combination and concurrent unity ensures the appropriate perception of a problem and the ability not just to work with it, but to be objective (Uznadze, 2004, p. 50).

---

[31] The most prominent representatives of the cognitive approach to creativity are *Margaret Boden, Robert Steinberg,* and in particular *Howard Gruber.* These researchers explored the creative process and creative personalities in terms of problem-solving, artificial intelligence, and computer technologies.

In the ***first case***, after assessing a problem and adopting an objective attitude towards it, we may simply ignore it and go on with our day-to-day life. There is a problem, but there is no need to solve it. The imbalance or discomfort it creates is quite acceptable and lies within bounds which allow us to coexist with it. Life is basically a way of coexisting with problems, and in this sense the role and significance of the first type of attitude towards a problem is difficult to overestimate.

In the ***second case***, a person recognizes the existence of a problem. He does not want to solve it, yet it exists and requires a solution, making itself known at regular intervals. The person is prepared to fake a solution, speak of the importance of a solution, and do everything except change his attitude towards the problem. In this case, we can see discomfort that significantly affects a person's psychological state, but not to the extent that it forces him to truly solve the problem.

And finally, the ***third way*** of relating to a problem is the desire to solve it. The solution of a problem becomes an urgent necessity. In this situation it is impossible to close one's eyes to a problem, let alone fake a solution. Both the problem and the person become hostage to a situation which can only be resolved by solving the problem. This situation is encountered in life quite often; of course, not as often as the first and second cases, but nevertheless quite often.

If a person manages to cope with the problem and find a solution, he returns to his everyday life. *If a solution cannot be found, the person enters a specific psychological state that is extremely important for understanding the nature of creativity: a state of awareness of the impossibility of solving the problem and of the failure to recognize ways out of it.* This state cannot last for long, because the level of personal involvement and the person's affected value structures is extremely great. It is quite logical to assume, as Festinger did, that in this situation a person will change his attitude towards the problem by adding additional elements of information to his cognitive structure.

If we cannot find the solution we need to a problem, then we, by changing its subjective value, change our attitude towards it. But this perception can only change the way we relate to it, i.e., replace the desire to solve a problem with the desire to fake a solution or the desire to ignore the problem altogether. A change in subjective attitude towards a problem does not always mean a real solution. In the literature we can find quite a few examples where a change in attitude towards an event, problem, or person, even the complete "remaking of oneself," does not produce the desired effect. For most people in a similar situation, creativity becomes the last resort for finding inner and outer harmony. In other words, *when a person cannot resolve the questions and problems facing him, or recognizes an inner conflicted state when the search for acceptable types of behavior does not produce results and he is unable to make his values consistent with the standards, rules, and values of his social environment, the person exhibits creative activity by producing a solution and changing the environment, himself, and his values.*

Such scenarios constitute additional evidence that creativity is essentially a *higher-order psychological protective mechanism that makes it possible for a person not just to protect himself from the destructive effect of his environment, but to boldly tackle the discovery of new secrets of nature without any fear of the problems that might arise along the way.* This approach lifts the veil of secrecy, inaccessibility, and uniqueness from creativity. There is no doubt that creativity is inherent to all people as a psychological phenomenon closely related to the development and character of the personality.

3.   The Personality and
Its Structure

The Concept of the Personality in Psychology

By 2010 the Earth's population came close to the seven billion mark. This figure, which is mind-boggling by itself, produces an even greater impression when you imagine the power of nature that made it possible to create approximately seven billion one-of-a-kind, irreplicable, and totally unique people. Their differences from each other are determined not just by biological and physiological characteristics, but by individual psychological traits. People differ not just with respect to the color of their eyes, the timbre of their voices, their EEG rhythms and fingerprints, but in their specific personality traits. Of course these differences are not as distinct as differences in skin color or eye shape, but they ultimately determine human behavior and a person's orientation towards achieving specific goals.

The word "personality" in many languages has a quite interesting and in a certain sense similar etymology. For example, in the Azerbaijani language, the word for "personality", *şəxsiyyət*, originates from the Arabic word *şəxs*, which means a specific individual. The origin of the word for "personality" in the Russian language is also related to the word "person" or "persona," which means the difference between one individual and another. In English, French, German, Italian, and Spanish, the word "personality" originates from the two Latin words *per* and *sona*, whose semantic meaning may be conveyed as "speaking by means of." In ancient Greece and the Roman Empire, these words were used to mean the masks/faces that actors used in theatrical productions. Then the word "persona" acquired the semantic weight that it now carries, namely, it came to represent the word "personality." As we can see, in most languages the word "personality" is used to identify an individual and his difference from other people, the uniqueness of his face, or the "mask" he puts on his face.

The human face, of course, is an individual's main identifier. We use the lines, shapes, contours, and other features of the face to distinguish one person from another and to determine his age. It is no accident that all personal identification documents require a facial photograph. Facial expression reveals our emotions, feelings, moods, states, and desires, and gives us the capability of non-verbal communication as well as verbal communication. The importance of the face in human life is difficult to overestimate, but it is not a reliable source for ascertaining an individual's personality traits. The exact opposite might be true, in that the physiological features of the face most often conceal an individual's true personality traits. Not everyone will agree with this, claiming that physiognomy, the doctrine that posits a correlation between a person's outward countenance and his personality traits, has been able to find sufficient evidence of the truth of its propositions.[32] Nevertheless, we do not plan to debate the evidence of face-personality relationships. Our area of interest is the personality itself, its structure, psychological features, and basic characteristics. We are interested in the personality as it reflects a person's spiritual life and all the manifestations of his mental state. In other words, we are interested in the "face" of the human soul.

Psychology contains a very large number of definitions of personality. Certain definitions emphasize the physical, or more precisely, individual physiological characteristics of a person, while others stress mental traits, and still others prioritize aspects of the personality that allow it to identify itself in society. This diversity of definitions forced one of the pioneers of research in the field of the personality, Gordon Allport, to devote an entire chapter of his book *Personality: A Physiological Interpretation* (1937) exclusively to definitions of the personality. Of course this makes its study much more difficult and often compels researchers to look for completely new approaches or attempts to integrate that which already exists. For example, the American researchers Robert Kreitner and Angelo Kinicki, who analyzed a very large number of definitions of the personality, formulated it as follows (2008, p. 133): "Personality is defined as the combination of stable physical and mental characteristics that give the individual his or her

---

[32] *Physiognomy* is the doctrine which claims that there is a definite relationship between a person's outward countenance and personality type, which means that external traits can be used to determine an individual's psychological characteristics. This doctrine originated in antiquity on the basis of the idea of the predetermination of the psychic (moral) and corporal in an individual, i.e., what was originally prescribed to him by nature. Over the centuries, physiognomy has served as the starting point for many character typologies (*Dictionary of the Practical Psychologist*, 1998).

identity." And in a book by the American researchers Daniel Cervone and Lawrence Pervin (2008, p. 8), *the personality is defined as a psychological characteristic that allows an individual to have stable behavioral, thinking, and sensory patterns that distinguish him from other people.* But these definitions, which are quite often used by researchers, cannot claim to be universal. They are too general and merely emphasize the personality's function as a social identifier, without allowing us to understand its entire depth and true role in human life. We can imagine how difficult it is to define personality if the interpretation of the personality as a psychological phenomenon is even more confused and contradictory. In our opinion, the difficulty in understanding it adequately may be attributed to several factors:

- An individual's personality is not material and tangible and is a complex psychological entity formed under by a large number of factors, conditions, premises, and determinants.

- An individual's personality, which experiences the effects of a large number of factors, cannot be interpreted solely on the basis of these factors, because it, like any complex psychological phenomenon, is not reducible to its constituent elements.

- The importance of the personality and its special role in determining human behavior have given rise to a huge number of often mutually contradictory theories and conceptions of the personality.

- The many theoretical and experimental studies of the personality can be neither unequivocally accepted nor rejected. Each of them may reflect real aspects of the multi-faceted phenomenon of personality or may interpret one and the same characteristic in different ways.

- An analysis of personality traits inevitably leads to the adoption of a particular psychological theoretical schema, which in turn will start to affect further studies.

Nevertheless, the aforementioned difficulties have not stopped researchers from looking for answers to questions concerning the nature of the personality and its role in human life.

Basic Theories of the Personality

By now the number of theories of personality, according to psychologists, has passed the 100 mark and continues to grow rapidly. An explanation of the "personality boom" should be sought both in the greater role of the personality in modern society and the greater capabilities of modern psychology. These myriad theories and conceptions include fundamental research that has determined the basic orientation of all other views of this phenomenon. According to Robert Ewen, one of the best-known students of personality theories, the basic conceptions that interpret the phenomenon of the personality can be divided into five groups: *classical, clinical, experimental, humanistic or existential, and behaviorist theories* (see Figure 2.1).

Figure 2.1

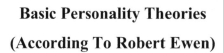

Basic Personality Theories

(According To Robert Ewen)

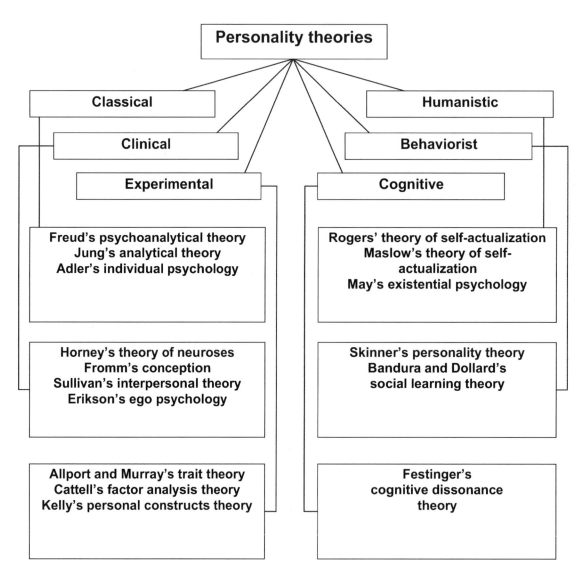

The *classical* group includes: Freud's psychoanalytical theory, Jung's analytical psychology, and Adler's individual psychology; the *clinical* group includes Karen Horney's neurosis theory, Erich Fromm's conception, Harry Stack Sullivan's interpersonal theory, and Eric Erikson's ego psychology; the *experimental* group includes the trait theories or personological theories of Gordon Allport and Henry Murray, Raymond Cattell's factor analysis theory, and George Kelly's theory of personal constructs; the *humanistic* group includes Carl Rogers' and Abraham Maslow's self-actualization theories and Rollo May's existential psychology; and finally, the *behaviorist* conceptions include B. F. Skinner's personality theory and Albert Bandura and John Dollard's social learning theory (Ewen, 1993).

A similar point of view in the classification of personality theories may be found in the study of Hjelle and Ziegler (2006, p. 600), who divided 15 personality theories among the following categories:

- The psychodynamic category represented by Freud's theory;
- A modified and revised psychodynamic category reflected in the works of Adler and Jung;
- Ego psychology and its associated currents in personality theory (Erikson, Fromm, and Horney);
- The dispositional category in personality theory (Allport, Cattell, and Hans Eysenck);
- The conditioning-behaviorist school in personality theory (Skinner);
- The social cognitive school in personality theory (Bandura and Julian Rotter);
- The cognitive trend in personality theory (Kelly);
- The humanist school in personality theory (Maslow);
- The phenomenological trend in personality theory (Rogers).

Another interesting classification of personality theories is given by Cervone and Pervin (2008). This book is unique in that the basic personality theories in psychology are considered from the standpoint of their development. "We focused our attention on the theoretical prospects for the 'great theories.' But while presenting information on the classics (such as Freud and Rogers) and their contribution to science, we nevertheless gave priority to modern studies of the personality," the authors wrote (Cervone & Pervin, 2006, p. 8). On this basis, they classified personality theories as follows:

1. ***Psychodynamic theory*** – Freud's psychoanalytic theory of the personality
   - ❖ Classical theoretical conceptions associated with Freud's theory:
     - – Freud's first two critics – Jung and Adler;
     - – Horney and Sullivan's cultural and interpersonal theories;

107

❖ Contemporary theories associated with psychodynamic personality theory:

  – Object relations theory[33];

  – The psychology of selfishness and the narcissistic personality;

  – Attachment theory[34];

2. ***Phenomenological theory****:* Carl Rogers' persona-oriented theory of the personality

  ❖ Concepts associated with Rogers' theory:

  – the humanist trend – Maslow's theory of self-actualization;

  – the positivist trend – studies of personal potential (Martin Seligman); and virtue and positive emotions (Barbara Fredrickson);

  – the existential trend – creation, non-existence, freedom, and responsibility (Jean-Paul Sartre);

  ❖ Contemporary theories:

  – Terror management theory, TMT (Sheldon Solomon, Jeff Greenberg);

  – Discrepancies theory[35] (E. Tory Higgins);

3. ***Personality trait theory***

  ❖ Allport's trait theory;

---

[33] *Object relations theory* is based on the postulate that the psyche consists of elements taken from the external, primary aspects of the functioning of other people. In part this approach comes from Freud's observations concerning the effect of objects on the development of the "Self." But in contrast to the Freudians, the advocates of object relations theory did not interpret all aspects of the personality in terms of the conflict between biological needs and social pressure (Smirnova, 1995).

[34] *Attachment theory* is currently one of the most popular trends in both American and European psychology. Originating in depth psychology, attachment theory became a separate scientific school. Like psychoanalysis, it emerged from clinical practice. Its founders, John Bowlby and Mary Ainsworth, were clinical psychologists and their early research focused on hands-on work with patients. Subsequently this trend became a full-fledged psychological concept that went far beyond the bounds of childhood psychology. Now attachment theory has applications in a very wide variety of fields in psychology: social, age, educational, and general psychology, and so forth. This theory is based on the relationship between two people and their interpersonal relations, which determine the entire mental and psychological structure of a person – an individual's attitude towards himself and the world, diverse experiences, cognitive and creative abilities, etc. Because the first relations with another person originate at an early age, the school's research focuses on early childhood (Smirnova, 1995).

[35] *Discrepancies theory* (theory of discrepancies among parts of the Self) of Higgins and his colleagues is devoted to an understanding of how violations of personal standards affect people's emotional and motivational states. This theory carefully examined the nature of the emotional suffering we experience when we realize that we have not lived up to our own ideals and standards. This discrepancy confirms the hypothesis that in addition to psychological arousal, dissonance also leads to psychological discomfort.

❖ Cattell's factor analysis trait theory;

❖ Eysenck's three-factor trait theory;

❖ Big Five theory[36];

4. ***Behaviorist personality theory***

❖ Skinner's operant conditioning theory;

5. ***Cognitive personality theory***

❖ Kelly's theory of personal constructs;

6. ***Social cognitive personality theory***

❖ Bandura's and Walter Mischel's personality theory;

❖ Hazel Markus's self-schemas theory;

❖ Carol Dweck's theory of learning and performance goals.

We can also cite other classifications of personality theories as examples, but for the most part they will fit within the framework of the theories cited above. We encounter a certain paradox when the growing number of personality theories does not in any way mean the emergence of a new trend in personality psychology. In fact, when you encounter a description of the next "new" theory of personality in the literature, you can quite easily come to an understanding of its philosophical and methodological foundations and its relationship to a specific existing personality theory. This is quite evident from the latest classification of personality theories, where new trends clearly fit within classical conceptions.

Personality specialists are not the only ones who complain of the lack of new trends in personality psychology. Researchers are starting to speak of a crisis in psychology as a whole, not just in the study of the personality. A unique sense of an invisible barrier which separates us from the unknown and which cannot be crossed or obliterated is well known to scientists. Édouard Claparède (1873–1940) was the first to mention this "taboo" for the study of the psyche, when he asserted that we do not know and will never know all its mysteries. Nevertheless, most psychologists have not abandoned their attempts to explain the complex and mysterious aspects

---

[36] The *Big Five theory* was developed by American psychologists P. T. Costa and R. R. McRae and became known by this name because of its focus on five factors: neuroticism (N), extroversion (E), openness (O), agreeableness (A), and conscientiousness (C). The NEO-PI survey was designed to measure the degree to which each factor is expressed. The Big Five model became quite popular in organizational psychology and management psychology, not just by virtue of its simplicity, but because of its validity and prognostic reliability.

of the human psyche, among which the problem of the relationship between the conscious and unconscious is the most complex.

From Jung
to More Jung

It is difficult to overestimate Carl Jung's legacy. His studies of dreams, the unconscious, the structure of the personality, the psychological role of myths, spiritual secrets, and much, much more have not only become classics of modern psychology and psychotherapy, but are also extensively employed by researchers today. Perhaps it would be hard to find a more successful attempt to interpret the relationship between the conscious and unconscious elements of the psyche than Jung's. Among all of the diverse theories and concepts of the personality, his analytical psychology has attracted particular attention. Originating at almost the same time as Freud's theory, for a long time it, like many other theories, experienced the impact of the tremendous success of psychoanalysis. But the more Freudianism faded into the past, the more attention Jung's theory attracted; and the more psychoanalysis was criticized, the more scientists were inclined to accept Jung's theory. Now the number of studies related to his works or based on his ideas has grown significantly and continues to grow.

Our focus on Jung's theory is no coincidence. From our point of view, *the personality is a system of interactive phenomena that determine the orientation of a person's behavior in society and that form its unique style, type, and mode of living and communicating.* A person's value orientations play an exceptional role in the phenomenology of the personality. Their importance in human consciousness has now become of such great interest to psychologists, sociologists, and social scientists, that the number of studies in this field has grown steadily. In speaking of values, we mean those of which a person is conscious. And while the study of unconscious values originated with Jung, the subsequent research of Kelly, Maslow, Rogers, Festinger, Bandura, and other outstanding psychologists led to interest in the importance of values, attitudes, and stereotypes as the basic conscious "regulators" of behavior.

Profound research in the field of value orientations and the identification of different types of values, such as terminal and instrumental values, have allowed psychologists to make quite detailed studies of their role in human life. But these studies usually proceeded from the premise that values are conscious convictions whose preservation and social realization is desirable. For example Kelly, in his debate with representatives of the psychodynamic school, generally abandoned the concept of *motivation*, considering that conscious goal-setting is a necessary and sufficient condition for the determination of human behavior. A huge layer of unconscious values, whose right to exist, as we have already mentioned, was proven by Jung, disappeared from view.

In speaking of unconscious values, we obviously have in mind the archetypes that Jung discovered, by which a person's unconscious tendencies are reflected in his life. This process, which Jung described quite well, made it possible to establish an unbreakable relationship between the unconscious and the conscious, a relationship that is considered the touchstone in many theories. The study of the structure of the personality and of the interaction of the unconscious and conscious and archetypes and value orientations within it, requires an analysis of the basic principles of Jung's theory and how they can be applied to contemporary interpretations of the personality.

According to Jung, the structure of the personality consists of three basic elements: *the conscious, the personal unconscious,* and *the collective unconscious.* Despite the fact that there are two unconscious elements and one conscious element, Jung assigned a great deal of importance to the conscious, believing that man is controlled not just by his latent tendencies, but to an equal degree by his desires, goals, dreams, and values.

In his view, ***consciousness*** embodies the *ego* as a complex of conscious ideas and goals that form the center of self-consciousness, while the *PERSONA* is a mask that we put on when we associate with other people. Quite often this mask is completely unsuited to our moods and desires, but we put it on nevertheless, in an attempt to respect the standards of morality and behavior accepted in a given social setting.

The ***personal unconscious*** originates from the moment a person is born and develops throughout his entire life. It includes a variety of experiences, sensations, and remembrances that a person has already experienced, but which were either forgotten or discarded. The personal unconscious can be recognized if necessary and has a certain regulatory effect on the conscious, by forcing a person to believe in his own strength or weakness. For example, Jung wrote: "It includes all mental contents forgotten over the course of life. Their traces permanently remain in the unconscious, even though their conscious perception becomes impossible. Moreover, the personal unconscious contains all subconscious impressions and perceptions that do not have enough energy to reach the consciousness…. Finally, the personal unconscious includes all psychological contents that are incompatible with a conscious attitude. They seem inaccessible mainly because of their moral, aesthetic, or intellectual flaws. A person cannot constantly feel and think in a lofty, proper, and moral way, and in an attempt to maintain an ideal attitude, he automatically discards everything that is not suited to it. If any function, such as thought, is highly developed and dominates the conscious, the function of feeling will naturally be discarded and descend into the unconscious" (Galperin & Zhdan, 2005, p. 623).

The ***collective unconscious*** can rightly be considered one of Jung's most outstanding discoveries which immortalized his name. He asserted that "The second compartment of the unconscious is the so-called super-personal or collective unconscious. The contents of this collective unconsciousness are not personal but collective; in other words, they belong not to any one individual, but to a lesser extent to an entire group of individuals; and usually they are the property of an entire people, or finally, all mankind. The contents of the collective unconscious are not acquired over the lifetime of a single person; they are innate instincts and primitive forms of comprehension – so-called archetypes or ideas" (Galperin & Zhdan, 2005, p. 624).

Thus a newborn infant is far from a *tabula rasa*, because it reflects innate tendencies which in adulthood will shape the orientation of its behavior. Similar tendencies called *archetypes* were defined as extremely complex relationships among images, desires, and modes of behavior, which are passed on from generation to generation and are directly reflected in human consciousness. According to Jung, it is archetypes that determine our attitude towards the social conditions in which we live and towards ourselves and the people with whom we associate (the ego), our animal needs (the Shadow), and our masculinity (Animus) and femininity (Anima).

For example, the "Shadow" archetype incorporates the most primitive and shadowy aspects of the personality; it originates, according to Jung, from our animalistic, amoral passions, and is absolutely unacceptable for normal social life. It is true that despite its amorality, the "Shadow" is the source of many of our creative inspirations and profound emotional experiences.

The importance of the idea of human archetypes has been proven by a large body of subsequent research by psychologists, philosophers, cultural researchers, anthropologists, and everyone who has been involved in the study of similar topics. Moreover, the discovery of archetypes stimulated the study of the ethnic psychological and cultural factors that affect human life. One example of such a study is the work of the remarkable Azerbaijani philosopher Hasan Guliyev, who in his book *Archetypes of the Gorgut Clan* (1998, p. 12), tried to describe several Azerbaijani archetypes.

In analyzing Jung's theory, we should place special emphasis on the ***transcendent functions of the psyche***, which he discovered and which upset contemporary notions of the relationship between the conscious and the unconscious. The fact is that the contents of the conscious and unconscious do not just affect each other and flow into each other, but may also lead to tension between them. This situation, which is quite often encountered, would lead to an intolerably grave condition were it not for the transcendent function of the psyche, which integrates opposites and creates a new quality of their manifestation. In fact the transcendent function of the psyche is a unique mechanism for the unity of opposites, which gives a personality its integrity and stability. "It is called 'transcendent' because it makes a transition from one attitude to another organically possible without the loss of the unconscious," wrote Jung (2006, p. 10).

The transcendence of the psyche, the collective unconsciousness and archetypes, the social dependence of behavior, and the creative potential of the personality – this is far from a complete list of the categories of Jung's theory on which the author of this monograph has relied in developing his own approach to the structure of the personality. Of course there will be quite a few critics of this approach, first of all those who did not comprehend Jung's ideas in the first place. But in our view, it is his ideas which, while very general and abstract, enable a quite specific and thorough description of the structure of the personality.

The Structure of the Personality

So what is the personality? If a personality is a system, as we have already mentioned, what are its constituent elements? What lies at the foundation of the "structure" known as the personality? All of our preceding analysis quite clearly demonstrates that in the current phase of development of psychology, it is doubtful that any one conception could answer these questions completely. At the same time, it was demonstrated that Jung's ideas were the best suited to the spirit and letter of our ideas of the nature of this phenomenon. On the basis of these premises, we will try to identify what we consider the most important ***elements in the structure of the personality***:

- The collective unconscious, whose most general and invariant elements are expressed in archetypes;

- The personal unconscious, which consists of information that a person has discarded or simply forgotten;

- The personal conscious, as the combination of feelings, ideas, convictions, values, and attitudes that determines and guides human behavior;

- The collective conscious, as invariant forms of a person's social existence reflected in neotypes.

Let us examine these concepts in greater detail.

Archetypes, as "definite relationships between images, desires, and forms of behavior passed down from generation to generation," have become firmly embedded in the psychological lexicon. They went beyond the boundaries of the semantic content that Jung gave them a long time ago, because the development of psychology has made it possible to discard their most mystical aspects and add real characteristics. Psychologists have added other archetypes that also exist in the human psyche (the Elder, the Parents, the Wife, and so forth) to the Jungian archetypes of the Shadow, Anima, Animus, and Persona as manifestations of the collective unconscious.

Archetypes have also been revised in terms of their commonality. The collective unconscious no longer refers to the invariant forms of behavior and living that are inherent to the entire human race, but rather to the invariants of a specific clan, nation, or generation. In other words, the presence of archetypes that is postulated for all people can vary significantly from nation to nation, from clan to clan, and from people to people, in their content. No matter what similarities exist among people, they differ from one another in the content of their cultures and ethnicities. Consequently they differ from each other in the content of their archetypes. The only thing that does not change is the fact that archetypes are not recognized. A person who lost his parents in infancy and who was not raised by them cannot recognize how, over the course of time, he exhibits the archetypal invariants of the behavior of his clan. A person cannot recognize how he starts unconsciously using the dialect of his ethnos when he does not even know it. Thus, archetypes, in our understanding, are invariant images, judgments, desires, and forms of behavior of any cultures, ethnicities, and clans which are passed down from generation to generation and remain unrecognized by a person, but determine his behavior.

The *human unconscious* is a domain which has always attracted the attention of psychologists by virtue of its mystery and mysticism, which contributed to the emergence of a large number of theories and conceptions.

Scientists have also turned to the unconscious when they have been unable to identify the true cause of a particular phenomenon. The unconscious only started acquiring a specific structure and levels and become an integral part of the psyche and personality with Sigmund Freud. By expanding the boundaries of the unconscious to the limit, or more precisely to the unlimited, and making the unconscious boundless and all-encompassing, Freud turned the personality into its hostage. He took it to absurd lengths, and consciousness came to be ignored altogether and was dismissed as "elements of perception infiltrating from the unconscious."

We should point out that it was Freud's aggressive expansion of the unconscious that became one of the main causes of his conflict with Jung. Jung not only could not agree with Freud's interpretation of the unconscious, but could not accept the total sexual determination of human behavior, as Freud insisted. By giving the libido the meaning of vital energy and by introducing the conscious into the structure of the personality, Jung limited the unconscious, but preserved the infinite variety of forms of its manifestations. The unconscious is infinite, but is not unbounded and its proper understanding is directly dependent on what we include in its content. Consequently, we, following Jung, believe that the unconscious has two layers, including the unconscious behavioral tendencies of our ancestors (the collective unconsciousness expressed in archetypes), and events, desires, needs, ideas, and forms of behavior forgotten and discarded by a person.

Strange though it may seem, psychology is obligated to modern physics, not its own research, for the greater role of the conscious in determining behavior. Modern physics abandoned the idea of absolute objectivity as the possibility of making an absolute distinction between an object and a subject, between the external world and an observer. Physicists recognized that it is impossible to observe an object and at the same time have absolutely no effect on it and not alter its characteristics (Einstein, Bohr, Heisenberg). Thus, the problem arose of constructing some kind of artificial bridge between the observer and the object, the internal and external worlds, and the world of consciousness and world of matter (Schultz & Sydney,

1998). To a large extent this gave rise to interest in the role of conscious experience in acquiring information about the external world. The research of cognitive psychologists, especially Bandura and Rotter in the field of social cognitive processes, constitutes clear evidence of this.

The Collective Unconscious and the Neotype

Giving consciousness special significance in the structure of the personality, we believe, allows us not just to reflect but to change reality. Traditionally the content of consciousness has been represented as information that a person has about himself, his environment, and the external world. This information is active and is constantly supplemented with new information, which enters into a relationship with elements already present in consciousness. In this sense, human consciousness is variable and changes with changes in the conceptions that are important to it. At the same time, a person's conscious system, which is variable as we stated above, contains invariable elements that we call **neotypes**, which reflect a person's **collective consciousness**. Thus human consciousness, like the unconscious, has two layers and includes categories that vary over time, as well as the invariant elements of the collective consciousness. The two-layer nature of consciousness, in our understanding, is not much different from the generally accepted approach in psychology, whereby consciousness is divided into individual consciousness and social consciousness. "Consciousness has at least two forms of existence," wrote the prominent Russian psychologist V. V. Nikandrov, "the individual and the social. Quite often group consciousness is interposed between them. General psychology studies the individual consciousness. Social psychology is mainly group and social consciousness" (Nikandrov, 2008, p. 563). But if individual consciousness is similar to our understanding of the personal conscious, then social consciousness as a term carries a semantic weight that is somewhat different from the weight we assign to the concept of collective consciousness.

Collective consciousness is a reflection of social invariables of our existence in the consciousness, which exist independently of individual consciousness. In terms of its semantic weight, our concept of collective consciousness includes both the characteristics of group mass consciousness once described by Gustave Le Bon, and Emile Durkheim's interpretation of collective consciousness as the spiritual unity of society.

As we have already mentioned, human consciousness may change with a change in its content, acquiring a personal meaning, i.e., it manifests a relationship to elements of its own content. A. N. Leontyev pointed this out in an attempt to distinguish the categories of "significance" and "meaning" in the structure of consciousness. For example, he wrote: "In contrast to significances, personal meanings as the sensitive tissue of consciousness have no 'supra-individual' or 'non-psychological' existence. While external sensitivity in the consciousness of the subject connects the significance and the reality of the objective world, personal meaning relates them to the reality of life in that world, with its underlying motivations. Personal meaning gives rise to the passion of human consciousness" (Leontyev, 1975, p. 153). While agreeing with this proposition, we must consider that consciousness contains special invariant forms that remain unchanged not just over the course of an individual's life, but continue to exist (in the consciousness of groups, nations, and peoples) after the individual's death. These forms of collective consciousness are manifest mainly in the form of invariant values, traditions, standards, feelings, and attitudes, which, in contrast to archetypes, are quite recognizable. They must be considered from two points of view: *that of a particular social group, people, nation, or ethnos, and from a common human point of view*. In the second case, the collective consciousness is reflected in sacred texts, the declarations of human rights and freedoms adopted by modern civilization, etc.

Consequently, *collective consciousness means invariantly existing group, ethnic, and social feelings, conceptions, ideas, values, and attitudes, recognized by a person and serving as a unifying spiritual force*. At the level of collective consciousness, invariance is both absolute and relative. The absolute nature of invariance applies to common human values, because they will remain invariant as long as humanity continues to exist, while the relative nature of invariance is directly applicable to the values of a specific social milieu, nation, or clan. In this case, values are also unchanged, but only at a certain point in time, and may change with changes in relationships with the environment.

From our point of view, the collective consciousness expressed in forms of collective conceptions and collective feelings in the individual consciousness is reflected as **neotypes**, which have the same content from generation to generation and are discovered and perceived by the individual during his lifetime. We have identified two such neotypes, called the "God" and "Prophet" neotypes. While the "God" neotype is recognizable as a combination of quite definite contents which are the same for all people, the "Prophet" neotype is only invariable within a given specific group, social milieu, nation, or people. Let us describe them in greater detail.

The "God" neotype. No one has ever cast doubt on the existence of common human values; these are the result of thousands of years of development of man's social ideals. In their most general and concise form, they become unique standards of human social behavior. These standards of behavior are highly moral and most of them originate from sacred scriptures such as the Koran, Bible, Talmud, etc. They have been invested with a certain divine aura, as sent from above. In the process of individual development, a person discovers for himself the existence of these norms and highly moral standards of behavior and life. It is not important how this discovery takes place: through the rules of behavior instilled in him by his parents or guardians or independently – in either case the individual is aware of their existence and value. They become neotypes of his consciousness, and their acceptance or rejection cannot disturb the "independence" of the existence of these values. Evidence of this may be provided by a survey of Americans concerning their acceptance of and belief in the Ten Commandments. It turns out that only 11% of the total number of Americans surveyed accept, believe, and order their behavior on the basis of the standards "thou shalt not kill," "thou shalt not steal," "love thy neighbor," and so forth, even though everyone knows of their existence (Patterson & Kim, 1992, p. 205).

As we mentioned above, a neotype that reflects common human values (the "God" neotype) becomes an element of consciousness, regardless of its acceptance as a personal value by an individual. This factor is extremely important for understanding the functioning of consciousness and the psyche as a whole. It indicates the presence of contents (standards, values, attitudes, etc.) in consciousness that are latently present and are not manifested outwardly, but have an effect on an individual's personal consciousness. Using A. N. Leontyev's terminology, a neotype in human consciousness acquires meaning and becomes "supra-individual." It is strange but true that in human consciousness, "impersonal" and "supra-personal" values coexist, along with the values of personal consciousness. Personal and impersonal values are recognized by the person, complement each other, go from one state to another, and often conflict, precisely in the same way as the archetypes and unconscious contents described by Jung. The transcendence between personal consciousness and neotypes is just as important as is the conflict between a person's unconscious and conscious tendencies. Its manifestations affect not just the possibility of integrating conflicting personal evaluations and neotypes into an integral whole, but also of making sense of events and developing an attitude towards them.

Thus human consciousness is filled with meaning and significance, attitude and knowledge, personal and impersonal content, and self-consciousness and neotypes. Of course this contradicts the generally accepted canons of Soviet psychology, whose paradigms are still used even today. We cannot agree with V. P. Zinchenko's claim (1991, p. 22) that "individual consciousness is not reducible to impersonal knowledge; that it is always passionate because of its association with a living being and its involvement in his activity; or in short, that consciousness is not just knowledge, but also attitude." The error of this approach is most clearly evident in an analysis of extreme pathological states of consciousness and deviant individual behavior. For example, studies of patients suffering from different kinds of neurotic disorders revealed that the "number" of meaningful elements that have become personal completely dominates the consciousness of the patient, leaving no room for neotypes. A constant "passionate" attitude towards every event and the impossibility of "letting go" and relaxing, the hypertrophy of the personal approach, personal evaluations, and personal interpretations, distinguish neurotics from normal people more than anything else. The exact opposite takes place in deviant behavior, when personal consciousness is fully dependent on neotypes, forcing a person to live according to "concepts." In both cases we observe deviations from the norm, which once again makes it possible to confirm the importance of unity in the consciousness of the personal and neotypal and the particular and the general, as the foundation for the normal functioning of the psyche and consciousness.

The "Prophet" neotype. In contrast to the "God" neotype, this neotype plays a major regulatory role in human consciousness, because it is a mandatory kind of behavior at the level where different groups of people have less in common. By representing the values of a certain social group, nation, or ethnos, the "Prophet" neotype is also a source of self-perfection and is similar in its semantic weight to Freud's concept of the superego and Jung's concept of the persona. The "Prophet" neotype is completely recognizable and embedded in the consciousness of an individual as a member of a given social group, in the form of stable convictions that "certain forms of behavior and goals of life are more preferable for an individual and his social environment than their opposites" (Rokeach, 1973, p. 5). An orientation towards the "Prophet" neotype allows a person to achieve not just social approval and reach a higher level in the hierarchy of a given social group, but to perfect his inner world and himself. But in social life, we often encounter people who reject this neotype for certain reasons. In this case, the social group starts to employ all its power to pressure the "heretic" by forcing him (at times physically) to follow the orders of the "Prophet" and adhere to accepted values. Because the "Prophet" neotype is relatively invariant and depends on social, economic, psychological, ethnic, and other environmental factors, which are themselves subject to change, a person sometimes succeeds in changing the attitudes of the members of a society, group, or nation. The neotype does not disappear, but is merely replaced by a new neotype with new content. "The King is dead, long live the King," is one case of a change in the content of a neotype which we mentioned above.

Neotypes are still a little-studied phenomenon of consciousness, but their role in regulating human behavior seems extremely important to us. As a direct expression of collective consciousness, neotypes are transformed by people into evaluative scales which they use to self-correct their social behavior. Collective values, standards, and traditions, regardless of whether they are common human values or group values, cannot affect a person if they are unknown to him. But by becoming familiar and significant, particular values are not automatically transformed into meaningful personal values, but exist latently in the consciousness and are actualized only when necessary. This "necessity" may be due to a number of reasons, including matters associated with the satisfaction or preservation of personal values. For example, in the event of a threat, in the broadest meaning of the word, the meaningful personal values that constitute the core of human self-consciousness are automatically associated with the entire structure of the value orientations of the person and his neotypes – *significant* (existing latently) and *personal*. While the structural association of a value makes it possible for a person to identify its place in his self-consciousness and thus form an attitude towards it, association with neotypes makes it possible to determine the type or manner of these attitudes. In other words, in human consciousness there is a constant process of not just the structuring self-consciousness, but developing the best possible modes of its operation in the social environment. It is this last quality that is made possible by neotypes as generalized subjective images of the collective consciousness.

The Schematic Structure of the Personality

We provide a graphic representation of the interaction of all the fundamentals of the structure of the personality that we have listed and analyzed (see Figure 2.2). Before we start analyzing the components of the diagram, we must say that the dividing lines are arbitrary. By identifying the "boundaries" of a particular component, we only intend to achieve greater clarity, which obviously might help us in our subsequent analysis. We emphasize this, because the transcendent function of the psyche not only makes it possible to "break" the boundaries of the unconscious and consciousness by going from one to the other, but also lays the foundations for the unity of opposites in the structure of the personality. From this point of view, special attention must be focused on the lack of a central component of the diagram, which in most theories symbolizes the nucleus of the personality. The "nuclear" approach to the structure of the personality cannot withstand criticism, because the personality itself claims this role. The search for a nucleus or central element may prove endless, because inside any nucleus there may be still another nucleus. Therefore we have depicted a structure of the personality in which each element corresponds to another complementary element. The mutual correspondence of the structural elements allows us to more adequately reflect the characteristics of their interaction and to avoid unnecessary speculation concerning the primary or secondary importance of particular elements. Thus, the priority is the interpretation of the interaction of **the unconscious** and **consciousness**, not the superiority of one or the other, in a situation where earlier attempts to establish this superiority in the history of psychology have not been crowned with success.

We have already stated that the interaction of the unconscious and consciousness, the transition from one to the other, and the conflict and tension between them are essential for their unity. But the transcendence of their mutual relationship would be incomplete without an understanding of aspects of the orientation of consciousness and unconscious. The term "orientation," which at present is more often used to describe the personality, was first used to describe psychological phenomena by Franz Brentano (1838–1917), who introduced the concept of "intentional orientation." In the process, an in-depth analysis of the intentionality of consciousness per se was conducted by Brentano's student and disciple Edmund Husserl (1859–1938), a German philosopher and the founder of phenomenology. He made one of the first attempts to guide human consciousness by means of intentions towards a temporal stream of experiences (Husserl, 1994, p. 37). Subsequently his ideas were developed in existential philosophy and psychology (Martin Heidegger, Jean-Paul Sartre, etc.), in personalism, in phenomenological sociology (Alfred Schutz), and so forth. The orientation of consciousness not just to spatial elements of being, but also to temporal elements, could hardly be doubted by any modern researcher. Psychologists have studied awareness of the future, anticipation, and a near-term and long-term orientation towards success as features of consciousness over time.

The situation is more complicated with respect to an understanding of the orientation of unconsciousness. Of course from the standpoint of psychoanalysis, there should be no doubt about this, because unconscious tendencies are always intentional. Nevertheless the orientation of the unconscious to any object is not so easy to represent because of the nature of the unconscious itself. In other words, if the unconscious is unconscionable (and may the reader please forgive me for the pun), the specific object towards which it (the unconscious) is oriented cannot be conscionable. But if this is so, at the very least, it is strange to speak of an orientation towards what looks unconscious. We should presumably try to find a way out of this situation in an approach which originates from Husserl's theoretical analyses. A scientist who basically denies the existence of anything that lies beyond the bounds of consciousness and who orients the intentions of consciousness towards time, has, in our view, also indicated the possibility of the intentionality of unconsciousness. In reality, the lack of a direct object of the orientation of the unconscious makes it possible to represent the intentionality of the unconscious towards time. From this standpoint, concepts such as "the unconscious tendencies of the past" and "dark, forgotten contents" acquire a specific meaning and orientation.

Thus, the orientation of the unconscious and consciousness towards the past, present, and future becomes one of the basic characteristics of our proposed structure of the personality. Figuratively speaking, *the personality becomes a means of expressing in the present the results of a comparison of the unconscious tendencies of the past and conscious aspirations for the future.* By expressing themselves in the personality, which apparently combines the incompatible – the past and the future, consciousness and the unconscious, our darkest sides and our brightest ones – we speak, socialize, live, and work.

Figure 2.2

The Structure of the Personality

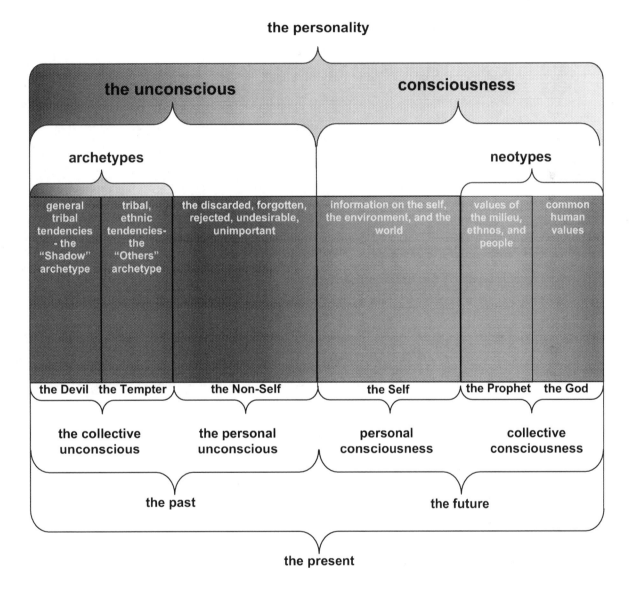

The next component of Figure 2.2 is the **structure of the unconscious** and **consciousness**. At first glance it might seem that the structure of these phenomena is three-layered: for the unconscious – common tribal archetypes, ethnic archetypes, and the personal unconscious; for consciousness – common human values, the values of a specific milieu, and personal consciousness. But this is not the case: The structures of the unconscious and consciousness are identical and consist of the collective plus the personal unconscious and the collective plus the personal consciousness. There are *absolute* and *relative* elements within the collective unconscious just as there are inside the collective consciousness. The absolute elements include the "Shadow" archetype (the darkest and most undesirable side of our personality) and the "God" neotype (common human values as the most desirable forms of behavior). The relative elements include unconscious tendencies expressed in the "Others" archetype and the recognized values of a specific social group expressed in the "Prophet" neotype.

The structuring elements of the personality, located on a continuum from the most undesirable in the unconscious to the most desirable in consciousness, have their own names:

- Animal instincts, shameful tendencies in the unconscious that deprive us of our human face – the "Devil";
- The tendencies of our tribe and ethnic group that we do not recognize but that attract us – the "Tempter";
- Events, desires, motives, and knowledge that we have forgotten, that are unimportant, and that we have discarded and rejected and constitute the contents of the personal unconscious – the "Non-Self";
- The cognitive elements of consciousness of oneself and one's environment and world – the "Self";
- Values recognized by a person, moral standards, moral principles, and attitudes accepted in a given social milieu, nation, people, and society – the "Prophet";
- Common human values that are the same for all people and are actually embedded in consciousness as the cultural heritage of mankind – "God."

The presence of each of these structuring elements in the personality is a condition for its integrity, but in reality we see the domination of one or more elements. This process leads to the construction of a subjective hierarchy of personal preferences or values. If the "God" or "Prophet" neotypes dominate in the values hierarchy, we are dealing with one type of personality; if the "Self" dominates, we are dealing with another type; and if the "Tempter" or

"Devil" archetypes dominate, then we are dealing with a completely different type. Consequently, *the domination of archetypal, unconscious, conscious, or neotypal tendencies presumes the formation of different types of personalities* (which are analyzed in the following sections of this monograph).

4. Feelings, Will, and Activity

*T*he sequence of the title of this section, "feelings – will – activity," was not chosen randomly. We are profoundly convinced that human *activity begins with an emotional experience that evokes certain feelings, whose projection onto the object of the experience leads to its association with a person's values, which in turn actualize efforts of the will to take specific actions.*

The origins of an emotional experience are associated with a change or violation of stereotypes, precepts, and attitudes, i.e., the developed forms of reflection of reality, and this is what evokes certain feelings. The relationships between the concepts of "emotion" and "feelings" are among the most complex and contradictory problems of psychology that have still not found a clear-cut solution. In his book *Emotions and Feelings*, Prof. Ye. P. Ilyin identified four approaches to this study that exist to this day:

1. The equation of feelings and emotions;
2. The study of feelings as one kind of emotional phenomenon;
3. The study of emotions as a form for the manifestation of feelings;
4. The separation of feelings and emotions (Ilyin, 2001, p. 136).

Our views are closest to the fourth approach, in which emotions and feelings are separate. We, like Professor Nikandrov, consider emotions and feelings to be "two different psychological phenomena which constitute a dialectical unity in which, first of all, emotions are the genetically original form and the primary level of the organization of affect, … and secondly, both forms are interwoven and interdependent in each affective experience" (Nikandrov, 2008, p. 443).

Feelings that originate on the basis of emotional experiences are multi-faceted and manifested at different levels of human life and hence are difficult to classify. Differing in their modality, intensity, depth, and other criteria, feelings accompany any manifestations of a person's activity, which ultimately serve to satisfy his needs. The emotional "companion" of human activity is determined by the very nature of the feelings, their subject matter, and their orientation towards an object. In other words, exhibited feelings are always projected onto an object. We do not experience joy for no reason at all; we are happy for a reason, and we are not just sad and we grieve for a reason. The negativity or positivity of our feeling world is determined by subjective or objective factors. This orientation or projection of feelings is very important, because the process allows a person to determine the objects of his experiences. Thus, if there are feelings, there is always an object that reflects them.

Let us consider an example. In most cases, what we experience emotionally when the quality of our work is criticized causes us to feel dissatisfaction, anger, or disappointment. After hearing criticism directed at us, we start to experience these feelings, which are immediately projected onto personally significant objects. They could be anything: the circumstances under which we were criticized, the type of work that was criticized, the person who was criticized, or the critic. At any rate, the feelings of dissatisfaction and anger are projected and find an object. In the situation described here, most often the object that reflects these feelings is the person of the critic. This phenomenon is well known at the level of common-sense psychology and is quite firmly embedded in ordinary human consciousness. It is no accident that as we start to criticize someone, we often use the phrase "Don't get mad, but…," stressing that the person we are about to criticize should focus his attention on the substance of the criticism and not take it personally. Thus, there are no such things as "unprojected" feelings. They are always projected and always find an object.

Two Types of Association of Feelings

In the next phase, projected feelings (objects of experience) are associated with the orientation of our values. By experiencing, feeling, and projecting our feelings onto personally significant objects, we always associate them with our own values. But in this case we must elaborate the concept of "association," because it can be manifested in two ways.

The first type (so-called *outward association*) occurs when projected feelings (the objects of experience) are associated and evaluated by a person with respect to his exterior world and are "not given access to" truly personally significant values. Of course, the use of the phrase "not given access to" is quite arbitrary, because "access" does take place, even though it has absolutely no effect on personally significant and "specially protected" values in the pyramid of the value-oriented unity of a personality. Quite often outward association is manifested in a person's greater verbalizing, which in its own way takes the place of all other kinds of activity, limiting a person in his actions. How many times have we witnessed hyperactive verbalizing accompanied by the phrases "Are you kidding me?" "He should be ashamed of himself," "This is unbelievable!", which, if these led to subsequent action, would have had absolutely nothing to do with the subject of verbal dissatisfaction? Strong rhetoric, with many stock phrases like these, plus the outward comparison of projected feelings, are perhaps inconsistent with the person's true intentions, goals, and values. *Thus insincerity and lying are the means by which a person engages in a socially approved type of behavior, regardless of whether he actually accepts the forms and standards of behavior of a given social milieu.*

The custom of mourning the deceased, which has been adopted by practically all nations and peoples, can serve as evidence of this. For example, in Azerbaijan, wakes include inviting relatives and acquaintances to accompany the deceased on his last journey. Quite often in the process of this activity (especially in rural areas) a group of women is organized for the purpose of mourning the deceased fervently and emotionally. This group usually does not consist of close relatives, but of persons who are acquainted with the deceased and his relatives, but do not have close ties to him or his family. The emotional experiences of the group, which are vividly presented to the public (shouting, crying, tears, lamentations, stock phrases, and so forth) are intended to evoke feelings of sadness, grief, and hopelessness among the other participants in the ceremony. They release the emotions of the people and cause all the participants to shed tears, thus turning it into a kind of "theatrical production." While setting aside the psychotherapeutic nature of this "production" (the fervent and free exhibition of emotions helps to eliminate stress), we should mention that the association of the projected feelings of the "initiating" group with their own values occurs only on the external level, which explains the demonstrativeness and at times theatricality of their expressions and actions. The object of the experiences, in this case the deceased, does not "disturb" the profound personal values of the professional mourners, forcing them to portray the deceased as a person close to them in order to play their roles professionally.

The insincerity and falsehood of the feelings of these people has nothing in common with the genuine grief of a person who has suffered a loss. That person's emotional experiences, exhibited in feelings of grief, loneliness, and melancholy, are also projected and associated with the personally significant values of the individual, as in the first case, but in this case the association is genuine and forces him at times to sacrifice himself and his health in an attempt to recover the loss of the person who was dear to him. Thus, an external association of projected feelings must be clearly distinguished from *a genuine association to the core values of a person,* which actualizes his willingness to act.

The Orientation of the Personality

Among all the mutually determined phases of the transformation of emotional experiences into concrete actions, the final phase of associating projected feelings (objects of experience) with values that are significant to a person is the most important, because the final phase explains the orientation of human behavior. This phase makes it clear why a person reacts to certain events in a certain way and how his orientation is formed. In the broadest understanding of the words, "human values" – their interaction, co-subordination, urgency, significance, and meaningfulness – become the basic determinants of our purposeful behavior. By representing this graphically, we can use a specific example to explain it (see Figure 2.3).

Waiting for a person who is very late, who is close to us or whom we badly need, for example, leads to the experience of certain feelings (disappointment, alarm, etc.), which are immediately projected onto the object of personal significance to us (the person we are waiting for). "Why didn't he tell us?" "What could have happened to him?" "Is he being irresponsible, or was he delayed by circumstances?" By asking ourselves these questions, we trigger the "mechanism" for associating projected feelings (objects of experience) with the hierarchy of our values. Depending on whether the association is merely outward or is genuine, we behave in a particular way. For example, if the person or our relationship to him occupies a leading position in our values hierarchy, we engage in deliberate efforts to find him (looking around, calling various phone numbers, etc.). If the association of projected feelings occurs only at the outward level, without affecting our deep personal structures, the response will most probably be determined by one's individual psychological traits and social environment.

Figure 2.3

**The Mechanism of Transformation of Emotional Experiences
into Concrete Actions**

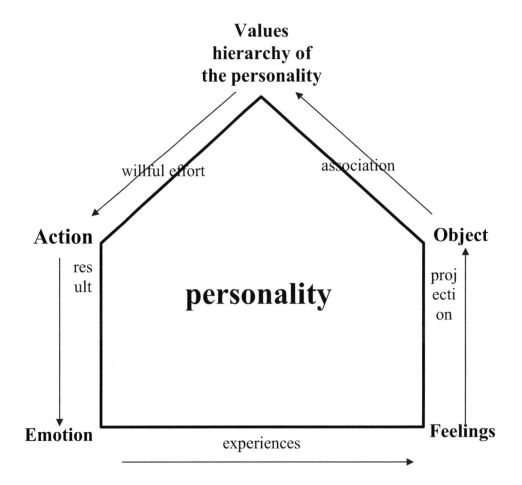

This example of the contraposition of projected feelings allows us to identify the cause of our actions. It is not just the fact of the contraposition of projected feelings and one's values that is important, but its result. If the contraposition is urgent and significant for a person and brings him satisfaction, then his willful efforts and actions will be focused on maintaining his present state; whereas if the contraposition does not bring him satisfaction and is not consistent with his values, as is the case with negative feelings, willful efforts will be focused on neutralizing the factors that evoked those feelings. This may be expressed in different ways – from a change in one's living environment to a change in attitude towards the source of the negative experiences and the feelings that correspond to them. For example, if a person feels uncomfortable in new company, he may exhibit different kinds of behavior, starting with the comical and ending with the aggressive.

Fear as a State of Threat to Personally Significant Values

It is totally different when the association of projected feelings is not just inconsistent with but threatens a person's values. In this case the person experiences *fear*, which most researchers still consider an emotion or feeling. From our point of view, fear is a state that occurs when the contraposition of projected feelings (objects of experience) and one's personally significant values starts to threaten these values. And the more significant the threatened value is, the greater the fear. But the *danger level or threat level* are quite subjective concepts, because to one man combat is everyday risky work, while for another person a walk in the park is a very hazardous undertaking. Consequently, the level of subjective danger is directly dependent on the position of the values in the overall values hierarchy and is determined accordingly. In short, we need to clearly understand that fear of the destruction or disappearance of a value will contribute to willful efforts to take actions to preserve and save the value itself. *And the higher the position a value occupies in the hierarchy, the greater the fear a person experiences about it and the stronger his willful efforts to "salvage" the value will be.* You be the judge.

As we know, the entire process of training a soldier proceeds in three basic directions. The *first* is the material aspect, learning to use his weapons; the *second* is physical training; and the *third* is fostering of high morale and love of country. The third and last one is reflected in the oath a soldier takes during his service. The assumption is that if the training has been successful, the values a soldier affirms in his oath will occupy a paramount position in the structure of his personality and will guide his behavior.

Now let us imagine that the same solider is in actual combat. His emotional experiences instill a feeling of hatred projected onto the enemy. At the same time, the people and country he is defending are transformed into objects of his experiences. In the soldier's consciousness, the enemy becomes treacherous and perfidious, while the people he is defending become aggrieved, humiliated, and injured. This projection of feelings, as we have already mentioned, is associated with his values hierarchy. We see here a case of genuine inner, not outward association, which actualizes the higher levels of the person's hierarchy of values. This association may, as we stated above, be consistent or inconsistent with a person's aspirations; but if it threatens the stability of his core values, he will start experiencing fear not for himself, but for the value he affirmed in his oath and which is at the very top level of his values hierarchy. As a result, the situation brings all of his will to bear, to act to protect that value: The soldier charges a machine-gun nest and falls on a live grenade, not out of any thought of his own well-being, but out of fear for his higher values – his country, his friends, his relatives, and so forth. *Heroism becomes the highest manifestation of fear, not for oneself, but for one's values.* It is exhibited where a person, by force of will, takes actions to "save" his aspirations, hopes, desires, and values.

This example of heroism is based on thinking about the dominance of the value of country in a soldier's values hierarchy; but it is quite possible to speculate that an extremely wide variety of values may occupy the top spot in a values hierarchy, depending on an individual's personal aspirations, his upbringing, the requirements of his environment, etc. The hero of the movie *Ballad of a Soldier* (1959), after knocking out two enemy tanks, admitted that he was "very afraid for himself," thus confirming that his personal safety occupied first place in his values hierarchy. *We may conclude that the content of a value is not as important as the place in the values hierarchy that it occupies.* And if it occupies first place, the actions to preserve it will be the most energetic.

We have tried to explain the mechanism and causes of a person's actions and the orientation of his behavior. It has become clear that the determinant of willful effort is a contraposition of projected feelings; and it is obvious why it is not the content of the values but their place in a person's values hierarchy that determines the degree of effort that will be expended to achieve them; and finally, we succeeded in demonstrating that the highest level of human activity is nothing but the highest manifestation of a person's fear for the preservation of his values, with the continuum of differences in values being quite large, perhaps including both self-valuation (valuing one's own life, well-being, health, etc.) and love for one's friends, near and dear ones, work, and country.

5. *Personal Creativity, Freedom, and Degradation*

(the Sociopolitical Aspect)

*H*aving shown that the level of activity is determined not so much by the substance of values as by their place in a person's values hierarchy, we should mention that activity in and of itself is just one of the psyche's three basic functions. In addition to stimulating activity, the psyche also enables psychological reflection and communication with other people. Depending on the person's prevailing reflections, and with whom he communicates and how he communicates, his activity may lead to degradation of the personality, loss of the socialization of the personality, and a disintegrative and destructive type of behavior. This proposition is quite provocative when we consider that certain researchers proceed from the absolutization of activity as a value that makes it possible for a person to reflect and communicate. Setting aside scientific debates on the role and effect of activity in shaping the personality, we will say that revealing its inner potential is related to, on the one hand, the person's creative talents, and on the other hand, the opportunities for their free manifestation and development in society. Ideally, values that are shaped on this basis and occupy a dominant position in an individual will require his maximum effort for their preservation and possible realization. In reality, personal activity, reflecting real social relations, is designed in most cases to sustain and develop values that are not a priority for the person himself, but for the society around him.

Thus, the formation of the personality cannot be imagined outside the social processes in which a person lives, works, exists. Society, by "painting" human activity in the colors it needs, by giving a person's psyche "material" for reflection, and by creating "favorable" forms of communications for the personality, can serve not just as a source of development of the personality, but can also contribute to its degradation. Of course, degradation as the gradual disintegration of the personality may have a variety of causes.

The most common idea of the degradation of the personality is associated with psychopathological processes, which have been quite thoroughly studied in medical psychology and psychiatry. But we have not encountered any studies that dealt with the interrelationship of the degradation of the personality and social processes. More often scientific journals and monographs contain information on how society affects the formation of the personality, what role it plays in raising the new generation, or conversely, what role the personality plays in the development of social processes. Despite all their importance, these studies presume that society *a priori* has an advantage over the personality, and that it is the personality that must integrate into society. And the more profound this integration is, the more important and valuable a person becomes to society. Although obvious, this approach is dangerous in that the social processes that require the involvement of persons may be, at the very least, inadequate. If in addition we assume that the adequacy or inadequacy of social processes is quite difficult to determine, the danger of mistaking the degradation of the personality for its formation and development becomes even more obvious.

The Appropriateness of Social Processes and the Personality

It is difficult to assume that any society, especially a nation, would call itself inappropriate. It is no less difficult to find criteria for the appropriateness of social processes. But these difficulties have not stopped scientists, who are conducting studies in this field at a rapidly growing rate. The use of the term "appropriateness" to describe social processes, society, and authority has become more and more popular in the world of political scientists and social technologists. For example, the outstanding American scientist Noam Chomsky entitled his most recent book *Failed States* (2006, p. 26). He made extensive use of the term "appropriateness" in his discussions, understanding it as one of the basic characteristics of "successful states." Another American researcher, Fareed Zakaria, in his book *The Future of Freedom* (2003, p. 33), also analyzed the issue of appropriateness in politics, studying "non-liberal democracies" and comparing them to the liberal democracies of the West.

In the opinion of most researchers, appropriateness in relation to social phenomena means conformity to the specific criteria, values, or standards of a democratic society. It is hard not to agree that democracy is the only form of social structure that allows people to live normally and to develop their personalities in society. In all other cases, the risk of destruction and degradation of the personality is much higher. I have no intention of exaggerating the importance of democracy and unjustifiably denigrating the role of all other types of social formations. Recent world events have demonstrated that to absolutize democracy and accept it as "manna from heaven" and a panacea for all the ills of modern society would be badly mistaken (Seyidov, 2009e, p. 320). In reality, outstanding individuals, creators, writers, artists, public figures, military leaders, and brilliant scientists have been present at all times and in societies of all types. Our logic could not withstand any criticism were we to deny this.

Democracy and the Ability of an Individual To Oppose the System

At the same time, in contrast to all other forms, types, and modes of social relations, democracy gives an individual official and genuine rights affirmed in law to oppose the system in which he lives. Moreover, the possibility of intervening in, influencing, and refusing to accept the social system has become a basic condition for the system's existence. In a speech to the Council of Europe Parliamentary Assembly in April 2008, German Chancellor Angela Merkel (2008) said the following: "We must do everything we can to make it possible for the citizens of the United Europe to sue Brussels. What is a desire and dream today must become a reality tomorrow."

As we can see, it is not a particular form of social order, but the possibility and right to oppose it that acquires paramount importance. Most of the breakthrough discoveries and achievements that have changed the world order were created as a reaction to the micro-order in which they were created. The conflict between the *individual and society* has become a necessary condition for the development of the individual, and the kind of sociopolitical system a person lives in is absolutely irrelevant. From the standpoint of personal development, it is not the system in which a person develops that is important, but the possibility of opposing the system.

By putting the question this way, the advantages of democracy are obvious: Only in this system is there the possibility of opposing it without negative consequences for the individual who opposes it. In all other systems, such opposition, while it may be possible, is dangerous and often considered illegal. Moral and physical violence against a person who is not afraid to oppose a system that does not tolerate this type of behavior most often ends quite sadly for the individual. History has plenty of examples of society's inadequate reaction to an individual who protests and refuses to accept the forms and manners of behavior or thought imposed on him. Withstanding pressure and defending one's own point of view has never been an easy task for an individual in any era or in any form of social relations. But democracy was the first to utilize personal protest as an essential element of social relations. In turn we know that creativity is the most "protesting" type of activity that rejects the prevailing morality (see *The Paradox of Morality*). Creativity has become one of the foundations of a free, democratic society. Thus studies of "personal protest," non-conformism, field independence, and unusual or taboo fields of activity, along with other "creative" phenomena, have acquired a special significance. By ensuring the opposition of the person and society, these phenomena have been transformed into critical factors for development of the creative personality and into conditions for the adequate functioning of society. Any restriction or prohibition of these phenomena if they materialize leads to the degradation and disintegration of the personality and ultimately to the degradation of society.

6. The Opposition Between the Creative Person and Society (Psychological Aspect)

The opposition between *the individual and society* is an age-old problem that is not only of interest to us. It has long troubled, continues to trouble, and will probably long continue to agitate psychologists, sociologists, political scientists, and other social scientists. There is no doubt that in studying the psychology of creativity, we are most interested in the conflict with society that is exhibited by gifted people. We previously stated that opposition becomes one of the basic types or modes of the relationship between a gifted person and the world around him. The characteristics of the relationship between a creative person and society, the roots of his conformist or non-conformist behavior, dependence or independence on external circumstances, and his self-confidence or lack thereof have been studied quite well. For example, there are a vast number of studies that have identified particular traits of a creative person and his talents and cognitive characteristics. By analyzing certain traits, we will gain a better understanding of the causes that impel a creative person to unusual, unconventional behavior.

The Aptitude for Metaphorical Thinking

Most researchers who study creative aptitudes have identified the capacity for metaphorical thinking as one of the most important. And in fact, the ability to use a single object, word, gesture, or image in an unusual way is a distinctive trait of the creative individual. The objects around us, what happens to us, and the people with whom we associate are multi-faceted and extremely complex. Everything we come into contact with has many aspects and nuances, but not everyone can see even a few of them. Most people see what immediately catches their eye. But with metaphorical thinking, a person not only sees an object better than others, but can find a way to portray it that no one had even thought of before. Scientists proved a long time ago that metaphorical thinking, as the capacity to represent ordinary items of existence and phenomena in new and untraditional ways and relationships, has a significant impact on the productivity of creative thinking.

Flexibility

Another generally accepted capability of a creatively active person is flexibility. The outstanding American psychologist J. P. Guilford studied it in particular detail and understood this capacity as the ability to make a relatively quick cognitive transition from one class to another (Guilford, 1967a). This allows a person, if necessary, to go from considering one problem to studying a completely different problem that seems totally unrelated to the first. Many researchers believe that a creatively active individual is relatively free of associative responses and is capable of denying them, not experiencing them, or greatly neutralizing pressure from them.

Another aspect of the flexibility of a creative person is his adaptability, which allows him to adjust well to problem solving and become a "professional" in devising solutions. This ability allows him to use past experience in a new situation in the best and most productive way.

The Capacity for Inner Vision

As Frank Barron has observed (1969, p. 45), this capacity very much distinguishes a creative nature and is the amazing "tool" that allows a creatively active person to grasp the essence of a subject even before achieving a final analysis. A person with this capacity intuitively senses the direction in which his thinking must proceed. The capacity for inner vision is often associated with intuitive decision-making ability; but while an intuitive decision arises directly in the process of solving a problem, the capacity for inner vision distinguishes the creative person in his day-to-day experience.

The Neutralization of Visual Cues

The capacity for inner vision is closely related to the creative individual's ability to *neutralize visual cues* (Sternberg, 1994, pp. 607–677). This allows him to clearly recognize the most essential attributes of an object that cannot be noticed right away. We know that the essence of any problem is quite frequently hidden, and it is visual cues and illusions that prevent a person from arriving at a solution. It is extremely difficult for an "ordinary" individual to neutralize these cues and illusions. Back in 1923, Karl Jaspers wrote that "*Illusions* is the term for perceptions which in fact are transpositions (or distortions) of real perceptions; here, external sensory stimuli unite with certain transposing (or distorting) elements so that in the end we cannot differentiate the one from the other" (Jaspers, 1997, p. 65). For a gifted, creative person, the neutralization of illusions and the ability to see what is most essential in a studied event or fact is a distinctive trait.

The Ability to Find Order in Disorder and Chaos

Another distinctive trait of the creative individual is *the ability to find order in disorder and chaos* (Gruber, 1981, p. 65; Davis & Restle, 1963, pp. 103–116; Sternberg, 1994, p. 609). The concepts of *order and chaos* are quite subjective. What is order to one person is total chaos to another, and vice versa. The concept of harmony, which a creative person can create from disharmonious elements better than other people, helps resolve this conflict. The phenomenon of improvisation, which is most vividly expressed in music, confirms this. "A person sits down at a piano and pensively plays with the keys. There's still nothing – no idea, no theme, no concept. Nothing specific. There's only a mood and its associated sadness, in a melodic recognition of oneself in the world and the world in oneself. Just a vague need for creative self-realization. By playing with the keys, the person feels the point of application of this need, the direction of this feeling, the contours of this musical state. An unintended combination of sounds gradually gives rise to the logic of their movement. It carries within itself a rhythmic picture, flashes of an idea, and the seeds of a melody. And it already seems as if the very process of aimless, random playing of the keys has miraculously given birth to music" (Runin, 1980, p. 45). But musical improvisation is the province of highly gifted and talented musicians, not just anyone who participates in the art form.

The following characteristics of the creative individual that are most often represented as his personality's cognitive traits are verbal agility, a fertile imagination, intelligence, originality, and activity in unusual fields. But in identifying specific cognitive traits, we must not confuse them with personality traits *per se*, which in creative persons are quite contradictory. For example, Ellis Torrance initially identified traits such as a lack of self-confidence, shyness, reticence, love of solitude, and unpopularity, but subsequently cited the desire to dominate, boldness in defending one's ideas, need for social contact and social activity, and gregariousness and popularity (Walbeg, 1972, pp. 340–361).

Intelligence or Relatively High Intelligence

This cognitive personality trait has many interpretations, and its role in creativity depends on the definition of the concept of "intelligence." We understand a relatively high intelligence as a trait of a creative personality in connection with such qualities as "intuitiveness," "quick-wittedness," "mental agility," etc. It is difficult to overestimate their role in human creativity, because they allow us to speak of an intelligent person.

Nevertheless, the relationship between intelligence and creativity is not so clear-cut. Wallach and Kogan's studies (1972, p. 42) demonstrated that the correlation between measures of creativity and intelligence is almost zero. A high level of creativity does not prove that a particular person possesses a high level of intelligence or vice versa.

Originality

Any creativity, in no matter which field of human endeavor it occurs, presupposes originality, i.e., dissimilarity to others, unconventional solutions, new ideas, etc. Originality as a creative personal trait is manifested in two ways: the *first* is related to the product of the creator's activity, his creation, which bears the imprint of originality, while the *second* is related to the behavior of the creative person, because he exhibits creativity not just in his work, but in his dress, tastes, mannerism, speech, and so forth. Some researchers have even identified eccentricity as a separate creative personality trait and have stated that creative persons do not object to being described as eccentric.

Verbal Facility

We should not understand this in the literal meaning that a creative person talks rather fast; the exact opposite might be the case. Verbal facility as a creative personality trait is understood as the rapid comprehension of words, in the phenomenon of "catching on the fly," etc. We are well aware that a thought is difficult to separate from its verbal shell. On the other hand, any word carries a certain semantic weight; but an abundance of words and terms does not mean an abundance of ideas. It is often true that words serve as an extremely strong barrier that prevents an understanding of the essence of a subject under study or the meaning of a word or idea. Verbal facility allows an individual to "sense" the falsehood of words and "feel" the meaning of an event or phenomenon, which is so important in the process of creativity

Rich Imagination

It is undisputed that imagination plays a huge role in human creativity. This does not mean that only creative people have imaginations and fantasies, because everyone has them, insofar as they are an integral part of human mental processes. "There is a bit of fantasy in any abstract thought that rises above the immediate facts; and there is a bit of fantasy in every action that changes the world in any way; there is a bit of fantasy in every person who, by thinking, feeling, and acting, contributes even a grain of something of his own…" (Rubinshteyn, 2002, p. 372). A rich imagination and a wealth of fantasies are distinctive traits of a creative person. The level and quality of the transformations a person makes by virtue of his imagination distinguishes this individual from "ordinary" people. And the power of the creative imagination and its level are determined, as Rubinshteyn claimed, by the correlation of two indicators: "The extent to which the imagination adheres to the restrictive conditions on which the meaningfulness and objective significance of his creations depend, and the extent to which his creations are new and original and different from that which gave rise to them. An imagination that does not meet both conditions at the same time is fantastic but creatively infertile" (Rubinsteyn, 2002, p. 365).

Activity in Unusual Fields of Endeavor

A creative person is unusual by nature and is significantly different from the people around him in the richness of his inner world. A creative person cannot be interested, caught up, or engaged in humdrum, routine work. He is always looking for the new and unusual. Even in activity which is not in any way unusual, a creative person can find, or more precisely create, something that makes the activity creative. Activity in unusual fields of endeavor as a personality trait is manifested in two ways:

The *first* involves a constant search for new, original, fascinating, interesting, and unusual fields of endeavor.

The *second* involves the transformation of routine work into creative work. In discussing the characteristics of the creative person, we cannot ignore the person's cognitive styles, i.e., the person's relatively stable individual cognitive traits, which most often include *a tendency to generalize and a broad outlook, a predisposition to non-verbal information, and the construction of new structures from old elements, constantly asking "why?", sensitivity to gaps in knowledge, the use of existing knowledge as the basis for creating new ideas, field independence, etc.*

Of the aforementioned cognitive styles, a predisposition to non-verbal information and field dependence are the most interesting from the standpoint of the relationship between individual and society.

Predisposition to Non-Verbal Information

The non-verbal information used by a creatively active individual presupposes several semiotic systems. The *first* must be called the *optical kinetic system*, which includes gestures, facial expressions, and pantomime. There is no doubt of its significance in the communications process. There is even a special field of study of these phenomena known as kinetics. A creative person uses this channel for acquiring information to the greatest benefit and advantage for himself and his work.

The *second* is the *paralinguistic and extralinguistic system* of signs. Paralinguistics is the vocalization system, i.e., the quality of the voice and its range and tonality. The extralinguistic system includes pauses and other modes of expression, such as coughing, laughter, the tempo of speech, etc. The paralinguistic and extralinguistic systems augment semantically significant information, which is extremely important for human creative activity.

Space and time serve as another semiotic system. How people position themselves in the process of communications and how they react to the timing of communications (delays, the length of conversations, and so forth) have a significant impact on the quality of the information acquired in this way (Andreyeva, 1980, p. 109).

A creative person is distinguished by the predisposition to non-verbal information and the ability to "read," experience, and feel that which does not exist for other people.

Field Independence

One of the cognitive styles of an individual which is studied more than other styles is field independence. Researchers have identified its relationship to the sociability, orientation, and attitudes of an individual (Seyidov, 1989, pp. 131–132). Also, the relationship of field independence – understood as a subject's orientation towards internal standards, when inadequate forms of reflecting the external world are imposed on him – to a person's creative activity is very important and interesting to us. This relationship is unique in its own way, because in our view, a field-independent person resorts to creative activity when the inadequate ways of reflecting reality that are imposed on him threaten his internal standards.

In order to prove this hypothesis, we conducted an experiment in which field-independent test subjects were subjected to a pressure technique that involved changing their internal standards of behavior. By using a "masked figures" test, which consisted of 30 composite complex figures, we determined the field dependence-field independence (FD-FI) indicators of a group of 200 students. The test subjects had to identify simple figures in the complex figures, and the time of identification and number of right answers served as FD-FI indicators. As a result, 61 individuals out of the total sample of test subjects were identified as field-independent. The other participants in the experiment were divided into two groups – an FD group and an extremely FD (EFD) group. The test results are presented in Table 1. Here we can see that the FD group of test subjects included 107 persons, while the EFD group consisted of 32 individuals; that is, there were about two field-dependent subjects for every field-independent test subject. The EFD subjects were people who could basically not solve the "masked figures" assignment or who took an extremely long time to accomplish the task.

Table 1

The Distribution of Test Subjects in Terms of the FD-FI Indicator[37]

FI	FD	EFD	Total test subjects
61	107	32	200

In the next phase of the experiment, the FI, FD, and EFD students were divided into 10 groups, each of which included nine FD test subjects, five FD subjects, and two EFD subjects.

Thus we maintained the approximate ratio of FD to FI individuals in the total sample (two to one). We divided the groups into two categories of five groups each. The first five groups served as control groups, while the other five were the experimental groups. We should point out that all 10 groups were given the same assignment,[38] which the control groups completed without preconditions, while the experimental groups completed it with special instructions. Instructions in the experimental groups were only given to the FD subjects, who, in their collective discussions and solutions of the problem, were supposed to ignore as much as possible the solutions proposed by the FI group members.

The results were quite interesting. *First of all*, we acquired additional proof that the FD subjects were more oriented to external, socially approved standards of behavior. The activity of the latter in the groups (control and experimental) greatly differentiated them from the FI subjects, and often it was this difference that caused social tension between them. *Secondly*, the clear positive correlation between FI and success in problem solving found in our previous studies was reconfirmed. And *thirdly*, in the experimental groups, where the test subjects were instructed ahead of time to ignore the solutions proposed by the FI members, the productivity and originality of the solutions proposed by the FI group members improved dramatically. By

---

[37] *FI* – field independent, *FD* – field dependent, *EFD* – extremely field-dependent test subjects. Customarily studies of this cognitive style do not involve singling out extremely field dependent individuals as a separate group. But in our experiments, the EFD test subjects exhibited specific atypical forms of behavior which are more often observed in FI subjects. This served as the basis for a more careful consideration of this group and its identification as a separate group.

[38] For the group discussion, we proposed resolving the so-called barber's paradox, in which two mutually exclusive conditions make a formal logical solution impossible. But the formal insolvability of the paradox did not stop the students from devising original ways to eliminate the contradiction at the root of the problem.

comparison with the level of activity of the FI members in the control groups, the activity of the FI members of the experimental groups was on average 140% greater. These results are presented in Table 2. Only in one experimental group, the fourth, did the effectiveness of the FI subjects decline by comparison with the control group, as a result of excessive pressure from the FD group members.

Table 2

Ratio of Answers of FI Members in the Control and Experimental Groups (%)

No. and type of group	Control	Experimental
1	33	47
2	40	90
3	30	64
4	45	21
5	50	70
Arithmetic mean (M)	39.6	58.4

The 'Masking' of an Extremely Field-Dependent Individual

The experiments revealed one more interesting fact: The EFD and FI members exhibited behavioral characteristics that were outwardly very similar. We were unable to find an explanation of this phenomenon in the literature, but our attention was drawn to a description of the types of psychological defenses employed by the FD individuals. Using the Rorschach method, incomplete sentences tests, and special questionnaires, scientists have concluded that FD individuals mainly employ suppression as a defense mechanism (Dunchev, 1985, p. 123). The scientific data led us to conclude that extremely FD individuals, aware of their marked failures in the "masked figures" test by comparison with the other subjects, tried to compensate for and conceal this failure. By suppressing field dependence as the root of their problem-solving failure, they acted as though they were capable of finding the right solution better and faster than anyone else, i.e., like the field-independent group members. By playing the role of "scorned geniuses" and getting angry and retreating into themselves, they were basically uninterested in solving the problems and their goal was to avoid losing their place in the group's social hierarchy and to draw attention to themselves.

This "masking" on the part of EFD individuals is extremely important for understanding several problems of the social psychology of creativity, because ungifted people who are the most short-changed in terms of creativity try to pass themselves off as genuine creators (see *The Paradox of Desirability*). But field independence allows a creative person not just to proceed from his own point of view, but is one of the determining factors of creative activity.

The ability of creative persons to withstand social pressure, their resistance to imposed social processes, and independence from the "field" around them, in the broadest meaning of the word, become necessary conditions for creativity. Once again we are returning to the idea of creativity as a phenomenon that makes it possible for an individual not just to actualize his inner world, but to withstand pressure and overcome the difficulties of the world around him. In the process, we should note that the opposition between the individual and society ultimately makes it possible to harmonize this relationship, until the next creator comes along and his inner world rejects the prevailing "harmony" and enters into conflict with it.

7. The Psychology of Culture and

the Typology of the Personality

Culture is the most "terrible" thing ever created by mankind. It was the root cause of all of the most tragic pages in human history. People have always tried to destroy culture. Culture has been and still is the source of envy and imitation, delight and hatred, love and disgust. Each new generation feels in its own life all of the horror of the destruction of Rome by the barbarians, and this is literally the curse of the human race. Some people create, and others destroy.

Culture is also the most splendid thing ever created by mankind. Human history is basically the history of the development of human culture. It is human culture that reflects all of mankind's deeds, thoughts, desires, and motives. Like Prometheus' fire, culture not only illuminates, but warms and nurtures all that is best in man.

Culture and psychology are just as much interrelated as man and his soul. Someone might imagine a soul without a man to carry it or speak of a man without a soul, but ultimately the one is impossible without the other.

Cultural Psychology and the Psychology of Culture

In posing the question of the relationship of psychology and culture, we should keep in mind that it can be studied from two points of view. The *first*, which has become increasingly influential, is *cultural psychology, a scientific discipline which, by examining culture as one component of psychology, reveals psychology's role in a person's mental life*. The *second* point of view studies the psychological aspects of culture and is directly related to psychological anthropology.

Both approaches have their own themes, priorities, and right to exist. But their current status and development are based on the general basic research of such geniuses of psychology as Wundt, James, Freud, Vygotsky, Leontyev, and many others. While cultural psychology can be interpreted as a definite entity like the personality, the psychology of culture is obviously a process, and a profoundly creative process at that.

The Personality in Cultural Psychology

The personality as man's most integral characteristic comes to the forefront in cultural psychology research. Many of its properties have become important elements in establishing the relationships between *the individual and society*. The deep, cognitive, and motivational mechanisms of the personality have been increasingly supplemented with social and psychological criteria by psychologists. As Ye. V. Starovoytenko writes (2007, p. 107), they make it possible to "reveal the attitudes of the personality to cultural values that are universal, unique, and specific to a given ethnos or social group." The study of the personality from the standpoint of cultural psychology makes it possible to answer many urgent questions that modern society asks us. Among them the most important is *the conflict between archetypal and neotypal elements in the structure of the personality*. In principle, this profound intrapersonal conflict most fully reflects the personality's cultural component and its ability not just to resolve conflicts, but to use them for its own development.

In the section "The Personality and Its Structure" we discussed the archetypal and neotypal characteristics of the personality in detail. The conflict between them is a typological conflict, which assigns a person to a certain group of people, who have a certain opinion and attitude towards culture and perception of it. We believe that a personality type, as a product of the interaction of its structuring elements, reflects the individual psychological aspects of cultural perception. The nature of the interaction of the internal elements of the personality is itself subject to the influence of a specific society's culture and subordinate to its foundations.

The idea that culture influences the formation of certain personality types is not new. Psychological typologies based on a study of the interaction of culture and personality began with the research of George Meade and are most vividly portrayed in the works of Theodore Adorno, Erich Fromm, and others. A systematic analysis of all these trends and theories that examine the typology of the personality in connection with the interrelationships of people in a society and culture is given in the work of S. M. Mejidova (2001).

148

Thus a differential approach to the study of the personality has acquired an additional opportunity to develop by analysis of the cultural influences on an individual. Cognitive styles, intrapersonal conflicts, values, orientations, and motivations, when examined from the standpoint of their cultural component, have become quite interesting and productive material for personality researchers. In turn this has made it possible to conduct intercultural studies that identify the specific characteristics of the personality among different social and ethnic groups, nations, or peoples.

Recent world events have served as the basis for a significant increase in the number of studies in this field. Clashes of civilizations, peoples, and ethnic groups in our time cannot leave people indifferent, not just members of other faiths or politicians, but also the scientists who are trying to find answers to the questions these clashes raise. The process of studying personality formation in a certain culture, which is by its nature complex, may help us understand why a person is so intolerant towards a member of another culture in one case and why he is tolerant in another.

The Psychology of Culture and the Development of the Personality

After a quite detailed analysis of cultural psychology as a new trend in psychology, we turn now to the psychology of culture. Earlier, in distinguishing the two trends, we compared cultural psychology with the psychology of the personality, and the psychology of culture with the psychology of creativity. This comparison is worthy of attention, because *the psychology of culture is essentially the psychology of the generation of psychological characteristics that influence people and society.*

The study of the psychology of culture is directly related to the *Paradox of the Product* of creativity described earlier in this chapter. Let us review this once again. *A product of creativity that is characterized by high value, beauty, simplicity, general availability, and desirability becomes so firmly embedded in our lives that it "destroys" the very personality of its creator, by leveling and dissolving in itself the entire inner world of its immediate creator.* There is another side of the *Paradox of the Product*. It applies to works whose authors are well known; in this case, the product of creativity "detaches" its creator from his immediate environment, elevates him, and "destroys" the crowd by dissolving all of its hopes, desires, and goals in the person of the creator.

Based on the *Paradox of the Product* of creativity, psychologists may interpret a culture from at least two points of view. The **first** is an analysis of a product of creativity that has become a cultural activity (artifact) in which the personality of the creator is "destroyed," i.e., the author is unknown. This is an analysis of cultural values that have dissolved the inner worlds of their creators into themselves and carry crucial psychological information on the ethnic environments in which they originated. Scientists started analyzing the psychological characteristics of individuals as well as ethnic groups and peoples, based on an analysis of their cultural heritage, a long time ago. This approach is the most productive in analyzing folk creativity.

The **second** point of view is an analysis of the personality of a creator who has been elevated and transformed into a cultural value by his creative product. In this case, the personality of a specific individual reflects all the richness of the culture of his time, and an analysis of his life and creativity becomes a study of the psychology of his people. A study of the personality of a creator who has himself become an artifact and a cultural value is different from the study of the personality of an "ordinary" person under the auspices of cultural psychology. This difference is quite significant, because the personality of a statistically average person who carries within himself cultural elements, merely reflects the state of the personality and its cross-section at a single point in time, while the personality of a creator as a progenitor of a culture reflects the process of its emergence, present state, and prospects for development.

'Local' Values and Global Culture

Any people and any nation are proud of not just their history, but the great personalities who made it. A study of the biographies, careers, and creativity of leading members of specific ethnic groups, nations, and peoples allows us to understand them better and penetrate their deep archetypal strata. This process is also important from the standpoint of the acceptance of a people by other ethnic groups. After all, it is well known that the only way to preserve uniqueness and autonomy in the current environment of globalization is to transform a "local" value of a specific people into a "global" value. The process of integration into world culture by means of the diversification of its global goals into specific values is a true effective way to preserve the values themselves.

That is why "local" jazz, as a manifestation of the creativity and autonomy of the African-American minority in the USA, became a global value of all mankind. Or take our national *mugam* (folk music), a kind of "local" culture that almost disappeared, but has not only been revived by the efforts of the First Lady of Azerbaijan, Mekhriban Aliyeva, but has become a global value of the Azerbaijani people.

The Personality as a Cultural Value

As we have already stated, it is not just a product, but the personality itself, that can become a cultural value. It is doubtful that anyone would dispute that a person who has become a cultural value not only carries and embodies the aspirations and hopes of his people, but also serves as a kind of "key" providing the access code for its ethnos to world culture and, conversely, provides the access code for world culture to the national cultural heritage. This mutual cultural enrichment is a process of the development of both and constitutes the basis for creating cultural values that are common human values, i.e., values on a global scale.

While assigning the lead role in the creation, enrichment, and spread of culture to the creative personality, we must not forget the specific nature of cultural perception as a problem of **ethnic psychology**, *an interdisciplinary field of knowledge that studies the ethnic characteristics of the human psyche, national character, patterns of the formation and functions of national self-consciousness, ethnic stereotypes, etc.*

Every people views the world in its own way by reflecting different world perceptions in the elements of its culture. Every culture carries within itself the characteristics of its people's mental activity, their national self-consciousness, and stereotypes. These basically simple propositions should not incite impassioned debates, but they do. At present "the curse of psychology" we described above has never been better suited to studying the processes underway in ethnic psychology. Despite all the diversity of approaches and currents in this field of knowledge, no single approach leads to a clear understanding of the causes and characteristics of phenomena such as "national character," "mentality," "ethnic stereotype," and so forth. Nevertheless the number of studies in this field is growing and interest in ethnic psychology is becoming deeper.

It might seem strange, but answers to several questions posed by modern investigators of ethnic psychology can perhaps be obtained by typologizing the personality. We have already stated that a personality type, as a product of the interaction of its structuring elements, reflects the individual psychological aspects of cultural perception. And the interaction of the internal elements of the personality is itself subject to the influence of and subordinate to the foundations of the culture of a specific society.

8. *Psychological Personality Types*

*T*he presented in this book (see Chapter 2, Figure 2.2) has made it possible to identify certain of its structural elements. We hypothesized that the psychological traits of an individual, which experience the effects of the structural elements of the personality, are transformed into certain personality types, which determine the directionality of a person's behavior in his socio-cultural environment.

We have identified four basic structural elements of the personality:

1. The collective unconscious, the most general and invariant elements of which are expressed in archetypes;

2. The personal unconscious, as information that has been discarded or simply forgotten by a person over his lifetime;

3. The personal conscious, as a combination of ideas, convictions, and values that determine and guide behavior;

4. The collective conscious, as invariant forms of the social existence of a person expressed in neotypes.

We have already mentioned that archetypes have two layers. They may be *absolute* and reflect our darkest animal instincts, or *relative* and express the unconscious tendencies of a specific society. Neotypes are structured according to the same principle. They consist of common human values as absolute and invariable priorities of civilization, and completely recognizable values of specific nations, peoples, and ethnic groups. Thus the two-layered nature of the unconscious, in combination with the two-layered nature of the collective consciousness, increases the number of basic elements of the personality to six. By defining them with symbolic names, we simplify their memorization and subsequent manipulation and analysis:

1. Animal instincts, which are shameful tendencies in the unconscious which deprive us of a human countenance – **the Devil**;

2. The tendencies of the tribe or ethnos to which we belong, of which we are unaware but which attract us – **the Tempter**;

3. Events, desires, motives, and knowledge that we have forgotten, are unimportant, and that we have discarded and rejected, and which form the contents of our personal unconscious – **the Non – Self**;

4. Cognitive elements of consciousness of oneself, one's environment, and the world in which we live – **the Self**;

5. Values, moral standards, and moral principles recognized by a person and accepted in a given social milieu, nation, people, or society – **the Prophet**;

6. Human values which are common to all people and are truly embedded in consciousness as the cultural heritage of mankind – **God**.

Let us reiterate that the presence of each of the aforementioned structural elements in the personality is a condition for its integrity. Every individual is characterized by the dominance of one or more elements, which ultimately determines his specific personality type. Of course we cannot say that the personality typology we have proposed is flawless (the "curse of psychology" is also applicable in this case), but these elements of the personality enable a very clear differentiation of one personality from another in terms of its orientation, desires, and aspirations.

The Devil

Jung called this type the "Shadow," Freud called it the *id*, and Karen Horney called it "the dark side of the personality." Researchers rarely agree in evaluating different aspects of the personality and so reduce them to a common denominator. But not in this case – in this case there is truly a commonality of approaches. The image of the "Devil," which incarnates the most hidden elements of our personality and comes from our ancestors, is extremely important for understanding the nature of the human being.

The "Devil" is contradictory. On the one hand he is associated with evil, pain, disease, death, and everything repulsive to human flesh, but is so naturally and frequently encountered in daily life. On the other hand, he is associated with sensuality, sex, money, power, satisfaction, pleasure, and other things that please him, which are always in short supply. A person who identifies with this type will do everything he can to avoid pain in the broadest sense of the word and to get the most satisfaction out of life. No one and nothing exists except for this principle. Such a person, while recognizing his own exceptional nature, does not recognize the individuality of other people. Craving constant satisfaction, he transforms this into the purpose of life and does everything he can to achieve it. His efforts to achieve and protect this goal know no moral bounds, and in most cases the goal conflicts with not just the activity of the people around him, but with prevailing morality.

Paradoxical though it may seem, a person of the "Devil" type is sentimental and experiences a very strong attachment to what he possesses. Every attempt to take away what he holds dear and is accustomed to, and to deprive him of his habitual type and circle of relationships, meets fierce and stubborn resistance. He may lie, dispense totally false information, blackmail others, and commit other acts, even illegal ones, for the sole purpose of protecting what he considers important and valuable to himself.

This personality type is not a hostage of culture, in the sense that his behavior and ideas do not correlate with generally accepted cultural values or those of a given social milieu. Of course he may adhere to generally accepted standards and rules of behavior, but only for the purpose of using this socially approved behavior to move closer to achieving his own goals.

The "Devil" is obsessive in pursuit of his plans. This sensual, hedonistic obsession indicates that this personality type has creative talents. His extreme ardor and unrestrained desire to get what he wants no matter what the cost, his deep inner conviction of the need to achieve his goals, and his field independence constitute explicit evidence of the creativity of a person with a dominant "Devil" type.

We reach the surprising conclusion that the destructiveness, amorality, stubbornness, obsession, excessive self-esteem, indifference to surroundings, and other characteristics of the "Devil" must be complemented by his ability to create the new and original. Earlier we said that the "Devil" is contradictory; and in fact he combines the ability to create as well as to destroy, to create a new morality in addition to destroying the old morality.

The creative element, vitality, spontaneity, and other creative properties in the deep layers of his personality are well established. And regardless of what this aspect of the personality is called, it undoubtedly plays a huge role in human creativity.

The Tempter

The psychological characteristics of an individual with the dominant "Tempter" archetype are quite diverse, but the central, pivotal factor is attractiveness in the broadest sense of the word. This trait embodies not just physical attractiveness, but also inner, spiritual, and profoundly personal attractiveness. This is the ability to charm, hypnotize, and persuade, to make people follow him and fall in love with him. A Tempter is eloquent and possesses a strong analytical mind, and his ability to make contact is impressive. People look for opportunities to associate with him and be with him. Without trying to become the leader of a group, he is often forced to play this role against his will. In the process, his allure and attention are more important than his opinions.

A person of this type has values which are desired, but which are often inaccessible to most people. Through the person of the "Tempter," and in association and contact with him, it is possible to realize that which is otherwise unattainable, prohibited, and attractive. While embodying the realization of desires and the possibility of success, the "Tempter" becomes cynical, arrogant, and emotionally rigid. In contrast to the "Devil," who is firmly attached to his sources of satisfaction, the "Tempter" is flighty and unstable. The most important thing for him is not to be at the center of *attention*, but to be the center of *attraction* and the man behind the scenes manipulating the audience.

These people achieve the greatest results in politics. Even though they rarely play the leading role, they may play a huge role in making major decisions. With their unique ability to sense the desires and moods of others, they manipulate them quite easily and guide them in the desired direction. And it is this insight into others that makes them quite cautious. If it is necessary to assume responsibility, the "Tempter" will find a way to shift the burden onto someone else's shoulders. He will do this in such a way that the person assuming the responsibility not only does not suspect anything, but derives satisfaction from it.

The inventiveness of this personality type is indubitable, but it does not rise to the level of creativity. This kind of inventiveness is more of an everyday quick-wittedness, cleverness, evasiveness, and nothing more. The ability to get out of a difficult situation is another distinctive characteristic of the "Tempter." Of course he tells lies, but he does so not to achieve certain deep-seated goals as in the case of the "Devil," but rather to protect his influence over others.

This "social" orientation of his prevarication greatly distinguishes him from the preceding personality type.

The "Tempter" is a social type, to a certain extent. In contrast to the first personality type, he lives not just for himself, but is part of society and lives by virtue of the society in which he manages to realize himself. But his social relations are controlled not by the desire to help or correct, but the desire to use, subjugate, capture, and thus control.

The Non-Self

This personality type is the most contradictory and ambivalent in its psychological characteristics. The career of a person with a dominant "Non-Self" complex consists of frequent disappointments, not in others, but in himself. It is true that disappointments do not stop him, and indeed when he encounters them, he gains strength and confidence and tries to surmount them again. The expression "my mouth is my enemy" best fits this personality type. He is constantly experiencing guilt for his words and actions. Such characteristics make these people very responsible, and punctual to a certain extent. The discipline and consistency of their actions do not come from their internal needs, but are related to their high level of caution and desire to avoid failure and criticism.

We know quite well that flight from failure is closely associated with the success motive and for all intents and purposes is its flip side. In the opinion of most psychologists, the motive of achievement and motive of avoidance are two opposite tendencies inherent to all people. Obviously the motive of avoidance is dominant in "Non-Self" personalities, but under certain circumstances, the motive of achievement may play a dominant role. The desire to be a leader, "untouchable" and immune to criticism, is developed as a compensatory reaction to failures and disappointments.

Artiness and melodrama, quite often excessive, frequently give away people of this type. Desiring to conceal their inner world and sensing a hidden threat in direct and frank communications, this category of individual prefers to don the mask of a certain role which he plays when communicating with others. This phoniness is quite easy to recognize. But "Non-Self" personalities quite often prefer to be seen as "actors" than to reveal their real inner world. In day-to-day life, when we encounter such a person, we exclaim, "I can't tell when you're serious and when you're joking!"

These individuals are deeply attached to their closest associates. Only among their closest, most trusted friends do they allow themselves to take off the masks they wear when they communicate with other people. For years, they allow their closest friends to read the "pages" of their souls like a banned book, and are incapable of hiding anything from them. Their social aloofness is in sharp contrast to their personal openness when they communicate with close friends.

Just like the "Tempter," the "Non-Self" personality does not like to take personal responsibility. If he is forced to nonetheless, he will do his best. If he does not get a good outcome and the problem that had to be solved has not gone away, while outwardly denying his culpability for the failure, the Non-Self personality will take inwardly blame himself. The dissonance of his outward reactions and inner experiences is one of the most distinctive traits of this type. His internal conflict, his constant struggle with himself, and his dissatisfaction with the current state of affairs are the motors of the Non-Self personality's behavior and give his life a creative character. This trait makes the "Non-Self" kin to the "Devil." But while the "Devil's" creativity stems from his obsession, the "Non-Self's" creativity stems from his internally unresolved problems.

The 'Self'

This personality type is the one most often encountered. In general, the presence of a strong and adequate "Self" in a person is an objective and normal phenomenon. Psychologists who study the personality even use the term "self-concept" for an individual, with the implication that he has an integral conception of himself as a personality. We must express reservations right away, however, because the "self-concept" and the "Self" personality type are quite different and should not be confused. In order to clearly distinguish these concepts, we shall briefly dwell on the basic principles of the "self-concept" in psychology.

The "self-concept" was first used by the distinguished American psychologist Carl Rogers (1902–1987). His theory of personality, which was subsequently called phenomenology, essentially became a kind of anthem to the human "Self." It is doubtful that anyone before Rogers had studied the "Self" so profoundly, its role, significance, structure, and so forth. But in addition to an in-depth study of the "Self," Rogers identified the sources of its development by first examining them in positive traits.

Rogers was harshly critical of Freud's dominant concept, that the personality's formation is pre-determined by the pressure of negative unconscious tendencies. In Rogers' opinion, the situation is exactly the opposite. A person starts out as positive, and the formation of his personality is determined by his fundamental tendency to actualization. The development of his own natural abilities contributes to the formation of his personality. In the initial phase of development a person does everything he can to actualize himself, and in the phase when he is capable of distinguishing himself from his environment, he proceeds to actualize himself. The processes of actualization and self-actualization are accompanied by a constant organismic valuation process, Rogers emphasized. This is an association or evaluation of the extent to which an organism, an individual, a person perceives the changes that occur as consistent with his personality. The valuing process by itself occurs over the person's entire lifetime and thus ensures an endless (within a finite human lifetime) process of self-improvement.

Self-improvement as a permanent process is manifested in all areas of human life and enables the formation of an integral, or as Rogers put it, a Gestalt personality. Only such an integral personality can speak of his selfhood or "self-concept." Thus the "Self" is a differentiated part of the person's phenomenological field or field of perception (determined as the universality of experience), which consists of a conscious perception and the values of the "Self." The "self-concept," a person's conception of what he is, reflects the characteristics that a person perceives as part of himself (Hjelle & Ziegler, 2006, p. 540). Rogers' discovery of the "self-concept" immediately fascinated other scientists and is still one of the most widely used concepts in describing psychological phenomena.

Having briefly explained the "self-concept," we shall now proceed directly to an analysis of the psychological characteristics of the "Self" personality type, which is often called the egocentric type.

Egocentrism is the inner conviction of the priority of oneself over others. An egocentric not only tries to be at the center of attention; he cannot imagine himself outside the center. The world around him begins with him and then extends to everything else. People with these characteristics often cause tension in their personal associations, because they do not allow people who could cast doubt on their views and convictions into their close circle of friends. In general, the tension, emotionality, or as psychologists are convinced, neuroticism of the egocentric are his calling card. This may be attributed to the nature of egocentrism itself, which was first described in detail by Jean Piaget. In his view, egocentrism is most clearly exhibited in the process of childhood development up to the age of seven. In this period when language and symbolic thinking develop, a child exhibits egocentrism by refracting the entire world around him through himself (Piaget, 2008, p. 35). But when adults exhibit this "childlike" manner of thinking and perceiving the world, it is impossible for them to communicate adequately, which presupposes mutual communication, interaction, and perception. Naturally in this case the situation becomes tenser, and the egocentric starts to focus more and more on his "Self." The expression "big baby" is best suited to him, because temper, vulnerability, and tearfulness are his distinctive features. But an egocentric can be abrupt, rude, and aggressive when he sees that the "childishness" of his behavior is not removing the threat to his "Self."

With his startling and contradictory qualities, an egocentric can be sociable and isolated at the same time, or reflective and deeply sensuous. This duality of the "Self" is another one of his integral traits. Getting re-energized by his feelings and under pressure of his own cognitions, an egocentric becomes simultaneously their hostage and their connecting link. This duality is clearly exhibited when one associates with an eccentric, because his expressive exhibition of his feelings may suddenly give way to abrupt inhibition and a retreat into himself, only to then be manifested as rude and aggressive behavior.

The Prophet

If the priority of the self over everyone else gives way to the dominance of ideas which a person considers true, genuine, and acceptable regardless of the individual who conceived them, we are dealing with the personality type we call the "Prophet." Ideas and values conceived by himself and others may dominate and determine his behavior and actions. What is important for the "Prophet" is not the authorship of an idea, conception, manner of behavior, or any other value, but its significance for himself and those around him. This trait is key in distinguishing the "Prophet" from all other personality types, especially the "Self" type.

People with the "Prophet" personality type devise their own schema for perceiving the reality around them. They do not find it especially difficult to evaluate an event or phenomenon from a moral and ethical point of view. They can answer the questions "What is good?" and "What is bad?" without hesitation or difficulty. This happens because a person with this personality type is constantly relating the events, ideas, and phenomena around him and happening to him to his own schema for perceiving reality. And if the association is appropriate, events or phenomena are evaluated as positive, while if not, they are evaluated as negative.

Research on the schema for perceiving reality as a special psychological phenomenon has become widespread among cognitive psychologists. In the psychology of the personality, this was reflected in the research of Kelly, Bandura, and Rotter. George Kelly occupies a special place among these leading psychologists. His postulate that a person has special "channels" which allow him to predict events served as the basis of the theory that subsequently became known as the theory of personal constructs. These constructs, as the basis for human mental activity, allow him not just to understand the events happing around him and to him, but also to manage them. In Kelly's view, a person "judges the world by means of his concept systems or models he creates and then tries to adapt to objective reality. This adaptation is not always successful. Nevertheless without such systems the world would seem so undifferentiated and homogeneous that a person could not make sense of it." The systems or models of perceiving reality that Kelly defined as personal constructs are ideas or thoughts that a person uses in order to perceive or interpret and explain or predict his experience (Hjelle & Ziegler, 2006, p. 438).

A person with a unique system of his own personal constructs as Kelly described them is better suited than others to the "Prophet" personality type. Of course, everyone, regardless of personality type, has a system of personal constructs that make it possible to live normally. But a keen ability to look at the present in order to see the future and the presence of specific and clear patterns of behavior and special decision-making models essentially distinguish the "Prophet" from all other personality types.

God

What could seemingly be easier than to list the characteristics we normally use in describing God: kindness, mercy, love of mankind, constancy, and so forth? But this process becomes extremely complicated when we speak of people. Imamedin Nasimi, who proclaimed that he was God, was perhaps one of the first persons to suggest that certain qualities in a person distinguish him and elevate him above those around him. Of course, as a poet and adherent of pantheism (Hurufism), Nasimi only deified man, but the *man-God* idea itself forced him to describe a certain personality type poetically. Thus he wrote that "The person who does not know God and is not recognized by God cannot know himself" and "Ultimately, the person who lived in order to embrace his lovers proved to be right" (Nashimi, 1973, p. 35). In these lines we see characteristics which modern psychologists call *reflexivity* and *sensuality*. In fact, these traits, in addition to profound spirituality and orientation to values and ideas, distinguish the man-God from others. While similar to the "Prophet" in terms of his values orientation, the man-God is socially much different than the "Prophet." The "Prophet" is a socially oriented type whose behavior is mainly focused on those around him. He is the disseminator and popularizer of ideas in his social environment and his behavior is determined not just by ideas, but by the desire to make them as attractive and accessible as possible. In contrast, the man-God is an introverted person on the periphery of society, who is completely indifferent to society's perception of his ideas and behavior. He is the creator of his own world in which he is omnipotent. Irrationality is another trait of the man-God which is fully manifested in the world he has created. His "universe" is unreal, illogical, irrational, and anti-intellectual. But to him it is perfect and gives him total satisfaction and happiness.

---

9. *Personality Theories as the Basis for*

a Personality Typology

*T*he structure of the personality that has allowed us to identify and briefly describe its types also makes it possible to formulate another interesting hypothesis: that *the basic personality theories in modern psychology may be interpreted as typological descriptions of the personality.* An idea which seems absolutely ludicrous at first glance acquires quite distinct contours when it is examined through the prism of the personality structure we have developed.

In our view, the personality is a means for expressing the unconscious tendencies of the past in the present and the conscious aspirations for the future. From this standpoint, the typology of the personality is a typology of means, the differentiation of the tools by which a person expresses himself. It seems to us that the personality typology described above most fully reflects the conceptions of the "means" that foster the unity of the unconscious and consciousness in the psyche in real time.

In fact, most, if not all, personality theories have turned to the unconscious/conscious dilemma in an attempt to find a balance that would assure the accuracy of their theoretical analyses and the reliability of their research applications. Depending on their philosophical and methodological preferences, authors have given preference to either the unconscious or the conscious in the psyche. Researchers have rarely ignored one or the other, even though for all intents and purposes B. F. Skinner reduced the human personality to the level of reactions to environmental stimuli. More often the battle between the unconscious and conscious ended with the "victory" of one side, which led researchers to almost completely ignore either consciousness in human life (Freud) or unconscious motives (Kelly). Of course, there are theories that account for both the unconscious and conscious tendencies of the human psyche; however, each of them ultimately resolves the *unconscious/conscious* dilemma in favor of one or the other, tending towards either Freud's or Wundt's interpretation of the personality.

Realizing that a successful resolution of this dilemma is unlikely, we have tried to find the key factor that would make it possible to integrate the unconscious tendencies of the psyche with the conscious manifestations in our lives. Of all the known phenomena of psychology, only two could contend for this exclusive role: *creativity* and *personality*. In creativity there is always a place for both unconscious and conscious tendencies, but they compete more than they cooperate. The personality, which functionally reflects a person's existing tendencies regardless of whether they are unconscious or conscious, is another matter. The personality is an instrument that can combine the entire depth of the unconscious and the boundlessness of the conscious better than any other human phenomenon.

If the personality is a means of expression, then personality theories describe different modes of the expression of the personality's psychological phenomena. This basic principle makes it possible to formulate the hypothesis that the many personality theories developed by psychologists are essentially descriptions of different personality types or modes of personal expression.

To illustrate this, we will use an example of the types identified according to the personality structure we have developed. Thus six structural elements have been identified in the human personality: the "Devil," the "Tempter," the "Non-Self," the "Self," the "Prophet," and "God." Each of them, which is at the same time a personality type, has its own characteristics, which, according to our hypothesis, should conform to existing psychological theories. And furthermore, if our hypothesis is true, then personality psychology should have theories that will allow us to describe the elements of the structure we have developed.

The Hedonistic Personality Type

Even a superficial glance at the history of psychology makes it possible to speak of a certain connection between personality theories and the types listed above. For example, the "Devil" as a *hedonistic personality type* can be examined from the standpoint of Freudian theory more clearly than any other type. In fact, Freud's psychodynamics, with the dominance of the unconscious libido and the minimal influence of consciousness in human life, can serve as a theoretical explanation of this personality type. This conception, which unambiguously resolved the "unconscious/conscious" dilemma in favor of the former, revealed in a very detailed way the psychological traits of a person for whom the role of consciousness is infinitesimal or practically speaking zero. For example, Freud wrote (1991, p. 352) that "Psychoanalysis cannot consider the conscious the essence of the psyche and must look at consciousness as a quality of the psyche that may be combined with other qualities or may be lacking altogether."

A Freudian personality living by the principle of enjoyment and encountering reality and his inner unrealized tendencies acquires the features of a type that we quite often encounter. We described in detail this personality type, which was affirmed by Freud's brilliant discoveries. Thus, in our view Freudian psychoanalysis is not just and not so much a theory of psychology as it is an amazing, original, but real means for a personality's self-expression.

The Seductive Personality Type

It is well known that Jung, Freud's best student, completely shared his teacher's ideas at the beginning of his scientific and creative career. But their views started to diverge over time, and Jung could no longer agree with the Freudian interpretation of the unconscious. He believed that the unconscious had a much broader and deeper content than Freud had depicted. It consists of not only repressed sexual and aggressive urges, but also contains "the entire spiritual legacy of human evolution reborn in the structure of the individual brain" (Campbell, 1971, p. 66). This hypothesis, which subsequently became the theory of the collective unconscious and archetypes, became Jung's best-known idea. Without going into the details of his theoretical investigations, I would simply like to note that the idea of archetypes as entailing unconscious psychic tendencies made it possible not just to socialize man and represent him as a real member of society, and not just to abandon the all-devouring Freudian principle of satisfaction, but also to make the personality an object of inspiration and imitation.

While a Freudian person lives for himself and social relations are unimportant to him, the personality, according to Jung, which is originally archetypal, becomes an integral element of society, and the more archetypal it is, the more attractive it becomes. In fact, if we accept Jung's hypothesis that archetypes are the quintessence of historical experience in each particular individual, we can image how necessary a person is who not only possesses them more than other people, but who vividly exhibits this valuable experience. And which archetype is dominant (the anima, animus, shadow, elder, etc.) is no longer important; what is important is that a person meets the expectations of those around him that society perceives as most valuable. That is how *the "Tempter" behaves, a personality type which can also be called "seductive."*

The Evasive Personality Type

The next type we identified in our six-component personality structure was the *"Non-Self" type. It can be called "evasive."* According to our hypothesis, the basis for the evasive personality type is reflected in Erich Fromm's concept. While Jung could introduce the social determinants of human behavior into the human unconscious and thus reveal new facets of the personality, Fromm went further and stated that the interpretation of human behavior without an analysis of contemporary culture is impossible. His concept of the personality was the first in the history of psychology to so clearly affirm the role of socio-cultural factors in determining behavior, which later became impossible to deny. He analyzed contemporary society from the standpoint of the effect of freedom on people. Freedom, after becoming one of man's most magnificent achievements, turned into a source of profound conflict between the individual and his environment.

According to Fromm, the more freely and independently a person acts, the more defenseless, isolated, and vulnerable he becomes. These feelings, which are contrary to human nature, compel him to seek a way out of the situation and an opportunity to evade the "consequences" of freedom. Fromm (2003, p. 82) believed that "an individual uses 'escape' mechanisms to overcome the sense of his insignificance by comparison with the overwhelmingly powerful outside world" of modern industrial society. Fromm attributed special significance to one of the many methods of "escape." For example, he wrote that "It is this mechanism that is the salvation for most normal individuals in modern society. In short, an individual ceases to be himself, he fully assumes the personality type offered to him by the generally accepted stereotype, and becomes exactly what everyone else is and the way they want to see him. The distinction between the 'Self' and the surrounding world disappears, along with the conscious fear of isolation and helplessness."

If we follow this logic, then quite a few people in modern society have voluntarily renounced their own "Self" and their own individuality, and in our terminology have become "Non-Self" people who evade both freedom and responsibility. In this case evasiveness becomes paramount and determines the orientation of a person's behavior and thinking. The "Non-Self" or evasive personality type "grabs his own song by the throat" (as the poet Mayakovsky wrote) and turns into a gray mouse who can feel confident and calm in a huge crowd. In contrast to the seductive personality type, in which a person expresses the desires that most people cannot attain, the evasive type reflects what is available to everyone.

As we demonstrated above, the evasiveness of a personality may be exhibited not just in conformism, but in other forms of "escape from freedom": authoritarianism, renunciation of activity, destructiveness, and so forth. In all these forms of behavior, a person either renounces his own "Self" or associates his "Self" with something or someone outside him. In other words, a person transforms his "Self" into the "Non-Self" which is created by himself, but for which he assumes practically no responsibility.

The Egocentric Personality Type

The next *personality type that we must explain theoretically is the "Self" or egocentric type.* This task, which seems to be simple at first glance, becomes extremely complex and confusing when examined in detail. We should keep in mind that the "Self" is analyzed in all theoretical treatments of the psychology of the personality. Psychoanalysts, behaviorists, humanists, cognitivists, and phenomenologists have all raised the subject of the human "Self" to one degree or another. But each had his own personal answer, which at times was the exact opposite of what was known at the time.

Obvious though it may be, the contradictory nature of the "Self" may be attributed to the role and position of this element in the structure of the personality. The "Self" is not just one element of the personality structure; it is the central element, which interconnects and expresses in itself all the other elements and is a structural component of the personality. We have already mentioned that the personality expresses the unconscious tendencies of the past, combined into an integral whole with conscious aspirations for the future. Thus the human "Self" is the basic mechanism that enables the unity and reflection of internal and external tendencies in the life of the individual. At the same time all the aspects, elements, and diverse traits of the personality are reflected inside the "Self" as if in miniature. It is this characteristic of the "Self" that has often confused researchers, who have either equated the "Self" and the personality, thus dissolving the personality into the "Self," or have completely ignored the "Self" by entering into debates about the impersonal personality.

In this light, we can now understand how Eric Erikson's ego psychology, Albert Bandura's theory of social leaning, and George Kelly's Self-Concept, which are so different in their philosophical and methodological positions, were so emphatic in speaking of the role of the "Self" in the personality. In fact, each of these outstanding scientists, by emphasizing a certain aspect of the "Self," demonstrated its versatility, perhaps without being aware of it themselves. For example, Erikson, proceeding on the basis of Freud's psychoanalytical concepts, wrote (1963a, p. 116) that the " 'ego' lives between the 'id' and the 'superego.' By constantly trying to balance itself between these extremes and parrying their extremism, the 'ego' stays focused on historical reality by examining images of perception, by sorting memories, by guiding actions, and by using other means to integrate an individual's ability to orient and plan." As we can see, to Erikson (1963a, p. 118) the ego was a central and independent "internal institution" designed to preserve the individual order on which all external order depends. There is no doubt that as a scientist whose views developed under the very powerful influence of psychoanalysis, Erikson approached the interpretation of the "Self" from the standpoint of its sensual, emotional, energetic component, i.e., the component that permits the inclusion in the "Self" of the inner tendencies that predispose a person to a certain type of activity.

Bandura, who is considered the founder of the new social cognitive psychology, also placed the "Self" at the head of the list in the structure of the personality. But in his view, predispositional and situational factors are equally important in determining the "Self." Mutual determinism, as he called it, allows a person not just to shape the environment, but to be shaped under its influence. At times Bandura's approach is called social behaviorism, and this term contains a grain of truth. That which was obstinately ignored by adherents of the psychodynamic school, i.e., the role of the situation, the stimulus, and the reinforcement, not only got the right to exist from Bandura, but was also included in the structure of the "Self," as an integral part of it.

Bandura's social learning studies proved to be so viable and attractive that they elicited tremendous interest and forced scientists to rethink the significance of the external stimulus itself. The traditional behaviorist approach to the stimulation of human behavior was replaced with an understanding of the stimulus as a source of personal regulation. It is through observation, examples, and modeling reality that learning and ultimately the development of the personality take place, Bandura believed. In his book *Social Learning Theory* (1977, p. 50), Bandura wrote: "Shortening the process of learning behavior by observation is vitally important for both development and survival. Because errors can have costly and at times fatal consequences, the possibility of survival could have become very unlikely unless a person had another way of learning besides his own painful experience of trial and error. It is for this reason that no one would think of teaching a child to swim, a boy to drive a car, or a student to perform surgery by giving him the full opportunity to experience the consequences of his successes and failures on his own. The graver and more dangerous the consequences of a possible error, the greater the reliance on learning by observing the actions of competent people is. And even if we ignore the question of survival, it is very hard to imagine a process of the social transmission of information in which language, lifestyle, and cultural practice were taught to a new member of the community exclusively by means of random reinforcement of successful behavior without the use of models that provide examples of cultural behavior."

While Erikson explained the existence of a predisposition towards a specific type of behavior and Bandura succeeded in demonstrating the importance of situational factors, Kelly was able to lift the veil of secrecy hiding the cognitive constructs of the consciousness. His work is extremely valuable from the standpoint of understanding the human "Self" as a structure determined by cognitive processes of the psyche.

An analysis of these approaches allows us to formulate a hypothesis of the three-component structure of the "Self" within the overall structure of the personality. This hypothesis undoubtedly emerged not only and not so much under the influence of these theories as it did because of the lack of an integral theory that combined all other points of view on the nature of the "Self." The studies cited above as the most vivid examples of personality theories have allowed us to explain the integral structure of the "Self."

Thus, we believe that the structure of the "Self" is an integral entity which is key to understanding the entire human personality. While the personality expresses human individuality, the "Self" is the method and mechanism for this expression and the floodlight that illuminates and highlights special aspects of the personality, i.e., makes a person unique and irreplicable. The "Self," as we have already said, consists of three components:

- inner feelings, sensations;
- situations;
- cognitions.

The "Self" can be represented graphically by an oval divided into three parts, where the left part is responsible for differentiating the emotional and sensuous tendencies of person's inner world, the middle part is responsible for recording situations that are personally significant and allow a person to orient himself and develop in his environment, while the right part contributes to the formation of values and cognitive constructs that guides its behavior (see Figure 2.4).

Figure 2.4

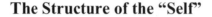

The Structure of the "Self"

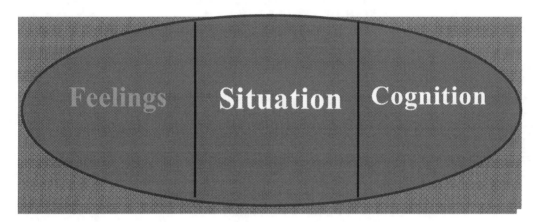

The three-component structure of the "Self" is nothing new in psychology. As we showed above, most researchers (Freud, Rogers, etc.) also identified three components of the "Self." Of the Russian psychologists, A. V. Petrovsky held this opinion. For example, he wrote (1988, pp. 142–143): "A person's conceptions of his outward appearance, talents, abilities, social significance, and so forth … are a result of a cognitive … process. A second essential aspect of the 'Self-Image' is the emotional aspect. And finally, the third aspect of the 'Self-Image' is the element of will…." But in contrast to all these concepts, we were the first to connect the elements of internal predetermination, external situational awareness, and cognitive outlook in the structure of the "Self."

The Convincive Personality Type

After conducting a quite detailed analysis of the "Self" personality type which is also known as the egocentric type, *we will proceed to explain the "Prophet" personality type, which we have called convincive*. The ability to convince and argue one's point of view is one of the most complex skills that psychologists today have identified. But in addition to in-depth knowledge and the ability to speak logically and correctly, certain other traits are required in order for a person to get others to accept the ideas he presents, defends, and proves.

These traits essentially make up the convincive personality type. Convinciveness, in our view, is based on three basic principles of effectiveness:

- a clear idea;
- a profound belief in its truth;
- the ability to convince and prove.

In fact, ideas plus belief are the basic characteristics of the convincive personality type, and in combination with a person's oratorical, organizational, intellectual, suggestive, and other talents, they make it possible to most clearly distinguish this personality type from the others.

The "idea orientation" of the convincive personality type has been confirmed in several theories and conceptions, notably in cognitive personality theories. As we know, the cognitive approach to the interpretation of the personality originated with the research of Kelly. Subsequently studies of the personality as a psychological phenomenon were developed in the so-called social cognitive approach, among the most outstanding representatives of which were Bandura and Rotter. Cognitive psychology, starting in the mid 20th century, became the leading approach that has allowed scientists to discover and interpret new phenomena of human life in general and the personality in particular. Kelly's personal constructs, Bandura's self-schemas, and Rotter's cognitive styles have determined the direction of the research of an entire generation of psychologists, and have not lost their importance decades later. Obviously the cognitive approach is no longer as attractive as it once was, but in our view, this is more related not to the weakness of its ideas, but to the emergence of new, quite interesting and still unstudied currents in psychology. Moreover, "cognitivism" as a type of behavior has been quite adequately and systematically studied by psychologists.

The next basic characteristic of the convincive personality type is *belief*, as a person's profound conviction of the truth of an idea. Studies of belief in psychology are quite extensive and diverse, but most scientists maintain that belief is inseparably linked to an idea, schema, or form of perception of subjective and objective reality (Granovskaya, 2004, p. 38). That belief is recorded in facts, ideas, and symbols and thus becomes a source of their existence. The strength

171

with which a person can defend the truth of his beliefs is directly related to his ***ability to convince***, which is the third basic characteristic of the convincive personality type.

The Reflexive Personality Type

We have tried to produce a theoretical explanation of the ***sixth and last personality type, which we call reflexive***. In this case we cannot help but agree with the Russian psychologist A.V. Surmava, that in its general form the theoretical psychological idea of the reflexivity of a person's attitude towards the world is set forth in the works of L. S. Vygotsky, A. N. Leontyev, and N. A. Rubinshteyn (Surmava, 2004, p. 12). In fact, the studies of these outstanding scientists, especially L. S. Vygotsky, laid the foundations for understanding reflexivity as a human conscious activity (Vygotsky, 1982, p. 222). At the same time, we cannot ignore the Gestalt understanding of reflexivity as self-analysis and self-development, which was elaborated in Fritz Perls' work (Perls & Goodman, 2001, p. 41). He approached the problem of self-analysis in a new way and associated it with a person's awareness of processes both within and outside himself. His conceptions of reflexivity (awareness) are clearly consistent with the phenomenon of "awareness of the unconscious" which we identified and described in 1994, and which, as we demonstrate, is the basis for development of a personal orientation towards creativity. But we should keep in mind that awarenessof the unconscious is the final phase of a person's perception of a problem before creative activity, and before this final phase, a person is conscious in the form of a direct reflection or an integral Gestalt self-analysis. Thus reflexivity is not just an intellectual analysis of events and phenomena happening to man and the world around him, but an integral, complex process that encompasses all spheres of an individual's inner world. These affective, volitional, and intellectual aspects interact and engender the special integral attitude of a person towards himself and the world around him.

We have noted two basic currents in psychology that assign special significance to reflexivity. In one case this is the semiotic, symbolic reflection which Lev Vygotsky and his followers spoke of as a process of "mediating psychic processes by means of psychological tools" (Leontyev, 1982, p. 41), understanding different semiotic systems as the psychological tools that a person uses in his life. In the second case this is deep self-analysis which presupposed an integral Gestalt approach to the interpretation of the personality.

Studies of reflexivity are not limited to these approaches. We have cited only the two most vivid examples of the interpretation of reflexivity in psychology. There are other kinds of studies of this intriguing phenomenon. But it is crystal clear that theoretical advances in the psychology of the personality, regardless of their methodological and philosophical bases, have singled out reflexivity as one of the fundamental features of the personality. Even the Big Five theory, which is one of the most controversial theories but has nevertheless gained more and more adherents with respect to the psychology of the personality, identifies awareness and reflexivity as basic features of the personality (De Raad et al., 2008, pp. 269–289). Reflexivity, if we identify its key characteristics that we find in different psychological concepts, makes it possible to speak of the existence of a certain type of personality in which semiotics, symbolism, a tendency towards permanent awareness of subjective and objective reality, consciousness of behavior, creativity, and imagination are dominant.

In conclusion, we shall present the aforementioned personality types in schematic form (see Table 3).

Table 3

Personality Types

Structural element of the personality	Author of explanatory theory	Personality type	Basic characteristics
The Devil	Freud	Hedonistic	satisfaction sentimentality obsession creativity
The Tempter	Jung	Seductive	attractiveness magnetism charisma sociability inventiveness
The Non-Self	Fromm	Evasive	avoidance of responsibility anxiety problematic character uncertainty submissiveness attachment punctuality
The Self	Rogers Erikson Bandura Kelly	Egocentric	activity narcissism neuroticism tension ambivalence of feelings and attitudes
The Prophet	Kelly Bandura Rotter	Convincive	orientation to ideas conviction morality eloquence desire to lead leadership
God	Vygotsky	Reflexive	irrationality introspection spirituality dreaminess marginality illogicality creativity

10. The Structural Typology of the Personality and

the Passionarity of Lev Gumilyov

Our typology of personality can be called a structure, because it is based on structuring elements of the personality. The ***structural typology of the personality (STP)*** is not just interrelated theoretical developments and discourses, but also a genuine tool for analyzing the human personality. It has opened up exciting new opportunities for the experimental study of the personality. The STP also permits an original interpretation of phenomena of the personality that are still disputed. For example, the theory of the "passionary" personality developed by Lev Gumilyov, which is quite contradictory, assumes fully realistic contours when we analyze it from the standpoint of STP theory. We believe that the reader will be interested in seeing the serviceability of STP first hand and at the same time gaining a better understanding of the creativity of Gumilyov, a distinguished scholar of Eastern and Turkic studies.

In the section "Paradoxes of Creativity," we described the *Paradox of Morality* as one of the most striking phenomena in human creative activity. As we have already mentioned, it essentially involves a constant struggle between the world views, ideas, and conceptions of a creative person and society's existing moral standards, generally accepted stereotypes of behavior, schematic images of the reality around us, algorithmic forms of thinking, and so forth. Using the language of the poet, the *Paradox of Morality* reflects the soul's ability to accommodate two worlds when the soul "cannot be accommodated" in even one world (Nasimi, 1973, p. 35).

We can state with full confidence that Lev Nikolayevich Gumilyov was referring to a category of people whose inner world was much richer, more diverse, beautiful, and original than the world imposed upon them. This proposition becomes more convincing when we consider that Gumilyov did his creative work at a time when Communist ideology "flourished" and persecuted any dissidence and freedom of creativity.[39] It is no coincidence that his doctoral dissertation, which was later published in the form of the monograph *Ethogenesis and the World's Biosphere*, despite his splendid defense of the dissertation at Leningrad State University, did not receive the certification of the Official Academic Degrees and Titles Commission of the Soviet Union.

What Did Gumilyov Do?

So what did this geographer, ethnographer, and historian do to so enrage the powers that be and their servile scholars and to so capture the hearts and minds of the millions of ordinary people who read his books and attended his lectures? We should look for the answers to these questions in the works of Gumilyov, who discovered new aspects of the phenomena of human existence. Like Jung, whose brilliance allowed him to discover archetypes in our psyche, Gumilyov, on the basis of historical facts and events, introduced the previously unknown phenomenon of "passionarity,"[40] a concept that Gumilyov was unable to analyze and study thoroughly. By providing several interpretations of the concept of passionarity, each of which differs from the others with respect to its depth and breadth, Gumilyov kept scholars and researchers "busy" for many years to come. As his student and follower M. I. Kovalenko (1999, p. 3) noted: "Gumilyov's interpretation of this phenomenon was multi-faceted and ambiguous. Passionarity and passionaries are repeatedly mentioned on the pages of his basic works."

Nevertheless Gumilyov's passionarity drew attention to itself instantly, because it reflected, at times at the level of intuitive knowledge, certain real layers, aspects, and nuances of human behavior and existence. We believe that its somehow interrelated characteristics constituted one of the basic reasons why scholars paid it such great attention. And the potential of this group of characteristics to provide an informative interpretation of intrapersonal and

---

[39] *Lev Gumilyov* (1912-1992) was the son of the famous poets Nikolai Gumilyov and Anna Akhmatova. His father was executed when he was nine years old; his mother was constantly persecuted; and Lev himself was sent to the camps from 1938 to 1956—editor's note.

[40] Unfortunately, we have not found any foreign studies of passionarity, besides the doctoral dissertation of the Canadian scholar Jamil Brownson (1988). Evidently in translating this term into English the word "passion" is used as the root word, which is completely inconsistent with the meaning of Gumilyov's term "passionarity."

interpersonal relations, as intragroup and intergroup processes as well as intraethnic and interethnic phenomena, made passionarity an especially valuable concept.

The universal applicability of passionarity to different fields of anthropology (Andreyev, 2008; Bogdanov, 2001; Zimina, 2007) was another attractive feature. It was this capability of passionarity that allowed Gumilyov not only to make extremely important scientific discoveries in the field of ethnogenesis, but also to develop an original typology of personalities.

Passionaries, Subpassionaries, and Harmonic People

Gumilyov divided all people into passionaries, harmonic people, and subpassionaries. In describing passionaries, he observed that "their number in an ethnos is insignificant" (Gumilyov, 2001, p. 293). But he believed that they are the ones who play a decisive role in the emergence of an ethnos. "We call people in whom this impulse is stronger than the instinct of both individual and species self-preservation *passionaries*" (emphasis added) (Gumilyov, 2001, p. 293).

Gumilyov classified most people as harmonic. In his words, a person who balances passionary and subpassionary impulses, who adapts to his environment, who is not hyperactive and is capable of in-depth intellectual and professional activity can be called harmonic (Gumilyov, 2001, p. 294).

And "finally, ethnic groups almost always include categories of people with negative 'passionarity.' In other words, their actions are controlled by impulses opposite to passionary intensity" (Gumilyov, 2001, p. 295).

Gumilyov and his student K. P. Ivanov tried to represent this proposed classification schematically in a more detailed form[41] (see Figure 2.5).

---

[41] http:// gumilevica.kulichki.net/fund/fund03.htm. This site asserts that "Gumilyov and his student K. P. Ivanov used this diagram as a graphic aid in giving a course of ethnology lectures."

Figure 2.5

Passionarity

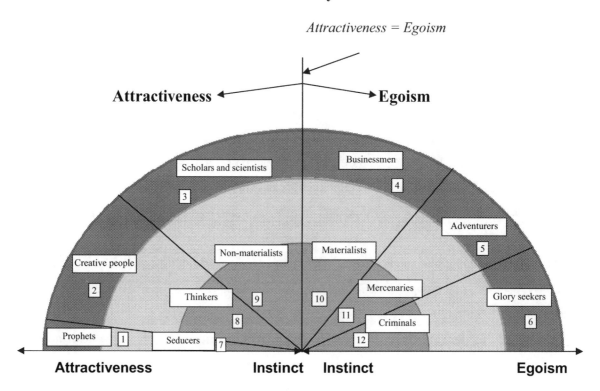

Although his figures and tables more graphically reflected his ideas, they were incapable of yielding a genuine typology. The passionary-attractive principle used as the basis for the classification could not serve as a criterion for identifying a personality type, because it did not identify an attribute that could integrate the diverse characteristics subsumed in the term "passionarity." Apparently recognizing the weakness of the passionary-attractive principle, Gumilyov started contemplating the levels of passionarity that people exhibit. In his and Ivanov's attempt to detail the typology of personalities, Gumilyov spoke of 100% passionaries or 100% subpassionaries. The use of percentages here is ineffective, however, because finding an effective criterion for distinguishing a 100% passionary from an 80% or 50% passionary is very difficult. This confirms Gumilyov's lack of a clear criterion for distinguishing one personality type from another, and the fact that these concepts existed for him solely on an intuitive, descriptive level.

The Psychology of Passionarity

From the moment Gumilyov's earliest works were published, his studies captured the interest of not only ethnographers, historians, and cultural studies specialists, but also of psychologists, who saw, as we have already mentioned, certain character traits of specific individuals in his discovery. Gumilyov himself noted this: "Passionarity is a special property of the human character" (Gumilyov, 1990, p. 33).

A search for the sources and specific characteristics of passionarity became one of the basic directions taken by the psychology of passionarity, although unfortunately there are not very many studies of the psychological traits of passionarity (Andreyev, 2008; Bogdanov, 2001; Kovalenko, 1999; A. A. Krylov & Kovalenko, 1993). Nevertheless, certain studies are worthy of special notice. For example, in the article "Passionarity as a Psychological Phenomenon," M. I. Kovalenko noted that "passionaries are characterized by a high overall level of mental activity and emotionalism … they are enthusiasts, movers, fanatics, and martyrs, and are also characterized by a dominant need for self-actualization." He also stressed that "passionarity is a very significant social characteristic. Its level has a decisive effect on the orientation of a personality…. This is the ability to change the environment and oneself and the need to prevail" (Kovalenko, 1999, p. 9). According to M. A. Abramov, passionaries are characterized by:

- Capacity for self-sacrifice;
- Creativity;
- Initiative;
- Ability to inspire the masses;
- Predictive ability;
- Heightened sense of responsibility;
- Dominance of consciousness over instincts;
- Organization according to the principle of the public interest (Frumkin, 2008, p. 123).

As we see, both authors have proposed quite a few psychological characteristics, without explaining why they are integrated into a specific "passionary complex" (Frumkin, 2008). This is not so simple to do, and Gumilyov himself stated that "the most difficult task is to account for and comprehend the diverse dominants engendered by passionarity..." (Gumilyov, 2001, p. 285).

Y. V. Bogdanov made an original attempt to analyze the personality types identified by Gumilyov. In his view, the psychological essence of passionarity/subpassionarity can be interpreted by raising the "question of the relationship between Lev Gumilyov's personality typology and psychological typology..." (Bogdanov, 2001, p. 2). For example, he tried to compare Gumilyov's personality typology and Carl Leonhard's well known "working" concept of accentuated personalities. He thinks that Leonhard's "well-structured" theory could help clearly distinguish the individual differences of the personality types identified by Gumilyov.

Bogdanov (2001, p. 7) arrived at this conclusion: "Hyperthymia[42] is the main symptom of passionarity." In contrast, dysthymia[43] and anxiety are symptoms of subpassionarity. Thus, according to Bogdanov the most "passionary" combination is a hyperthymic introvert, a kind of "generator of ideas," a nerve center, and a leader. The most "subpassionary combination is a dysthymic hysteric, while a harmonic personality is a non-accentuated personality whose behavior variations may be significant." Bogdanov's approach to Gumilyov's personality typology from the vantage point of accentuations allowed him to produce a quite original description of certain characteristics of passionaries/subpassionaries in terms of psychopathology and pathological psychology. But having demonstrated that passionaries are active (hyperthymic), he could not answer the question why activity makes some people passionaries and others subpassionaries. Why is "getting trapped," which he identified as a characteristic of the passionary type, encountered no less often in subpassionaries? Evidently Leonhard's concept is better suited to describe Gumilyov's personality types than to provide an explanatory mechanism for their origin.

---

[42] *Hyperthymia* is an accentuated character trait manifested in a person's almost always elevated mood, energy, and very high spirits. People with this trait usually try to be leaders, do not have stable interests, are not discriminating in their choice of associates, and have a hard time being alone.

[43] *Dysthymia* refers to mood disorders characterized by melancholy, depression, and sadness.

I. V. Andreyev has taken the same path as Bogdanov. He identifies activity as a manifestation of passionarity and adds a searching orientation to it. By using the Big Five personality traits model that is widely applied in modern psychology, he has tried to find a relationship between them and the searching activity of the personality as a manifestation of passionarity. He believes that a subject's high degree of searching activity is correlated with neuroticism, adaptability, emotionalism, and openness to experience (Andreyev, 2008, p. 1). Unfortunately, we see here yet another attempt to describe Gumilyov's types, this time in "Big Five" terms, without an explanation of their causes.

I. S. Zimina's article "The Development of Passionary Qualities in Children as a Means of Overcoming Laziness, Apathy, and Frailty" (Zimina, 2007, p. 1) is an interesting attempt to describe passionarity. In contrast to the preceding authors, she portrays passionaries not only as active people, but as people with active attitudes. This significant difference allowed Zimina to add characteristics such as goal-setting, social significance, and so forth to the definition of passionarity. She writes that "passionarity is an integrative characteristic of the personality whose qualities are directed at the improvement of self and society, is based on an individual's personal activity, and has social significance: goal-orientation, the ability to overcome obstacles and make extreme efforts, complementarity, adaptability, developed intuition, constructive aggressiveness, and mature emotionalism."

A brief overview of psychological studies of passionarity reveals a wide range of characteristics ascribed to this phenomenon, ranging from hereditary individual psychological traits to social characteristics that develop through social relations. But we still have not gotten an answer to the question of *what exactly is the basis for the combination, integration, and transformation into an integral whole of the diverse personality traits that Gumilyov called passionarity*. We believe that an appropriate answer can be found to this question if the role of passionarity in the overall structure of the personality is defined. After taking an interest in Gumilyov's discovery, we noted the surprising similarity between his conception of human types and the basic principles of our own approach to the personality. But none of the studies by Gumilyov or other researchers shed any light on the role assigned to passionarity in the structure of the personality. While in no way casting doubt on the existence of this phenomenon, we have tried to define its role by using the approach to personality that we developed. This approach, the

structural typology approach to the personality *(STP),* is distinguished by the following basic characteristics.

1. The personality's most significant so-called structuring elements are identified. In our opinion, there are four:

   a. the *collective unconscious*, whose most general and invariant elements are expressed in archetypes;

   b. the *personal unconscious*, information discarded or simply forgotten by a person over his lifetime;

   c. the *personal consciousness*, a combination of ideas, convictions, and values that determine and guide human behavior;

   d. the *collective consciousness*, invariant forms of a person's social existence expressed in neotypes.

2. The collective unconscious, like the collective consciousness, takes both "absolute" and "relative" forms:

   a. The *absolute form* of expression of the collective unconscious is found in the common tribal archetype the "Shadow," while the tendencies of a specific nation or group of people are reflected in the relatively invariant "Others" archetypes.

   b. The *collective consciousness* consists of invariant prevailing group, ethnic, and social feelings, conceptions, ideas, values, and relations that are recognized by a person and serve as an integrating force. Invariance at the level of the collective consciousness is also both absolute and relative in nature. The absolute nature of invariance refers to its common human contents, because they remain the same as long as mankind exists, while relativity is directly related to the feelings, conceptions, and values of a specific social environment, people, or tribe. In this case the contents are also invariable, but at a certain geographical and temporal level, and may change with changes in relations with the environment.

   The collective consciousness expressed in the forms of collective conceptions, collective feelings, and collective attitudes is reflected as neotypes in the individual consciousness. Neotypes are values that are unchanged from generation to generation and are discovered and recognized by a person in the course of his individual existence. We have identified two such neotypes, called the "God" neotype and the "Prophet" neotype. While we recognize the "God" neotype as a combination of definite values that are the same for all people, the "Prophet" neotype is invariant only within a specific group, social environment, nation, or group of people.

c. The relative invariance of the collective unconsciousness *(the "Others" archetypes) and the* collective consciousness *(the "Prophet" neotype) increase the number of structuring elements to six.*

3. The structuring elements of the personality, by interacting, form a definite structure of the personality that harmonizes the mutual interaction of its elements. The schematic structure of the personality was represented in Section 3 of Chapter 2 (see Figure 2.2). In analyzing this structure, we must keep in mind the arbitrary nature of its dividing lines. When we identified the "boundaries" of a particular component of the diagram, we merely intended to improve its graphic qualities.

4. The transcendent function of the psyche[44] plays an exceptionally important role in harmonizing the mutual influence of the structural elements of the psyche and not only makes it possible to "shatter" the boundaries between unconsciousness and consciousness by enabling a transition from one to another, but also creates the basis for the unity of opposites in the structure of the personality.

5. An important aspect of the structural typological approach is its consideration of the orientation of both conscious activity and unconscious tendencies towards the temporal aspects of life. In other words, the personality becomes a means of expressing in the present the results of a comparison of unconscious tendencies from the past and conscious aspirations for the future. Note that the word "persona," as we

---

[44] In analyzing the structure of the personality, we should especially emphasize Jung's identification of the transcendental function of the psyche, which overturned contemporary notions of the relationship between the **conscious** and **unconscious**. The fact of the matter is that the contents of the *conscious* and *unconscious* do not just influence each other and flow into each other, there can also be tension between them. This situation, which is quite often encountered in life, would lead to an intolerably grave condition were it not for the transcendent function of the psyche, which integrates opposites and creates a new quality of their manifestation. In reality the transcendent function of the psyche is a unique mechanism for integrating opposites that gives the personality its integrity and stability. "It is called 'transcendent' because it makes a transition from one attitude to another organically possible without losing the unconscious," Jung wrote.

have already mentioned, is a derivative of the two Latin words per and sona, which once meant "speak by means of." By expressing ourselves by means of the personality, which combines the seemingly incompatible – the past and the future, the conscious and the unconscious, our darkest and our brightest, most noble sides – we speak, communicate, live, and work.

6. Structural elements of the personality, on a continuum from the most undesirable in the unconscious to the most desirable in the conscious, have acquired symbolic names:

   a. Animal instincts and tendencies in the unconscious that are shameful and deprive us of our human countenance are the **Devil**.

   b. The tendencies of our tribe or ethnos that we are unaware of but that attract us are the **Tempter**.

   c. Events, desires, motives, and knowledge that we have forgotten, consider unimportant, have discarded, or have rejected constitute the contents of the personal unconscious are the **Non-Self**.

   d. Cognitive elements of awareness of ourselves and our environment are the **Self**.

   e. Values, moral standards, and moral principles that we recognize and that are accepted in our social milieu, nation, people, and society are the **Prophet**.

   f. Common human values that are the same for all people and are actually embedded in consciousness as the cultural heritage of mankind are **God**.

7. The presence of each of these structuring elements in consciousness is a condition for its integrity, although one or more elements is always dominant in a specific individual. This process constitutes the basis for construction of a subjective hierarchy of personal preferences or values.

8. The dominance of archetypal, unconscious, conscious, or neotypal tendencies in an individual presupposes the formation of different personality types. For example, if the "God" or "Prophet" neotypes dominate, we are dealing with one personality type; if the "Self" is dominant, we are dealing with another; and if the "Tempter" or "Devil" archetypes predominate, we are dealing with a completely different type.

9. On the basis of the dominance of one element in the overall structure of the personality, the structural typological approach makes it possible to identify six personality types:

    a. The "Devil" is a hedonistic personality type.

    b. The "Tempter" is a seductive personality type.

    c. The "Non-Self" is an evasive personality type.

    d. The "Self" is an egocentric personality type.

    e. The "Prophet" is a convincive personality type.

    f. "God" is a reflexive personality type.

10. The reasons for the dominance of a particular element in the structure of the personality and the main distinctive characteristics of each of these personality types can be explained by personality theories that already exist in psychology.

11. Combinations of the six personality types form certain ranges of types that can be adequately described if we account for all the basic principles of the structural typological approach.

Thus, we have presented the basic principles of our structural typological approach to the personality and have identified six of the most prominent types which, in combination, can produce a vast number of personality types. But in our view, of all the diversity of combinations, only one evokes a clear association with Gumilyov's passionaries. All we have to do is reread the characteristics of the convincive, egocentric, and most importantly, the seductive personality types to realize that it is a combination of these three types, which in a certain sense contradict one another, that is best suited for describing Gumilyov's passionary personality. The characteristics of the hedonistic, evasive, and reflexive personality types are also present in this range of types, but not in the dominant positions. The above can be represented schematically (see Figure 2.6).

Figure 2.6

The Personality Structure of Passionaries

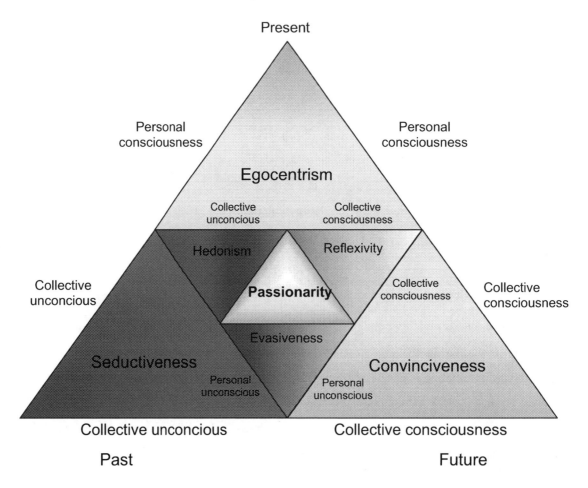

As we can see, the combination of unconscious archetypal tendencies and conscious neotypal aspirations in a highly neurotic and active individual are expressed in passionary behavior. The question is answered of why absolutely opposite characteristics are combined to form a single integral whole (which we specified at the very beginning). This integration is based on a unique combination of structural elements of the personality, which, by virtue of the transcendence of the psyche, form a range of types that embodies the convincive, seductive, and egocentric personality types all at the same time. This kind of unity and integrity means the development of a passionary. To put it in simpler terms, when a person can combine the past, present, and future into a single logical chain, and when others are attracted to him and he can convince and lead them, without forgetting his main role in the process, then we are dealing with a passionary, to whom all opportunities are open and to whom everything is accessible.

Our conception makes it possible to describe the personality structures of subpassionaries and harmonic people as well as passionaries according to Gumilyov. At first we will represent them schematically (see Figures 2.7 and 2.8).

Figure 2.7

The Personality Structure of Subpassionaries

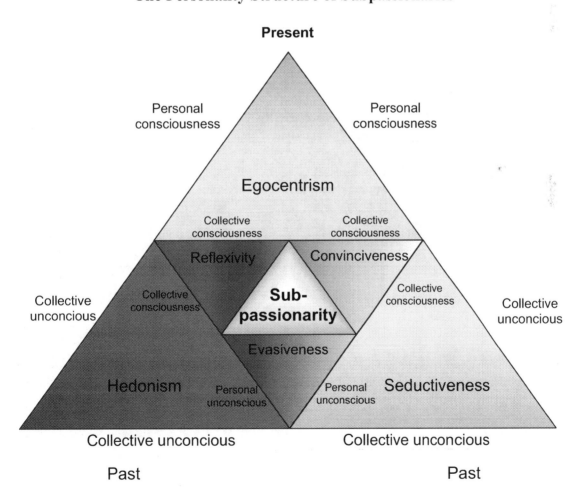

Figure 2.8

The Personality Structure of Harmonic People

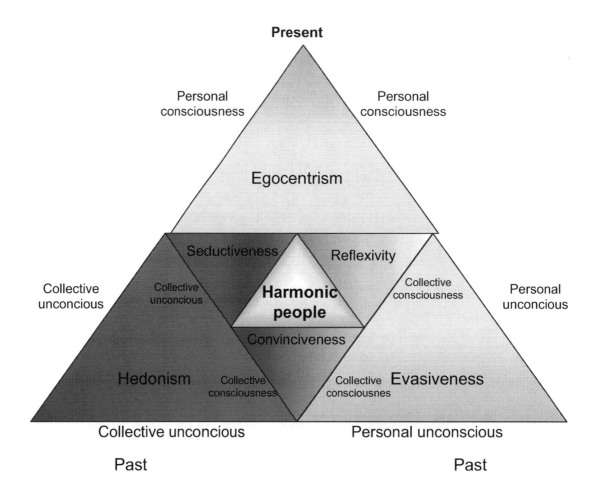

A subpassionary is the opposite of a passionary, in every respect: His personality has no unity of opposites, and the orientation of his behavior is determined by the past and present, not the future. Gumilyov noted (2001, p. 296) that "A subpassionary believes, according to his own invincible logic, that no one can predict the future, because he, the beneficiary of bread and circuses, is unable to make predictions on the basis of probability." The very idea of a future frightens him, forcing him to live not just for today, but to safeguard and protect "today" from any attempts at change. A subpassionary is a destroyer of a future he cannot understand and which he simply does not have. Living by the principle of satisfaction, the subpassionary does everything to attract attention to his "Self." The unconscious tendencies from our animal forebears, mixed with the unconscious tendencies of the ethnos in which the subpassionary lives, fill up his personal consciousness and leave no room for the rational, noble, and dignified. This is quite evident from the diagram, where hedonism from the most ancient tendencies of the psyche, in combination with the seductiveness determined by the history of his ethnos, is manifested at the level of the subpassionary's ego.

The personality structure of normal people who constitute the majority is no less interesting. In normal people, as Gumilyov wrote, "both impulses are balanced, which creates an intellectually capable, efficient, and adaptable, but not hyperactive, personality" (2001, p. 294). In fact, most people who want to have a "pain-free" existence do not want to shoulder the burden of social responsibility, but at the same time are always prepared to stand up for themselves. To a certain extent they may be attractive, idealistic, and persons who organize others around them. But in them these characteristics are always subordinate to the main characteristic, namely the desire for security, a comfortable life, and self-sufficiency.

They generally have no aspirations for the future and their plans are always focused on the present. And if they make plans, these are more short-term intentions than long-term horizons.

Thus, passionarity, subpassionarity, and harmony are combinations of the different structural elements we identified in the personality; but only passionarity arises from a unique combination of diverse elements, while subpassionarity and harmony are unidirectional.

The typology of the personality we have developed makes it possible to identify a large number of ranges of prominent personality types based on the dominance of a combination of structuring elements. For example, yet another range of type can be identified when the convincive, reflexive, and egocentric personality types are dominant in an integral whole. In contrast to subpassionaries, this category of individuals is definitely oriented towards the future, no matter what happened in the past. These characteristics are quite often typical of revolutionaries, anarchists, maximalists, terrorists, and everyone to whom the past has no value. For them, the past can and must be destroyed, because the past threatens their self-actualization in the future. They have no personal attachments, and feelings of kinship and friendship are meaningless to them. Profound reflection, the desire to show one's "Self," and convinciveness as a conscious tendency to lead, direct, convince, and demonstrate, constitute the combination of characteristics of this range of type. We could cite a large number of examples of these personality types, but perhaps the examples of the people who carried out the coup of October 1917 in Russia are the most eloquent. And today we see among us such people, who are so carried away with ideas about the future that they have lost touch with reality. The schematic structure of the personality of this kind of person is illustrated in Figure 2.9.

Figure 2.9

The Revolutionary Personality Type

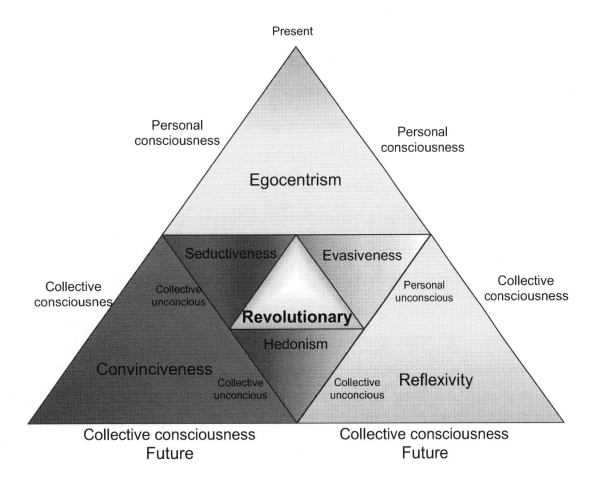

It seems to us that the idea of the dominance of certain elements in the personality structure is quite productive and merits additional study. We would be glad if any of our colleagues who have become interested in the ideas presented here would continue this research. For our part, we will be obligated to do so in our subsequent work.

CONCLUSION

More on the Role of Historical Analysis of the Subject of Creativity

At the very beginning of this study, we found that one of the basic features of psychology is its multi-facetedness, diversity, and at the same time integrity and systematization. The mutually exclusive conditions, contradictory nature, and paradoxical quality of certain principles of psychology become especially clear when we study creativity. But it is practically impossible to understand the reason for this without an historical analysis of the problem. History, with its marvelous "wisdom" and "information value," demonstrates that all major discoveries and research have historical underpinnings and pre-histories. The study of the historical past often gives us a quite objective and clear picture of present and future discoveries and advances. By approaching the subject of creativity from this historical standpoint, we have tried to find the basis for modern conceptions of the psychology of creativity. We think this approach can be applied to other fields of the humanities and in fact to any branch of science. It is quite obvious that without an historical foundation it is impossible and even unreasonable to discuss the causes of current events and phenomena and their possible consequences.

For example, by turning to Indian, Chinese, and ancient Greek philosophy, we discovered the amazing conceptions, theories, and viewpoints of the leading thinkers of antiquity, who had already laid the foundations on which the entire modern science of human creativity was built. In their tracts, books, and manuscripts, we discovered a striking connection between creativity and certain personality traits, and man's irreplicable individual qualities, abilities, temperament, thinking, perception, and imagination – i.e., everything that is known as man's psychological or spiritual world. In these sources is depicted the truth that creativity, although present in every act of human mental activity, remains an independent phenomenon. The diversity of creativity illuminated in the studies of ancient scholars and philosophers impelled us to make a more detailed study of their legacy.

Ancient Philosophy and Creativity

We started our analysis of the history of the study of creativity with ***Indian philosophy***, in which the doctrines of the Vedas provide very valuable material on topics of creativity. Of the many tracts that reflect the essence of Vedic knowledge, we chose the Bhagavad Gita, which is a great human monument. The Bhagavad Gita succeeded in finding the greatest number of characteristics and patterns of human behavior that are directly relevant to creativity and self-perfection. The creation of the self and a new "I" and the ability to renounce the material, change one's actions, and eliminate or partly cancel out the effect of the environment are the main factors in the behavior of a person who wants to perfect himself. In the understanding of Indian philosophy, creativity is manifested in a person's inner world and does not affect the external material world. This is creativity over creation; this is creativity as the creation of a new man. From this point of view, Indian philosophy is a quite specific and genuinely unique approach to the study of creativity.

Further exploration for the roots of creativity led us to ***Chinese philosophy***, where, as in Indian philosophy, we discovered a vast number of characteristics that reflect the features of creativity. Of course, in our discourse on Chinese philosophy, we mainly referred to the teachings of Confucius. Confucianism made it possible to look at the nature of human creativity in a somewhat different way. While Vedic philosophy represented creativity as a problem of self-perfection, i.e., the creation of the self, Chinese philosophy moved it in the direction of creative action in the reality around us. The role of self-perfection was not ruled out, but this was already a different approach to the subject of creativity than that taken by Indian philosophy.

While in Indian philosophy the problem of creativity is a matter of self-perfection, and in Chinese philosophy it is a matter of creative behavior based on self-perfection, ***ancient Greek philosophy*** was the first to approach creativity as an independent psychological phenomenon. In this sense it would be difficult to overestimate the contribution that the two Greek giants, Plato and Aristotle, made to the study of creativity. The *Phaedrus* dialogue provides vivid proof of the strength of the relationship between most modern studies of creativity and Plato's ideas. And Aristotle's views marked the beginning of the study of creativity as an independent mental process.

Sufism and the Psychology of Creativity

Further study of the history of ideas about creativity impelled us to analyze medieval **Arabic philosophy**. The term "Arabic" philosophy, which refers to a combination of the philosophical teachings of the peoples of the East who converted to Islam and used the Arabic language, is a very arbitrary concept, because after the Arab conquests, Persians, Azerbaijanis, Caucasian Persians, Jews, Tajiks, Uzbeks, and other peoples made their own contributions to its development, in addition to the Arabs. This fact, which greatly complicated the study of our topics of interest, at the same time allowed us to choose from among a multitude of currents a concept which represented a completely original and new approach to the interpretation of creativity: **Sufism**. While incorporating all pre-existing ideas of the study of creativity, Sufism also identified a divine talent in man, namely the ability to create. Creativity thus became an integral part and quintessence of the soul. By deifying man and transforming him into a Demiurge of the Universe, Sufism elevated creativity to the highest value which any person striving for it must and can exhibit. In our view, Azerbaijani philosophy and poetry, as reflected in the works of Nizami, Haghani, Shabustari, Nasimi, and Fizuli, represent splendid examples of the heights which a person can attain if his talents and directionality are mediated by creativity as the supreme value.

The modern understanding of creativity, which was influenced by all historical schools and currents, began to emerge in the West. Evidence of continuity in Western psychology is found in the relationship between psychoanalysis and Sufism that we described in this book. It is no coincidence that Freud and especially Jung repeatedly stressed that Eastern mysticism was one of the sources of their creativity. Western psychology in turn influenced Russian psychology, which, after becoming part of Soviet psychology in the early 20th century, determined the development of psychology in Azerbaijan. Thus ideas of creativity, by moving from one continent to another, from one doctrine to another, became a definite system of phenomena whose study became our primary objective.

The Paradoxes of Creativity

The phenomenology of creativity begins with paradoxes, which most clearly and brightly shed light on the basic distinctive feature of creativity, namely its paradoxical nature. In this study we focused attention on only a small number of paradoxes – 10 – but this number was sufficient to understand the irreducibility of creativity to "ordinary" mental processes or to the elements that constitute an act of creativity, i.e., to everything of which, figuratively speaking, creativity consists. In this sense, the paradoxical nature of creativity is creativity itself. We must understand that if creativity is truly exhibited, it is paradoxical, and if we encounter a paradox, we can only resolve it by means of creativity. History shows many examples of the solution of "insolvable" problems, and all of them reconfirm the premise that only creativity can fathom the unfathomable, solve the insolvable, and combine the uncombinable.

A Psychological Protective Mechanism

Creativity has another surprising attribute: It plays the role of our seeing-eye dog in the world of insolvable problems around us, a seeing-eye dog that leads us through the darkness to the light, allowing us to live a normal life. Evidently this trait is inherent to all mental processes. You'll agree that it would be difficult to imagine a person who would be competent without the proper level of development of thought, imagination, memory, and perception. A person's individual psychological traits and mental processes allow him to get his bearings in the environment and solve problems facing him. At times we might get the impression that creativity is unnecessary, because after all, various mental processes – thought and imagination in particular – can do what is often attributed to creativity. But this is a profound misjudgment.

All of a person's mental processes, properties, and states are oriented to ensuring a normal life when problems arise. By working together, they allow us to solve problems and escape the difficult situations that life confronts us with. But when all other methods of resolving a situation and escaping a problem are ineffective, creativity is activated and a solution to the problem is literally "created"; creativity finds a way out when a way out just does not exist; and it creates that which did not exist before. In other words, the ability of creativity to not just find a way out of a difficult situation, but to find it where it does not exist, qualitatively distinguishes it from all other psychological phenomena. This is not just a unique feature of creativity, but its protective function.

The "insolvability" of the problems people face has different levels, of which we can identify at least three. The *first* level of insolvability of a problem is the *individual level*, which arises when a problem is insolvable for a specific individual, but can be solved by others. The *second* is the *collective level*, where a problem is insolvable for a large group of people, but can be solved in principle. And finally the ***third*** level is the *universal level,* where a solution to a problem is non-existent or unknown at the current phase of social development.

A person most often encounters the first level of insolvability. Here the role of thinking, imagination, and other mental processes is clearly evident, and creativity in our meaning of the word is also exhibited. This is the so-called common level of creativity, everyday creativity, or "normal" creativity, strange though that phrase may sound. This is a person's discovery of what was known to others a long time ago, but which had been unknown to him.

Finding ways out of a particular problem when it is insolvable at the collective level is a difficult task. Creativity begins to clearly prove its social value when it "rescues" a group from the adverse effects of an unsolved problem. In essence, creativity at this level also "protects" the person himself, who otherwise feels himself to be the carrier of the problem, from degradation, spiritual malaise, and depression.

There is a third level of insolvability, the universal, where we witness a high-order exhibition of creativity, as the creation or discovery of the absolutely new, something that was heretofore unknown. In this case creativity manifests itself in pure form as scientific discoveries, splendid works of art, inventions, and so forth. By promoting progress, creativity in this phase protects us and all mankind from degradation and stagnation.

As we can see, in the first, second, and third cases, creativity performs a protective function for our psyche, our "Self," our personality, and our society. Yes, creativity is our innate method of improving ourselves and elevating the individual. After all, we are not simply looking for a way out of the situation in which we find ourselves, but we are creating a solution, creating it every second, every minute, and every hour from day to day, from year to year, and over our entire lives, by improving ourselves and the world around us.

The Structure of the Personality, the Collective Consciousness, and Neotypes

Studying creativity without a thorough analysis of the personality would be impossible. These two phenomena are not just interrelated; in a certain sense they constitute an integral whole. After analyzing the most important conceptions of the personality in psychology, we concluded that Carl Jung's conception merits special consideration. The fact that one subsection of this monograph is entitled "From Jung to More Jung" suggests the importance of referring to his theory from the standpoint of personal creativity. Jung's conception, which was presented to the court of the 20th-century psychology community and is still important to this day, permitted a new look at the problems of creativity, the personality, individual development, a person's distinctive features, and other phenomena. We assigned a special place to the structure of the personality, which includes the concepts of the collective unconscious and the archetypes. Many treatises by philosophers, literary critics, and psychologists have been devoted to the study of these terms, which Jung was the first to put into circulation. Their discovery overturned our conceptions of the nature of the human psyche. But our attention was mainly drawn to the asymmetry of the structure of the personality. For example, according to Jung, the personality consists of three basic elements: the *conscious*, the *personal unconscious*, and the *collective unconscious*. Thus for him there are two "unconsciouses" for one "conscious." This asymmetry also led us to approach the analysis of the structure of the personality more scrupulously from the standpoint of not just its unconscious tendencies, but also the structure of the conscious.

We have proposed a somewhat modified structure of the personality, which is nevertheless based on Jung's ideas. In it we have identified the collective conscious in addition to the collective unconscious. This approach completely changed our conception of the personality, by leading us to formulate yet another new concept, namely *neotypes in the structure of the human collective conscious*. It is well known that archetypes play the key role in the structure of the collective unconscious. The primary role in the structure of the collective conscious is played by neotypes, which are values that remain the same from generation to generation and are discovered and recognized by a person in the course of his individual development. We identified two basic neotypes – "God" and the "Prophet." While the "God" neotype seems to be a recognized system of values that remain unchanged and are completely determined for all people, the "Prophet" neotype is invariant only within the confines of a specific social group, nation, or people. By comparing the new elements of the personality structure that we introduced and the elements proposed by Jung, we obtained a structure which, in our opinion, most completely and effectively reflects the human personality.

198

From Emotion to Creativity

The personality structure will remain just a schema unless we proceed to analyze it from the standpoint of the activity a person exhibits during his life. But if we raise the issue of the role of activity, yet another question arises: On what basis and how does activity itself arise? This is a fundamental question of not just the psychology of creativity, but of psychology as a science. We are deeply convinced that a person's activity begins with an emotional experience that evokes certain feelings, whose projection onto the object of the experience leads to its association with a person's value orientations, which in turn actualizes willful efforts to take specific actions. In this sequence of phases that transforms emotional experiences into specific actions, the association of the object of the experiences (projected feelings) with an individual's value orientations plays the central role. It makes it possible to determine the place of the object of experience (projected feeling) in a person's values system. This complex process may be manifested on two levels: the *external* level, which is mostly inconsistent with a person's true goals and values, and an *internal*, true correlation with the person's core values. In the first case, a person may exhibit a socially approved type of behavior, regardless of whether he really accepts the forms and standards of behavior of a given social milieu, while in the second case, a person's behavior is sincerely designed to preserve and protect his values.

Creativity, Freedom, and the Degradation of the Personality

In the section on "The Personality and Its Structure," we presented a structure that reflects our concept of the *collective conscious*. In fact, the social values expressed in the "God" and "Prophet" neotypes have a significant impact on human behavior, but these values become priorities in life only when they occupy the top rungs of the personality's values hierarchy. In other words, a person's value orientations determine not only his activity, but the directionality of his activity.

In this book we have asserted that a person is willing to defend and fight for his values and in the process exhibit a high level of activity. But we should agree that activity to maintain and protect values, in and of itself, is still not the basic condition for personal development. We know that certain kinds of activity may also lead to the degradation of the individual, if the goals

199

of activity are not constant or clearly defined or are accomplished under duress. We must keep in mind that only creativity and the quest for freedom and autonomy, by occupying the leading position in a person's values hierarchy, will enable his self-improvement and development. In a democratic system these values become paramount, not just for the development of the individual, but for society as a whole. For example, in his speech to the House of Commons in 1947, Winston Churchill said that "Indeed, it has been said that democracy is the worst form of Government except all those other forms that have been tried from time to time" (Churchill, 2005, p. 509). In fact, this is the only form of government in which an individual feels that his liberties and opportunities for self-expression are not infringed. The Western world owes its current progress mainly to the democratic system of government, which protects human rights, the rule of law, and the freedom of self-expression and creativity. We must understand and remember that any restriction on human freedom means a restriction of human creativity. And because creativity, as we have emphasized, is the way a person improves himself, then by restricting freedom we limit the opportunities for personal self-improvement and development, which ultimately leads to personal degradation. A degraded person cannot serve as a source of development for the society in which he lives. Moreover, the person becomes a factor that retards social development and ultimately contributes to the decline of society as a whole.

The Conflict Between the Creative Personality and Society

We should keep in mind that a creative person will always strive for more than he has, even in the best sociopolitical system, namely democracy. In other words, irrespective of the environment and conditions in which he lives, a creative person will always oppose them. If a personality truly has creative characteristics, the person cannot and should not accept the prevailing morality in the broadest sense of the word (see *The Paradox of Morality*). His talents, perception of the world, world view, and methods and types of communication are significantly different from other people's. Of course under conditions of severe pressure on a creative person, such opposition will be very difficult. The history of science provides plenty of examples of the unjustifiably harsh treatment of outstanding scientists, artists, and poets whose creativity rejected the social morality of their times. But even when there is no pressure and there is complete freedom of creativity, a creator's personality will seek a new truth and reject that which exists. After analyzing the personal qualities, talents, and characteristics of the cognitive activity of creative people, we were once again convinced that the qualities possessed by creative people will not allow them to look at the world as other people do and accept it as it is for others, or to live as other people live. In this sense, the opposition of the creative person to the society in which he lives is itself creativity.

Culture and the Typology of the Personality

The relationship between the personality and society has another manifestation, related to the influence of culture on a person. The perception of culture and its personal interpretation have a significant effect on the organization of a person's social behavior and activity. The specific nature of this perception and the method of responding to social processes, or as it is often described, the type of human behavior, may be determined by the dominance of one or more elements in his personality structure. As we have already discussed, the personality structure consists of six structuring elements, all of them interconnected into an integral system that allows a person to live normally. But in reality there are always dominant, leading elements and also secondary elements. And the distinctive features of a person's behavior, thinking, and activity will be determined on the basis of which structural element is the leading one.

The Devil, Tempter, Non-Self, Self, Prophet, and God as the basic structuring elements can in combination yield a huge number of personality types. We identified only six of the most prominent and illustrative ones:

- the *hedonistic type*, which is manifested when the "Devil" element is dominant in the personality structure;
- the *seductive type*, which is manifested when the "Tempter" element is dominant;
- the *evasive type*, which is manifested when the "Non-Self" element is dominant;
- the *egocentric type*, which is manifested when the "Self" element is dominant;
- the *convincive type*, which is manifested when the "Prophet" element is dominant;
- the *reflexive type*, which is manifested when the "God" element is dominant.

These types are quite often encountered. In describing their psychological characteristics to students, friends, and colleagues, we saw that many of them mentioned specific names, recognizing these types by their reactions and behavior. Thus, the typologization of the personality on the basis of the dominance of structural elements has proven to be an effective and promising idea.

Personality Theory and Typology

Another feature of the personality types we have developed is that they were explained theoretically not within the framework of a single concept, but using different approaches to the interpretation of the personality in modern psychology. For example, the hedonistic personality type can be more easily described from the standpoint of Freudian theory than any other personality type. The seductive type can be described in terms of Jung's analytical psychology. The evasive type directly reflects the psychological characteristics of a person according to Fromm. The egocentric type fits within the conceptual framework of Erikson, Bandura, and Kelly. The convincive type is reflected both in the ideas of Bandura and Kelly and in Rotter's cognitive approach. And finally, the reflexive type is that attitude of man towards the world treated in the works of Vygotsky.

The Structural Typological Approach to the Personality

The structural typological approach to the personality (STP) which we developed is distinguished by the following basic characteristics:
1. The most significant so-called structuring elements are identified in the personality. From our point of view, there are four:
   a. The collective unconscious;
   b. The personal unconscious;
   c. The personal conscious;
   d. The collective conscious.
2. The collective unconscious, like the collective conscious, takes "absolute" and "relative" forms. The relative invariance of the collective unconscious (the "Others" archetype) and the collective conscious (the "Prophet" neotype) increase the number of structuring elements to six.
3. By interacting with each other, the structuring elements of the personality form a personality structure that enables harmonization of the mutual influence and interaction of its constituent elements.

4. The transcendent function of the psyche plays an exceptionally important role in harmonizing the interaction of the structural elements of the personality.

5. An important aspect of the structural typological approach is the fact that the personality becomes a means of expressing in the present the results of a comparison of unconscious tendencies of the past and conscious aspirations in the future.

6. The structuring elements of the personality have acquired symbolic names: the Devil, Tempter, Non-Self, Self, Prophet, and God.

7. The domination of a structural element in the overall structure of the personality is the basis for constructing a subjective hierarchy of preferences or values.

8. The domination of archetypal, unconscious, conscious, or neotypal tendencies anticipates the formation of different personality types.

9. The structural typological approach made it possible to identify six basic personality types: the hedonistic, seductive, evasive, egocentric, convincive, and reflexive types.

10. The reasons for the domination of a particular element in the personality structure and the basic distinctive characteristics of each type we identified can be explained by personality theories that already exist in psychology.

11. The combination of basic personality types leads to certain ranges of types that can be adequately described if all the basic principles of the structural typological approach are taken into account.

12. Creativity, paradoxes, the personality structure, the collective conscious, neotypes, the typology of the personality, and other phenomena analyzed in this book have opened up new avenues for investigation. The impossibility of analyzing them in one book forces us to stop here. But we are well aware that the incompleteness of an action, according to the well-known effect discovered by Blyuma Zeigarnik, will compel us to study these phenomena again. We would also like to see the readers of our book take an interest in studying them.

ODE TO CREATIVITY

I want, friends, the story of a problem to expose,
Which ages long ago within the soul arose.
Already then being immortal, it beckoned with its head
Those men who wished to grasp the tangled life's thread.

Then, at the dawn of history, not knowing one another's motto
The Chinese sage[45], the guru,[46] and the follower of Plato,
Wrote treatises on how to reach the God in future,
And how to be a creator not second to Mother Nature.

In this world we come across a host of coincidence,
I presented one of these not seeing the evidence.
It's not always given to get the cause of revelation,
But yet we have to search for it without reservation.

We try to gaze from jungles, forests full of sensations,
Upon civilizations of the world and great creations,
Upon the emergence of science, and searches through hells
For celestial ideas, which arose in quiet cells.

INDIA

Let us begin with India – a country mysterious,
With every corner miraculous and imperious.
The souls seem strange there, at first glance,
They settle in separate bodies taking their chance[47].

Before our eyes a great and mighty river flows,
The savior of Hindu souls with holy banks glows.
Millions of lives hasten to give hearts in Salvation,
Before her Buddha pales in the hypostasis of creation.

Their own place in the universe attempting to acknowledge,
The Buddhist creates the system of Vedantic[48] knowledge.
The wandering ascetic points out within himself signs,
And further movements of the Sciences defines.

---

[45] *Chinese sage* is used in the meaning of a Confucian (of or relating to the Chinese philosopher Confucius or his teachings or followers)
[46] *Guru* is a teacher, esp. intellectual and spiritual guide of Hinduism
[47] *This phrase is used to render the meaning of reincarnation - a rebirth of a soul in a new human body.*
[48] *Vedantic* – of or relating to Hindu philosophy, to Veda

Inconceivable, that in the lines of Indian manuscripts
We manage to find traces of contemporary transcripts.
There we see the flaws of our inherent choices,
Their sounds run through centuries as the prophets' voices.

HUMAN FLAWS

Through the years to us they whisper that flawed is mankind,
Man makes mistakes consistently, he can not possess a true mind.
Impossible to trust him, as he is fatally imperfect,
But we don't listen to the whispers, so reiterated is our defect.

Man has evermore a tendency, as Guru made it clear,
For fibbing, shedding phony tears, and acting insincere.
After all, one can not simply look and see
The lies in human thoughts: they from sight quickly flee.

We look upon the world and see what simply is not there.
Under the spell of dreams, we live really so many a year.
It is so strong and sweet, that man from day to day
Having fallen into illusion, is ready to while his life away.

My free consciousness the Creator has locked into a jail,
It has windows, sounds and smells, and walls fine and frail.
I can see it, I can touch it, I can try,
But certainly I know that I will cast it off when I die.

How to preserve the human being, so weak and lonely the shell is?
Ask forgiveness for his faults, or hold a blade behind this back of his?
How to protect oneself? How spiritual peace to gain?
Don't wait for God to grant it. You yourself must try it to attain.

Training your reason, your flesh, you have to raise yourself above,
Forget your friends, your close contacts and always starve.
Reach for blessedness as a flower reaches for the sun's ray,
To earthly perfection this is your only and sole way.

205

CHINA

Four main faults of humankind described the Indian mage,
He did not know that almost by his side was the Chinese sage,
Attempting to explain the problems of existence that he sought himself,
The source of perfection in the knowledge of life and in good strength of self.

In his laboring the Eastern genius exposed for us a truth only –
For man to be worthy he must upon himself work stubbornly.
Not caring just for his own needs he has to leave all behind,
And shining as a light for all, he should raise the level of mankind.

In the course of life three times you'll love, he foretold your duty,
First for yourself you'll burn with love, as if you were a beauty.
Then for another you'll have a passion, this gift to you the fates did lend
Finally falling for the truth, you'll to the heights of knowledge ascend.

GREECE

From sacred rivers, from the wall of China with steeps without lea,
We turn our sails to the West, to the surf of the Aegean Sea.
Here two great Greeks, friends with one another, both noble and high,
Laid the foundations of the Science known to you and I.

They brought to Science formal logic's wonderful culture.
They wove a bunch of spiritual strength, uniting all in one structure.
They discovered the law of contradiction in everything, every part,
Thus encouraging reception of charming rhetoric's art.

In his treatise on the soul Aristotle, for the first time in high class,
Presented, straight on and in profile, the soul to us.
From his ideas, from his labors having cast away astrology,
The psyche came to its native house in the science of psychology.

THE MIDDLE EAST

Absorbing three streams and forming one mighty river,
The Arabic world coalesced and the East to shine for ever.
Within it love for Greece with mysticism entwined in all,
A new teaching was created there which Sufism we call.

In the golden sands of Arabia and in Persia, supercilious
Murshid[49]– the teacher crossed a line very dangerous.
He sang a hymn of perfection with the voice of the Creator of the universe,
His words – a creation which shall never perish or grow worse.

And the dervish, wanderer of desert dunes himself deified,
He changed the words "No Allah but Allah" to "I am Allah" as guide.
The whole world of the Middle East was in shock, thunderstruck
When great Nasimi[50] without fear exclaimed: "An al Haq".[51]

Yes, the skin fell off his body, but his life eternally shone.
He lives in poetry immortal, in hurufism[52], in disciples of his own.
The way to truth today is impossible to cover, it's true,
You'll behold God himself if you pass four stages through.

In the first stage a son of Adam must learn Shariah.
The second stage kindles in the heart, that's Tariqah.
Flowing into the depth of knowledge, you'll know Marifah,
And God you will become, when you understand Haqiqah.

But another source of inspiration was discovered to the full,
Opened with a mysterious key, it became a tumult soulful
Of movement, rhythm, words – ecstasy – mystical glory
And before you miracle – a poem or a story.

II.

So at such a gallop through centuries rushed the soul,
She promised the one who is worthy to reveal her goal.
But she has not lived up to her words to a dot,
And where to look for her as before, we still know not.

---

[49] *Murshid* (Ar.) - guide or teacher. Particularly in <u>Sufism</u> it refers to a <u>Sufi</u> teacher.
[50] *Nassimi* – 14th century Azerbaijani poet, a representative of Hurufism.
[51] *An al Haq* (Ar.) "I am God". This is used to intend God is found within one's 'self'.
[52] *Hurufism* was a mystical Sufi doctrine, which spread in areas of western Persia, Anatolia and Azerbaijan in later 14th - early 15th centuries, and it recognized the truth in the substance of letters rather than in the person.

Millennia have passed and the thread of action we have caught
How to create something new, and how to revive the old.
There's one phenomenon which we still can not explain:
How the soul fell into the body with a spark, life to obtain.

She is a divine flame that lights the path of strife,
Of forward movement, after all, this is the essence of life.
Although time's arrow will not turn the other way anyhow,
Before her even time itself would its head bow.

Within us burns a flame – a bright and strong one,
Overwhelmingly it burns, invisible to everyone.
You must take this flame out, to keep your inner world wholesome,
Otherwise it shall burn it down, reduce to ashes, and the flower will not blossom.

God gave a flame for warmth to each sensible soul,
And within us as a beacon it serves for all.
But often we put it out, embarrassed by its glow.
There can be no warmth without a light, but we don't follow.

The cold, dark, frightening world with all its frame
Is the offspring of the soul, where there's no room for the flame.
To give people warmth and dispel fear, to disperse darkness abroad
Is possible only with the blessed marriage of flame and thought.

III.

And so we've come to the present day an advanced race,
And the situation, so to say, is different at its base.
Today so much is created, that all is nearly new.
They loudly deny novelty – give birth to "déjà vu".

To create, of course, is not a task simple and minimal
Not for nothing are soaked in tears the sonnets by Shakespeare,
And it was no accident that Carl Jung and Freud – the geniuses
Gave their talents to mankind to find an answer to this.

Thus the master of dreams examining grief 's decay,
From spiritual sources drew the various veils away.
He found in the psyche for morality a haven natural,
From there cold winds blow, such as may blow from the Mistral…

Now we know: upon consciousness the Super – Ego weighs,
Its influence is strong, under it seething the Ego stays.
And further still below is the ancient Id, that ahead shoots,
Weaving the levels of the Babylonian gardens with roots.

So for creative activity, three reasons Freud saw under the Sun.
He related the demise of the libido to the first, major one.
When you can not fall in love and yet you burn with passion
It lives anonymously within your plain creation.

The source of all the biggest problems has been fear always.
One instance of its presence is the remains of hope's decay.
But the father of analysis proceeded a way differently known.
He brought fear and hope together under a wedding crown.
Once they were married, he declaimed: "At last, I have found
That deep longing – this itself is the creator profound".

But for a creative activity there is a third reason – truth.
Freud enjoined us to seek it in the psyche of a youth.
And the wish in him to excel and surpass father must extend.
It's a vector of personal growth from the beginning to the end.

IV.

Jung, Adler and Maslow all sought the same path of progress,
Attempting how to unfold the book, the creative process.
And from the pages of their studies they tried to blow away
Everything extraneous to creation, revealing its essence in that way.

PARADOXES OF CREATION

But in the action of the Creator, in all he created
Some strange foil of himself to us he related.
As oil distilled in the process of making coke[53], hence
Paradox is the human creations' essence.

How used we were to thinking of truth as a unity,
It's given to rovers, to provide in the dark a light of dignity.
But paradoxes of creation, revealing an approach different
Speak to us that two truths are in one embodiment.

---

[53] *Coke* – the residue of coal left after destructive distillation. It is used as a fuel.

THE PARADOX OF LOGIC

And so, creation with intellect is Kindred. It's no bruit,
Their bond long ago was proved to rise from a common root.
But at the same time creation in effect
Can not be justified by the way of the intellect.

Mental reasoning is a logical process. All know it best.
Logic and intellect have a mutual sound, interest.
If logic and creation are not bound always overall,
The alogic of creation is the logic of the creator, all in all.

THE PARADOX OF MORALITY

Logic and morality are brothers – twins in all connections,
Without them creators can not embody their reflections.
If creation against the canon of logic takes the floor,
Then the amorality of creation becomes law.

How could creation suddenly become amoral to the limit?
Who is entitled to be a high judge indiscriminate?
It is not the one who is noted for his wish to create
A world where it's impossible to rise based on evil and hate?
But this society must not forget this event
Or there misfortune will hasten, where creation is insolvent.

THE PARADOX OF QUANTITY

There is a paradox of quantity in creative occurrence,
With an obvious shortage in their manifestation's instance.
But the growth in creations, insights, clever aspirations
Increases the need for more of the same creations.

THE PARADOX OF DESIRE

Of the fact creation is desirable we often speak more,
Praising the artist's work, we his talent adore.
But turning creation into a prestigious instrument
We create a disincentive for worthwhile content.

Yes, we wish they to create miracles around us were able,
And that the heights of creation to all were available.
But if people suddenly uncover the secrets of the gods,
Shall we become slaves in fact, or shall we become gods?

THE PARADOX OF DETERMINANTS

Everyone has his own reason to create things plain
And from where it arose, it's hard to explain.
Having found the motive, you can not your wonder hide
That to another it could never be applied.

The motivation of creation is not a simple phenomenon,
It's a source of development, it does not allow for stagnation.
But having furnished creation with worthy fruit,
It will not push forward for labors new, maybe for good.

THE PARADOX OF THE PRODUCT

In order to understand the creator, you value his creative prestige,
Into the work he put his labor, skill and all his knowledge.
But the more accessible, the easier it is to handle in purity,
And the more the author is threatened in history with obscurity.

The works of creation, coming into our everyday life
Become a part of the current day, features of our strife.
We no longer think of the one who granted them, let alone
Within them, the creator who dissolved the world of his own.

Folk creations can be a clear example of all this:
Verses, stories, songs, dances known to us sans their genesis.
But if you look deeper into the people's epopee,
One particular person begot every idea, you may see.

The products of creation have still another aspect,
We know of their particular and strong effect.
They are able to detach the creator from the rest
By creating a Bacchic[54] ecstasy or a perturbation tempest.

This grief or laughter disappear not into the crowd,
Like roots into creation itself they grow about.
For raising the creator above the earthly throng
The product, the ideas of the people are absorbed right along.

---

[54] Bacchic – of, relating to, or suggestive of Bacchus of the Bacchanalia, figuratively: frenzied, cheerfully noisy

THE CREATIVE PERSONALITY

Paradoxical are in everything creative natures,
Within them can be combined different textures.
That which for the mortal is difficult and undesirable
For a creative personality is simple, easy and liable.

The creative personality is full of energy wholesome,
But at the same time it is peaceful and calm.
Like a dormant volcano in a greatness of its own,
Only to this one is the time of awakening known.

Yes, creative people have a gift of the mind.
Nature a great intellect has given them, being kind.
But at times how naïve are the rulers of destinies,
To cut them into two parts no hard task is.

For dreaming in everybody lies a peculiarity,
They give themselves to fantasy, disregarding reality.
But the creator has a way to unite in a moment
The power of imagination with the reality of judgment.

Of contradiction in the personality another source
Manifest is the atypical particularity in intercourse.
In creative people the playfulness of extroversion
Comes out united with the deepest introversion.

The creative personality has an odd, strange feature,
From the soul's secret rooms it sends us a messenger.
There the masculine, joined with the feminine of good stock,
Allows the personality to see to swim out from this dock.

V.

We could write about creation without end
Sans uncovering all of its mystic trend.
The curse of psychology will manifest again here,
That which is revealed, as a first love, will disappear.

With a sweet tinge of memory in me stays
The psychic laceration of that unquiet day,
When the ability to create was revealed to me
And on the spot dissolved there, not letting me grasp any.

It may be unimportant how proceeds the act,
In which creation is revealed as an inviolable fact.
It's much more important that Godliness is Creation,
That which Created Man has given us this Relation.

Oh, Good gracious! I know how I can find you,
Even if you are not in the flesh, faceless, divine, true.
It costs us up to the creation act ourselves to deliver
As a young maiden the soul will soon begin to shiver.

It seems to me that God has found a good haven
In human creation into which he has come from the heaven.
And if I say "May God bless you", I make mention
That I mean "May you save yourself by Creation".

References

Aliyaryy, S. (Ed.) (2008). *The history of Azerbaijan. From ancient times to the 1870s [Istoriya Azerbaydzhana. S drevneyshikh vremen do 70-gg. XIX veka]* (p. 558). Baku.

Aliyev, B. (2008). *The issue of personality in education [Tehsilde shakhsiyyat problemi].* Baku: Obrazovaniye.

Aliyeva, K. (2008). Psychological issues of the development of a person's creative potential: Author's abstract of a doctor of psychology dissertation. Baku.

Alizade, A. A. (2005). Talented children. Educational questions: essays, studies [Istedadli ushaqlar. Pedaqozhi meseleler: esseler, etudler]. Baku: ASPI.

Allport, G. (1937). Personality: A psychological interpretation. New York: Holt, Rinehart, Winston.

Andreyev, I. V. (2008). Searching activity as a possible manifestation of the passionarity of subjects and its personality correlates with the "Big Five." In *Passionary energy and ethnos in a developed civilization.* Transactions of an All-Russian interdisciplinary scientific and practical conference [Poiskovaya aktivnost kak vozmozhnoye proyavleniye passionarnosti subyektov i yeyo lichnostnyye korrelyaty s «Big five». *Passionarnaya energiya i etnos v razvitoy tsivilizatsii. Materialy Vserossiiskoy mezhdistsiplinarnoy nauchno-prakticheskoy konferentsii*] (Dec. 19, 2007, pp. 9–12). Moscow.

Andreyeva, G. M. (1980). *Social psychology [Sotsialnaya pskikhologiya].* Moscow: Moscow State University Press.

Aristotle (1976). *On the soul. [Traktat o dushe]* In *Works in 4 Vols. [Sochineniya v 4-kh tomakh]* (Vol. 1, pp. 50–448). Moscow: Mysl. English translation from: Internet Classics Archive. classics.mit.edu/Aristotle/soul.html

Bayramov, A. S. (1989). *Psychological studies. [Psikhologicheskiye etyudy].* Baku: Azerneshr.

Bandura, A. (1977). *Social learning theory.* Englewood Cliffs, NJ: Prentice Hall.

Barron, F. (1958). The psychology of imagination. *Scientific American, 3,* 150–170.

Barron, F. (1969). *Creative person and creative process.* New York: Holt, Rinehart Winston.

Barron, F. (1972). The disposition towards originality. In: P. E. Vernon (Ed.), *Creativity.* Baltimore, MD: Penguin.

Barron, F., Montuori, A., and Barron, A. (Eds.). (1997). *Creators on creating.* New York: Jeremy P. Tarcher/Penguin Putnam.

Bartold, V. V. (1966). *Works on the history of Islam and the Arab Caliphate. Works in 9 Volumes. [Raboty po istorii Islama i Arabskogo khalifata. Sochineniya v 9 t.]* (Vol. 6). Moscow: Nauka.

Bekhterev, V. M. (1926). *The foundations of human reflexology [Obshchiye osnovy chelevecheskoi refleksologii].* Leningrad.

Bekhtereva, N. V. (2007). *The magic of the brain and the labyrinths of life. [Magiya mozga i labirinty zhizni]* (p. 352). St. Petersburg.

Bertels, Ye. E. (1962). Nizami and Fizuli. In *Ye. E. Bertels. Selected works.* [Nizami i Fizuli. *Ye. E. Bertels. Izbrannyye trudy]* (p. 511). Moscow.

Beylerov, E. (2008). *Talent identification and development of children. The concept of employee talent [Ushaqlarda istedadin mueyyenleshdirilmesi ve inkishaf etdirilmesi. Istedadin ishchi konsepsiyasi].* Baku.

Bhaktivedanta, A. C. (1986). *The Bhagavad Gita as it is [Bhagavadgita kak ona yest'].* Moscow. In English: London: Macmillan, 1968.

Blagaya, D. D. (Ed.). (1980). *The psychology of processes of artistic creativity [Psikhologiya protsessov khudozhestvennogo tvorchestva].* Moscow: Nauka.

Bogdanov, A. V. (2001). *L. N. Gumilyov's typology of personalities from the vantage point of accentuation theory [Tipologiya lichnostey L. N. Gumileva s pozitsiy ucheniye ob aktsentsuaktsiakh].* Moscow.

Bogoyavlenskaya, D. B. (1983a). *Intellectual activity as a problem of creativity [Intellektualnaya aktivnost' kak problema tvorchestva].* Rostov: Rostov State University Press.

Bogoyavlenskaya, D. B. (1983b). *Intellectual activity as a psychological aspect of the study of creativity: A study of the issues of the psychology of creativity [Intellektualnaya aktivnost' kak psikhologicheskiy aspekt izucheniya tvorchestva: Issledovaniya problem psikhologii tvorchestva]* (pp. 182–195). Moscow: Nauka.

Bratko, A. L. (1969). *Modeling the psyche [Modelirovaniye psikhiki].* Moscow: Nauka.

Brownson, J. M. J. (1988). Landscape and ethnos: An assessment of L.N. Gumilev's theory of historical geography [Ph.D. dissertation]. Canada: Simon Fraser University.

Boulanger, P.A. (Ed.). (1991). *Confucius. His life and teachings.* In the series: *The lives and teachings of wise men [Konfutsiy. Zhizn' yego i ucheniya. Zhizn i ucheniya mudretsov].* Moscow: Book Chamber International.

Campbell, J. (1971). *The hero with a thousand faces* (p. 66). New York: Pantheon.

Cervone, D. and Pervin, L. (2008). *Personality: theory and research* (p. 8). Hoboken, NJ: John Wiley & Sons.

Chomsky, N. (2006). *Failed states.* New York: Holt, Henry & Company.

Churchill, W. (2005). *The sinews of peace [Muskuly mira]* (p. 509). Moscow.

Corsini, R. (1999). *The dictionary of psychology* (p. 407). Philadelphia, PA: Brunner/Mazel.

Cropley, A. Y. (1969). *Creativity.* London: Harlow-Longman.

Csikszentmihalyi, M. (1996). *Creativity: Flow and the psychology of discovery and invention.* New York: Harper Collins.

Davis, J. and Restle, F. (1963).The analysis of problems and prediction of group problem solving. *J. of Abnormal and Social Psychology*.

Delyusin, L. P. (1982). *Confucianism in China: Problems of theory and practice [Konfutsiantsvo v Kitaye. Problemy v teorii i praktike]* (1982). Moscow: Nauka.

De Raad, B., Sullot, E., and Barelds, D. (2008). Which of the Big Five factors are in need of situational specification. *Eur. J. Pers. 22*, 269–289.

Dictionary of foreign words [Slovar' innostrannykh slov] (1990). Moscow: Russian Language.

Dictionary of the practical psychologist [Slovar' prakticheskogo psikhologa] (1998). Minsk.

Drozdov, V. A. (2005). Mystical love in Iranian Sufism. *Oriental Studies: Philological studies.* [Misticheskaya lyubov' v irranskom sufizme. *Vostokovedeniye: Filologicheskiye issledovaniya]* [Collection of articles, No. 26]. St. Petersburg: St. Petersburg University Press.

Dunchev, V. N. (1985). *A study of cognitive styles in connection with the problem of creativity [Issledovaniya kognitnivykh styley v svyazi s problemoy tvorchestva]* (p. 123). Leningrad.

Erikson, E. H. (1963a). *Childhood and society* (2nd ed.). New York: W. W. Norton & Co.

Erikson, E. H. (1963b). Reflection on Dr. Borg's life cycle. In E. H. Erikson (Ed.), *Adulthood* (pp.1–31). New York: Norton.

Etkind, A. (1994). Foreword to Vol. 2 of Jung, C. *The libido and its metamorphoses and symbols* [Predisloviye ko 2-mu tomu knigi K. Yunga «*Libido, ego metamorfozy i simvoly*»] (p. 9). St. Petersburg.

Ewen, R. (1993). *An introduction to theories of personality* (4th ed.). Hillsdale, NJ: Lawrence Erlbaum.

Freud, S. (1912). *Leonardo da Vinci and a memory of his childhood [Leonardo da Vinchi: Vospominaniya o detstve]*. Moscow.

Freud, S. (1916). *The psychopathology of everyday life [Psikhopatologiya obydennoy zhizni]*. Moscow.

Freud, S. (1923). *Basic psychological theories in psychoanalysis [Osnovnye psikhologicheskiye teorii v psikhoanalize]*. Moscow, Petrograd.

Freud, S. (1991). *The ego and the id [«Ya» i «Ono»]* (p. 352). Tbilisi. English edition (1949). *The ego and the id.* London: The Hogarth Press Ltd.

Freud, S. and Bullitt, W. (1967). *Thomas Woodrow Wilson – the 28th President of the United States. A psychological study.* Boston: Houghton Mifflin. Russian edition (1992). Moscow: Progress.

Frolov, I. T. (Ed.). (1980). *Dictionary of philosophy [Slovar' filosofii]* (p. 21). Moscow.

Fromm, E. (2003). *Escape from freedom [Begstvo ot svobody]* (p. 82). Moscow.

Frumkin, K. G. (2008). *Passionarity: The adventures of an idea [Passionarnost: priklyucheniya odnoy idei]* (p. 123). Moscow: LKI.

Galperin, P. Ya. and Zhdan, A. N. (2005). *The history of psychology: The 20th century [Istoriya psikhologii. XX vek].* Moscow.

Gardner, H. (1993). *Creating minds* (pp. 19–45). New York: Basic Books.

Geyushev, Z. B. (Ed.). (1966). *Essays on the history of Azerbaijani philosophy [Ocherki po istorii Azerbaydzhanskoy filosofii].*

Granovskaya, R. M. (2004). *The psychology of belief [Psikhologiya very]* (p. 38). St. Petersburg.

Grigoryan, S. N. (Ed.). 1961. *Selected works of thinkers of the Near and Middle East [Izbrannye trudy mysliteley blizhnego i srednego vostoka].* Moscow.

Gruber, H. (1981). *Pervin on man.* Chicago: University of Chicago Press.

Gruzemberg, S. O. (1924). *Genius and creativity [Geniy i tvorchestvo].* Leningrad.

Guilford, J. (1965). *Three aspects of intelligence. The psychology of thinking [Tri storony intellekta. Psikhologiya myshleniya]* (pp. 433–456). Moscow: Progress.

Guilford, J. (1967a). Some theoretical views of creativity. In: H. Helson (Ed.), *Contemporary approaches to psychology.* New York: Van Nostrand.

Guilford, J. (1967b). *The nature of human intelligence.* New York: McGraw-Hill.

Guliyev, G. (1998). *The archetypes of the Gorgut clan [Arkhetipy roda Gorguta].* Baku.

Gumilyov, L. N. (1990). *The geography of ethnos in the historical era [Geografiya etnosa v istoricheskiy period]* (p. 33). Moscow.

Gumilyov, L. N. (2001). *Ethnogenesis and the Earth's biosphere [Etnogenez i biosfera zemli].* Moscow.

Hegel, G. W. F (1929). *Works [Sochineniya]* (Vol. 2, p. 32). Moscow-Leningrad.

Hegel, G. W. F. (1956). *Works [Sochineniya]* (Vol. 3, p. 256). Moscow. In English editions of Hegel, *The Philosophy of Mind,* §453(2).

Hjelle, L. A. and Ziegler, D. J. (2006). *Personality theories [Teorii lichnosti]* (p. 438). Leningrad: Piter. English edition (1992). *Personality theories: Basic assumptions, research, and applications.* New York: McGraw-Hill.

Husserl, E. (1994). *On the phenomenology of the internal consciousness of time [Fenomenologiya vnutrennego soznaniya vremeni].* Moscow: Logos. English edition (1990). *On the phenomenology of the consciousness of internal time (1893–1917).* J. B. Brough, trans. Dordrecht: Kluwer.

Ilyin, Ye. L. (2001). *Emotions and feelings [Emotsii i chuvstva].* St. Petersburg.

Itelson, L. B. (1972). *Lectures on modern problems of learning psychology [Lektsii po sovremennym problemam psikhologii obucheniya].* Vladimir.

Jaspers, K. (1923). *General psychopathology [Allgemeine Psychopatologie].* Berlin. English edition (1997) (p. 65). J. Hoenig and M.W. Hamilton, trans. Baltimore, Md.: Johns Hopkins University Press.

Jung, C. (1994). *The libido and its metamorphoses and symbols [Libido i yego metamorfozy i simvoly]* (p.12). St. Petersburg.

Jung, C. (2006). *The transcendent function [Trantsendentnaya funktsiya]* (p. 10). Moscow. In English: The transcendent function. *Collected Works,* 8, par. 145. Princeton: Princeton University Press.

Jung, C. (2008). *Psychology and the east* (p. 10). London-New York: Routledge Classics.

Kovalenko, M. I. (1999). Passionarity as a psychological phenomenon. In *Psychological issues of personal self-realization. A collection of scientific treatises* [Passionarnost' kak psikhologicheskiy fenomen. *Psikhologicheskiye problemy samorealizatsii lichnosti. Sbornik nauchnykh trudov]*. St. Petersburg: St. Petersburg University Press.

Kreitner, R. and Kinicki, A. (2008). *Organizational behavior* (8th ed.), New York: McGraw-Hill.

Krylov, A.A. and Kovalenko, M.I. (1993). Issues of ethnic psychology in light of L.N. Gumilyov's theory of ethnogenesis. [Problemy etnicheskoy psikhologii v svete teorii etnogeneza L.N. Gumilyova]. *Transations of St. Petersburg University [Vestnik S.-peterb. universiteta]* Series 6, edition 4. St. Petersburg.

Lazursky, A. F. (1924). *The classification of personalities [Klassifikatsiya lichnostey].* Leningrad.

Leontyev, A. N. (1975). *Activity. Consciousness. Personality [Deyatel'nost'. Soznaniye. Lichnost'].* Moscow.

Leontyev, A. N. (1982). On the creative career of L. S. Vygotsky: Introductory article. In *L. S. Vygotsky. Collected Works.* [O tvorcheskom puti L. S. Vygotskogo: vstupitelnaya statya. *L. S. Vygotskiy. Sobraniye sochineniy]* (Vol. 1). Moscow.

Luk, A. N. (1985). *Issues of scientific creativity [Problemy nauchnogo tvorchestva]* (No. 4). Moscow: INION.

Makovelsky, A. O. (1947). Nizami's thoughts on the power and objectives of artistic creativity. In *Nizami Ganjevi* [Mysli Nizami o sile i zadachakh khudozhestvennogo tvorchestva. *Nizami Gyandzhe-vi]* (pp. 13–34). Baku.

Mardanov, M. S. (2009). *Azerbaijan's education at the new stage of development [Azerbayjan tehsili yeni inkishaf merhelesinde]* (p. 513). Baku.

Maslow, A. (1971). *The farther reaches of human nature* (p. 57). New York: Viking Press.

Mejidova, S. M. (2001). *Psychological types. Typology 69 [Psikhologicheskiye tipy. Tipologiya 69].* Baku.

Merkel, A. (2008). Address by Angela Merkel, Federal Chancellor of Germany on the occasion of the second part of the 2008 Ordinary Session of the Council of Europe Parliamentary Assembly. Strasbourg, April 14–18, 2008). http//assembly.coe. int/Sessions/2008/speeches

Meylach, B. S. (1980). *The psychology of artistic creativity: Subject and avenues of investigation. The psychology of processes of artistic creativity [Psikhologiya khudozhestvennogo tvorchestva: Predmet i puti issledovaniya. Psikhologiya protsessov khudozhestvennogo tvorchestva]* (pp. 5–23). Leningrad: Nauka.

Nadirashvili, Sh. A. (1974). *The concept of attitudes in general and social psychology [Ponyatiye ustanovki v obshchey i sotsial'noy psikhologii].* Tbilisi.

Nadirashvili, Sh. A. (1987). The classification of forms of activity in light of attitudinal theory. In *The psychology of the personality and way of life* [Klassifikatsiya form aktivnosti v svete teorii ustanovki. *Psikhologiya lichnosti i obraz zhizni]* (pp. 23–27). Moscow: Nauka.

Nasimi, I. *The manuscript couch [Rukopisny divan]* (Code M 227/11671, Sheet 58). Manuscript Archives of the Academy of Sciences of Azerbaijan.

Nasimi, I. (1973). *Lyrics [Lirika]* (p. 35). Moscow.

Newman, B. and Newman, R. (1999). *Development through life: a psychosocial approach* (p. 37) Belmont, CA: Wadsworth.

Nietzsche, F. (1910). *Complete works [Polnoye sobraniye sochineniy]* (Vol. 9, p. 189). Moscow. In English editions of Nietzsche, *The Will to Power,* §430.

Nikandrov, V. F. (2008). *Psychology [Psikhologiya].* Moscow: Prospect Publishing House.

Patterson, J., Kim P. (1992). *The day America told the truth.* New York: Prentice Hall.

Perls, F. and Goodman, P. (2001). *The theory of Gestalt therapy [Teoriya geshtalt-terapii]* (p. 41). Moscow.

Petrovsky, A. V. (1966). The issue of the activity of consciousness in the history of Soviet psychology. In *Problems of consciousness* [Problema aktivsnosti soznaniya v istorii sovetskoy psikhologii. *Problemy soznaniya]* (pp. 170–175). Moscow.

Petrovsky, A. V. (1967). *A history of Soviet psychology [Istoriya sovetskoy psikhologii].* Moscow: Prosveshcheniye.

Petrovsky, A. V. (1988). *What we know and what we know about ourselves [Chto my znayem i chto my znayem o sebe].* Moscow.

Piaget, J. (1968). *Selected psychological works [Izbrannyye psikhologicheskiye trudy].* Moscow: Prosveshcheniye. In English (2001). *The psychology of intelligence.* M. Piercy and D.E. Berlyne, trans. London and New York: Routledge.

Piaget, J. (2008). *The language and thought of the child [Rech' i myshleniye rebyonka]* (p. 35). Moscow: RIMIS Press. English edition (2003). *The language and thought of the child.* London and New York: Routledge.

Pigulevskaya, N. V., Yakobovich, A. Ya. et al. (1958). *The history of Iran from ancient times to the late 18th century [Istoriya Irana s drevneyshikh vremen do kontsa XVIII veka]* (p. 157). Leningrad.

Plato (1989). *Phaedrus [Fedr]* (pp. 24–51). Moscow: Progress. In English: Internet Classics Archive. classics.mit.edu/Plato/phaedrus.html

Ponomarev, Ya. A. (1976) *The psychology of creativity [Psikhologiya tvorchestva].* Moscow: Nauka.

Ponomarev, Ya. A. and Gajiyev, Ch. M. (1990). The patterns of communication in a creative group. In *The psychology of creativity: General, differential, and applied* [Zakomomernosti obshcheniya v tvorcheskom kollektive. *Psikhologiya tvorchestva: obshchaya, differentsial'naya, prikladnaya]* (pp. 92–103). Moscow: Nauka.

Psychobox. A box of psychological games. (2004). (Card 36). UK: Shambhala.

Quluzade, Z. A. (1983). *Patterns of the development of 15th-16th-century Eastern philosophy and the West-East question [Zakonomernosti razvitiya vostochnoy filosofii XV-XVI vv. i problema Zapad-Vostok]*. Baku: Elm.

Quluzade, Z. A. (1989). On several aspects of the development of 15th-16th-century Eastern philosophy. In *The history of medieval Eastern philosophy* [O nekotorykh osobennostyakh razvitiya vostochnoy filosofii XV-XVI vv. *Istoriya srednevekovoy vostochnoy filosofii]* (pp. 25–41). Baku: Elm. Rokeach, M. (1973). *The nature of human values.* New York: Free Press.

Runin, B. M. (1980). The psychology of improvisation. In *The psychology of processes of artistic creativity* [Psikhologiya improvizatsii. *Psikhologiya protsessov khudozhestvennogo tvorchestva]* (pp. 45–57). Moscow: Nauka.

Rubinshteyn, S. L. (1940; 4th ed. 2002). *The fundamentals of general psychology [Osnovy obshchey psikhologii]*. St. Petersburg. Piter. http://yanko.lib.ru/books/psycho/rubinshteyn=osnovu_obzhey_psc.pdf

Schultz, D. P. and Schultz, E. S. (1998). *The history of modern psychology [Istoriya sovremennoy psikhologii]* (p. 486). St. Petersburg. English 9th ed. (2008) (p. 496). Belmont, CA: Thomson Wadsworth.

Schwartz, B. (2004). *The paradox of choice* (p. 265). New York: Harper Perennial.

Seyidov, S. I. (1989). The relationship of the orientation of the personality and cognitive style (using field dependence-field independence as an example). In *The activation of the personality in the system of social relations* [Vzaimosvyaz' napravlennosti lichnosti i kognitivnogo stilya (na primere polezavisimosti-polenezavisimosti). *Aktivizatsiya lichnosti v sisteme obshchestvennykh otnosheniy]* (p. 78). Moscow.

Seyidov, S. I. (1994). *The social psychology of creativity [Sotsial'naya psikhologiya tvorchestva]*. Baku: Azerbaijan Translation Center.

Seyidov, S. I. (1995). On the paradoxical nature of personal creative activity. In *Topics of psychology, education, and language instruction methodology.* [O paradoksal'nosti lichnoy tvorcheskoy aktivnosti. *Voprosy psikhologii, pedagokiki i metodiki prepodavaniya yazykov]* (pp. 59–71). Baku: Mutarjim.

Seyidov, S. I. (1997a). Management psychology in the system of higher education. In *Contemporary research problems in the liberal arts* [Psikhologiya menedzhmenta v sisteme vysshego obrazovaniya. *Muasir merhelede humanitar elmlerin tedqiqi problemleri kitabinda]* (pp. 76–77). Baku: Mutarjim.

Seyidov, S. I. (1997b). The history and current state of management psychology. In *Collection of articles on the liberal arts* [Istoriya i sovremennoye sostoyaniye psikhologii menedzhmenta. *Maqalalar toplusu (Humanitar elm sahibleri uzre)]* (No. 1, pp. 183–191). ADDI.

Seyidov, S. I. (1997c). *The paradoxes of creativity [Yaradijiliq paradokslari]* (No. 4, pp. 49–55). Baku: Mutarcim.

Seyidov, S. I. (1998a). Management psychology: Problems of personnel recruitment. In *Collection of articles on the liberal arts* [Psikhologiya menedzhmenta: Problemy otbora kadrov *Maqalalar toplusu (Humanitar elm sahibleri uzre)]* (No. 2, pp. 123–143). ADDI.

Seyidov, S. I. (1998b). Management psychology: Problems of interpersonal relations in organizations. In *Current topics of humanities studies* [Psikhologiya menedzhmenta: Problemy mezhlichnostnykh otnosheniy v organizatsiyakh. *Aktualnyye voprosy izucheniya gumanitarnykh nauk]* (No. 5, pp. 104–118). Baku: Mutarjim.

Seyidov, S. I. (1999a). Management psychology: The issue of creative activity in organizations. In *Current topics of humanities studies* [Psikhologiya menedzhmenta: Problema tvorcheskoy aktivnosti v organizatsiyakh. *Aktualnyye voprosy izucheniya gumanitarnykh nauk]* (No. 1, pp. 164–170). Baku: Mutarjim.

Seyidov, S. I. (1999b). A study of the issue of personal creativity in Soviet Azerbaijan. In *Collection of articles on the liberal arts* [Issledovaniye problemy tvorcheskoy aktivnosti lichnosti v Sovetskom Azerbaydzhane. *Maqalalar toplusu (Humanitar elm sahibleri uzre)]* (No. 3, pp. 89–101). ADDI.

Seyidov, S. I. (2000a). *Management psychology [Psikhologiya menedzhmenta]*. Baku: Chashyogli.

Seyidov, S. I. (2000b). F.A. Ibrahimbeyov: An innovative scientist. *Psychology Journal* [F.E. Ibrahimbeyov yenilikchi alimdir. *Psixologiya jurnali], 1–2,* 105–109. Baku.

Seyidov, S. I. (2008). Creativity as a psychic protective mechanism. *Scholarly Transactions* [Tvorchestvo kak okhranitelny mekhanizm psikhiki. *Uchenyye zapiski], 2,* 3–6. Baku: Azerbaijan Languages University.

Seyidov, S. I. (2009a). Psychological personality types, creativity, and culture. *Scholarly transactions* [Psikhologicheskiye tipy lichnosti, tvorchestvo i kul'tura. *Uchenyye zapiski], 1,* 3–12. Baku: Azerbaijan Languages University.

Seyidov, S. I. (2009b). Lev Gumilyov's passionarity and the convincive personality type. *Psychology journal.* [Passionarnost' L. N. Gumileva i konvincivnogo tipa lichnosti. *Psixologiya jurnali], 2,* 3–35. Baku.

Seyidov, S. I. (2009c). Personality theories as the basis for personality typologization. *Scholarly transactions* [Teorii lichnosti kak osnova yeye tipologizatsii. *Uchenyye zapiski], 1,* 13–23. Baku: Azerbaijan Languages University.

Seyidov, S. I. (2009d). Creativity in Sufism and psychoanalysis. *Scholarly transactions* [Tvorchestvo v sufizme i psikhoanaliz. *Uchenyye zapiski], 2,* 3–9. Baku: Azerbaijan Languages University.

Seyidov, S. I. (2009e). Democracy, human rights and foreign policy: From Winston Churchill to Heydar Aliyev. In *Azerbaijan in global politics: Crafting foreign policy* (pp. 299–322). Baku: Azerbaijan Diplomatic Academy.

Seyidov, S. I. and Hamzayev, M.E. (2007). *Psychology [Psixologiya]*. Baku: Nurlan.

Sheynman-Topishan, S. Ya. (1978). *Plato and Vedic philosophy [Plato i vediyskaya filosofiya]*. Moscow: Nauka.

Smirnova, Ye. O. (1995) Attachment theory: concept and experiment [Theoriya privyazanosti: kontseptsiya i eksperiment]. http://www.voppsy.ru/journals_all/issues/1995/953/953139.htm

Smullyan, R. (1981). *What's the name of this book? [Kak zhe nazyvayetsia eta kniga?]* Moscow: Mir.

Spengler, O. (1993). *The decline of the West [Zakat yevropy]* (Vol. 1, p. 477) (In English editions, Chapter IX: Soul-image and life-feeling: On the form of the soul). Moscow: Mysl.

Sri Upanishad [Shri Ishopanishad] (1991). Tver.

Starovoytenko, Ye. B. (2007). *The cultural psychology of the personality [Kulturnaya psikhologiya lichnosti]* (p. 107). Moscow.

Sternberg, R. J. (1985). Implicit theories of intelligence, creativity, and wisdom. *Journal of Personality and Social Psychology, 49* (3), 609–677.

Sukhodolsky, G. V. (1972). *Basic mathematical statistics for psychologists [Osnovy matematicheskoy statistiki dlya psikhologov].* Leningrad.

Surmava, A. V. (2004a). The idea of reflexivity in theoretical psychology: Author's abstract for a Doctorate of Psychology dissertation [Ideya reflektivnosti v teoreticheskoy psikhologii: avtoreferat dissertatsii na soiskanie uchenoy stepeni kand. psikhol. nauk]. Moscow.

Surmava, A. V. (2004b). *The idea of reflexivity in theoretical psychology [Ideya reflektivnosti v teoreticheskoy psikhologii].* Moscow.

Ternovsky, V. N. (1969). *Ibn Sina (Avicenna) [Ibn Sina (Avitsenna)].* Moscow: Nauka.

Uznadze, D. N. (2004). *General Psychology [Obshchaya psikhologiya].* Moscow: Mysl; St. Petersburg et al: Piter.

Verdiyeva, Z. N., Bayramov, A. S. et al. (Eds.). (1992). *F. A. Ibrahimbekov: 90 years [Ibrahimbekov F. A. 90 let.]* (pp. 7–58).Vichev, V. (1978). *Morality and the social psyche [Moral i sotsialnaya psikhika]* (p. 92). Moscow: Progress.

Vygotsky, L. S. (1982). *Problems of general psychology.* In Vygotsky, L. S. *Collected works [Problemy obshchey psikhologii. Sobraniye sochineniy* (Vol. 2, p. 222). Moscow.

Walbweg, H. J. (1988). Creativity and talent as learning. In *The nature of creativity.* Cambridge University Press. 1988.

Wallach, M. A. and Kogan, N. (1972). A new look at the creativity-intelligence distinction. In P. E. Vernon (Ed.). *Creativity.* Baltimore MD: Penguin.

Wertheimer, M. (1945). *Productive thinking.* New York-London: Harper & Brothers.

Yaroshevsky, M. T. (1985). *The history of psychology [Istoriya psikhologii].* Moscow: Mysl.

Yaroslavsky, V. (2004). *100 great psychologists [100 velikikh psikhologov].* Moscow: Veche.

Yarovoy, G. L. and Radayev, Yu. N. (2004). On a new reading of Whitehead's and Russell's *Principia mathematica. Transactions of Samara State University.* Natural sciences series. Mathematics [O novom prochtenii «*Osnovanii matematiki*» A. Uaytkheda i B. Rassella. *Vestnik Sam-GU.* Yestestvenno-nauchnaya seriya. Mathematika], *4,* 34.

Zakaria, F. (2003). *The future of freedom.* New York: W. W. Norton & Company.

Zalkind, A. (1924). *Freudianism and Marxism [Freydizm i marksizm].* Moscow.

Zimina, I. S. (2007). The development of passionary qualities in children as a means of overcoming laziness, apathy, and frailty. *Psychology.* [Razvitiye passionarnykh kachestv u detey kak sredstvo preodoleniya leni, apatii, boleznennosti. *Psikhologiya], 11,* 14–17.

Zinchenko, V. P. (1991). The worlds of consciousness and the structures of consciousness. *Topics of psychology* [Miry soznaniya i struktury soznaniya. *Voprosy psikhologii], 2.*

Index